WITHDRAWN
University of
Illinois Library
at Urbana-Champaign

D0207769

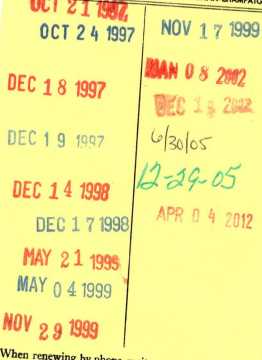
CENTRAL CIRCULATION BOOKSTACKS

The person charging this material is responsible for its renewal or its return to
the library from which it was borrowed
on or before the **Latest Date** stamped
below. **You may be charged a minimum
fee of $75.00 for each lost book.**

Theft, mutilation, and underlining of books are reasons
for disciplinary action and may result in dismissal from
the University.

TO RENEW CALL TELEPHONE CENTER, 333-8400

UNIVERSITY OF ILLINOIS LIBRARY AT URBANA-CHAMPAIGN

OCT 21 1997
OCT 24 1997   NOV 17 1999

DEC 18 1997   JAN 08 2002
                     DEC 19 2002
DEC 19 1997   6/30/05
                     12-29-05
DEC 14 1998
                     APR 04 2012
DEC 17 1998

MAY 21 1999
MAY 04 1999

NOV 29 1999

When renewing by phone, write new due date below
previous due date.
                                    L162

The Los Angeles Riots

URBAN POLICY CHALLENGES
Terry Nichols Clark, Series Editor

Cities are critical. From the Los Angeles riots of 1992 to the Hong Kong reversion of 1997, cities represent in microcosm the problems and potentials we face at all governmental levels.

Focusing on cities can help clarify our most challenging issues. Most key decisions affecting our lives are made locally. Although national governments collect the majority of funds, most welfare state programs around the world are provided by local governments. Urban leaders play key roles in encouraging economic development, maintaining quality public services, and mandating reasonable taxes.

And they are pressed to do more: provide attractive physical environments, improve amenities such as bike paths, help encourage recycling, assist disadvantaged groups to achieve broader acceptance and access to public facilities, keep streets safe, and fill the gaps in health and social services.

Books in the *Urban Policy Challenges* series will explore the range of urban policy problems and will detail solutions that have been sought and implemented in cities from around the world. They will build on studies of leadership, public management, organizational culture, community power, intergovernmental relations, public finance, citizen responsiveness, and related elements of urban public decisionmaking.

These approaches to urban challenges will range from case studies to quantitative modeling. The series will include monographs, texts, as well as edited volumes. While some works will target professional and student audiences, many books will elicit attention from thoughtful public leaders and informed citizens as well.

BOOKS IN THE SERIES

The Los Angeles Riots

Lessons for the Urban Future

EDITED BY

Mark Baldassare

Westview Press

BOULDER • SAN FRANCISCO • OXFORD

Urban Policy Challenges

All rights reserved. No part of this publication may be reproduced or transmitted in any form or by any means, electronic or mechanical, including photocopy, recording, or any information storage and retrieval system, without permission in writing from the publisher.

Copyright © 1994 by Westview Press, Inc.

Published in 1994 in the United States of America by Westview Press, Inc., 5500 Central Avenue, Boulder, Colorado 80301-2877, and in the United Kingdom by Westview Press, 36 Lonsdale Road, Summertown, Oxford OX2 7EW

A CIP catalog record for this book is available from the Library of Congress.
ISBN 0-8133-2391-6   ISBN 0-8133-2392-4 (pbk)

Printed and bound in the United States of America

 The paper used in this publication meets the requirements of the American National Standard for Permanence of Paper for Printed Library Materials Z39.48-1984.

10   9   8   7   6   5   4

979.494
L8962
cp. 2

Contents

Figures and Tables

Figures

Tables

About the Contributors

Allan Abrahamse is a mathematician in the RAND Corporation's Social Policy Department and a member of RAND's Statistical Research Consulting Group.

Mark Baldassare is professor and chair of the Department of Urban and Regional Planning, School of Social Ecology, University of California, Irvine. He is also the co-director of the Orange County, California, Annual Survey, University of California, Irvine.

Lawrence Bobo is a professor in the Department of Sociology and director of the Center for Research on Race, Politics and Society, University of California, Los Angeles.

Edgar W. Butler is a professor in the Department of Sociology, University of California, Riverside.

Regina Freer is a Ph.D. candidate in the Department of Political Science, University of Michigan, Ann Arbor.

Hiroshi Fukurai is an assistant professor in the Board of Studies in Sociology and Legal Studies Program, University of California, Santa Cruz.

James H. Johnson Jr. is a professor in the Department of Geography, University of North Carolina, Chapel Hill.

Richard Krooth is a visiting professor in the Department of Sociology, University of California, Berkeley, a lecturer at Golden Gate University, San Francisco, and a practicing attorney.

Ira S. Lowry is a housing and development consultant based in Pacific Palisades, California.

Peter A. Morrison is a demographer on the senior research staff at the RAND Corporation.

Melvin L. Oliver is a professor in the Department of Sociology, University of California, Los Angeles.

Joan Petersilia is director of RAND's Criminal Justice Program and a professor in the Department of Criminology, Law and Society, School of Social Ecology, University of California, Irvine.

James A. Regalado is an associate professor in the Department of Political Science and executive director at the Edmund G. "Pat" Brown Institute of Public Affairs, California State University, Los Angeles.

David O. Sears is a professor in the Department of Psychology and the Department of Political Science, University of California, Los Angeles.

Raphael J. Sonenshein is an associate professor in the Department of Political Science, California State University, Fullerton.

Kathleen J. Tierney is an associate professor in the Department of Sociology and research director of the Disaster Research Center at the University of Delaware.

Camille L. Zubrinsky is a graduate research fellow at the Center for the Study of Urban Poverty, University of California, Los Angeles.

Acknowledgments

I wish to acknowledge the contributions of many people who made this volume possible. First, there is Terry N. Clark, the Series Editor for "Urban Policy Challenges," whose initial support for this volume and helpful advice along the way were critical. I received constructive feedback from the editors at Westview Press, including Dean Birkenkamp, Jennifer Knerr, and especially Eric W. Wright. I was also assisted by the editorial efforts of Valerie Lorenz and typesetting by Stephanie Pas.

I am most grateful to the authors of this book for taking on the challenge of my call for chapters. Each approached the task with skill, hard work, and scholarly dedication as we went through several months of writing and revising each of the chapters. The high enthusiasm they expressed toward contributing to this collection was a major source of inspiration for me.

Scott Bollens, John Dombrink, Elaine Vaughan, Lois Takahashi, and Carol Uhlaner at the University of California, Irvine, were important sources of scholarly contacts, references, insights, and encouragement. I also wish to thank Cheryl Katz for providing, as usual, intelligent advice, honest feedback, and understanding.

Mark Baldassare

1

Introduction

Mark Baldassare

Why study the Los Angeles riots? There are several reasons for this inquiry into the April 1992 violence and unrest that occurred after a jury acquitted the police officers who were accused of using excessive force in the Rodney King beating. First, the Los Angeles riots are among the most violent, destructive and frightening episodes in twentieth century American urban history. Next, the Los Angeles riots have been regarded by some observers as a sign of a dangerous turning point in the history of U.S. cities. Lastly, many have said that there are lessons to be learned from the events that took place in Los Angeles for improving policies toward U.S. cities.

When I began this search for knowledge more than a year ago, however, there were few publications dedicated to increasing understanding of this important urban event (see for example Gooding-Williams, 1993; Hazen, 1992; Los Angeles Times, 1992). By contrast, the 1965 Watts riot has been reviewed, analyzed and interpreted in many places (Cohen, 1970; Cohen and Murphy, 1966; Crump, 1966; Fogelson, 1969; Oberschall, 1968; Sears and McConahay, 1973). What I discovered instead were recent studies that had not yet found their way into print, and scholars whose expertise made it possible for them to offer unique analyses of the riots. My task, then, was to organize and integrate new works by several authors into a collection of essays.

This book represents the first, comprehensive study of the Los Angeles riots. It is an edited volume of original works by urban scholars seeking to answer these basic questions: what were the causes of the Los Angeles riots, what actually took place, and what are the consequences of the riots for Los Angeles and other U.S. cities? The authors also offer suggestions for avoiding future unrest similar in size and scope to what took place in Los Angeles, and solutions for the problems which plague U.S. cities and race relations.

The Element of Surprise

I have noted with interest that many observers were initially surprised by the Los Angeles riots, including both the event itself and the circumstances around it. This was the response of many scholars and policy makers, as well as the media and the public. The unexpectedness of this tragic event was yet another compelling reason for a detailed analysis of what happened, why it occurred, and to what end.

The world was shocked by the video tape showing a black motorist being beaten by white police officers. No one had expected that a jury viewing this tape would find the four police officers to be not guilty of using excessive force against Rodney King. The Los Angeles Police Department was unprepared when the personal shock over the trial outcome turned into angry and violent crowd behavior. Koreans did not seem to anticipate that the black rage against the white establishment would be diverted into looting their grocery stores and burning their small businesses. City officials, the police and local merchants did not expect Hispanic immigrants, who were becoming known as the new "silent majority" on the Los Angeles scene, to be found in large numbers among the participants in the rioting and looting that took place after the verdict.

One reason that the Los Angeles riots were unexpected was the belief that too much had changed in the lives of urban blacks for a repeat of the 1965 Watts uprising. Certainly, Los Angeles in 1992 had a black mayor, an inter-racial city council, and a reputation as a multicultural "melting pot." Federal efforts such as civil rights laws and affirmative action would also seem to lessen the past racial problems in Los Angeles. Health, education and social service programs were in place to lessen the pain of poverty and despair in the ghetto. South Central had become a racially mixed area of Asians, Hispanics and blacks. The prospects of black residents burning and looting neighborhood stores once again seemed absurd.

Urban scholars can also count themselves among the surprised in April 1992. The 1990s perspective on inner-city problems focused on impoverished blacks in a deep depression facing poverty, chronic unemployment, welfare, broken families, teen pregnancies and school dropouts. This was a group appearing to harm itself more than others through gangs, violence, alcohol and drug abuse. The level of despair and hopelessness would seem to be too high to mount racial uprisings similar to the 1960s, when soaring hopes of the Kennedy and Johnson era were disappointed. The one recent exception was the Miami riot of 1980 and, after all, Miami with its explosive combination of Cuban expatriates, Haitian refugees, poor blacks and Southern whites was viewed as an anomaly.

Today, however, a look back at the circumstances surrounding the Watts riot and other 1960s urban uprisings does show some remarkable similarities with the recent Los Angeles riots. Black anger stemming from the mistreatment of a black man by white police officers was evident. Large numbers of young, unemployed and fairly desperate black males in the neighborhood were available and motivated to become part of the urban disturbances. Small businesses that residents perceived as treating them badly became the targets of rioting and looting.

In retrospect, the initial surprise about the 1992 Los Angeles riots reflects a failure to realize that the treatment of blacks and the living conditions of poor blacks had changed less than we had thought. Meanwhile, the potential for violence was heightened by a social and economic transformation that was occurring in and around the inner-city black neighborhoods.

The Defining Characteristics

There are three factors noted often in this book which I believe are the defining characteristics of the Los Angeles riots. First, the conditions of poor, urban blacks or the "underclass" have not improved and remain a critical source for urban uprisings. Next, black-white tensions remain high, as race relations are in a troubled state due to personal and institutional racism, and can easily explode into violent episodes. Third, the combined effects of foreign immigration and economic restructuring, present in many U.S. cities in the 1990s, are leading to inter-ethnic hostilities.

The authors in this book vary in the importance they place on these three urban themes. In my opinion, a comprehensive understanding of what happened, why it happened and what can be learned from the Los Angeles riots needs to include the issues of the underclass, black-white tensions and inter-ethnic hostilities. Any policy solutions that are proposed for U.S. cities must incorporate all of these three elements that will continue to shape the future urban experience.

First, the existence of an underclass has been noted for some time in the writings of sociologists who study cities and American blacks (see Wilson, 1978, 1987). Moreover, the fact that little has improved in the conditions of poor, urban blacks is a disturbing but a well-documented fact. That is, a large group of inner-city blacks continue to live an isolated ghetto life of poverty, chronic unemployment, crime, poor schools, violence and despair. That is, despite the outlawing of racial discrimination in housing, many poor urban blacks continue to live in highly segregated urban neighborhoods (Farley and Frey, 1994; Galster and Hill, 1992; Massey and Denton, 1987, 1989, 1993). Thus, while the explosive growth of suburban employment was taking place in recent decades (Baldassare, 1986, 1992, 1994; Kelly, 1989; Scott, 1988), poor urban blacks did not benefit (Kasarda, 1988, 1993). Moreover, this impoverished group has seen job opportunities around them dwindle even more as economic restructuring resulted in a decline in city manufacturing jobs (Sassen, 1990, 1991, 1994).

The presence of an underclass in U.S. cities was often noted as a causal factor in the riots in the 1960s. Unfortunately, many efforts with the goal of fundamentally changing the living conditions of large numbers of poor, urban blacks have fallen short. As a result, desperate acts of violence and destruction take place on a daily basis, and can escalate into events such as what occurred in Los Angeles in 1992.

Next, black-white tensions in the U.S. are still present, and race relations remain highly charged. The blatant expressions of racism by whites are less common now than in the 1960s. However, many whites continue to feel uncomfortable about living around large numbers of blacks, or busing white children for the goal of school integration, or supporting policies to improve the conditions of poor urban blacks (see Pettigrew, 1971, 1980, 1985; Kluegel, 1990; Schuman, Steeh and Bobo, 1985). Clearly, the economic conditions of blacks have improved and racial discrimination has declined. Yet, many blacks continue to feel the sting of prejudiced attitudes expressed by whites, while they may also experience mistreatment due to their race and color and, importantly, many perceive themselves as possible victims of discrimination when they encounter the criminal justice system or other societal institutions (Blalock, 1979; Blauner, 1889; Feagin, 1991; Jaynes and Williams, 1989; Sigelman and Welch, 1991).

Black-white tensions were potent forces in explaining the riots in the 1960s. For instance, the 1965 Watts riot began when a crowd turned violent as a white policeman arrested a black motorist. In a similar place and a different era, feelings of mistreatment by whites and distrust of the criminal justice system still run high in black communities. Today, a video of white police officers beating a black motorist, and a jury finding the police officers not guilty of using excessive force, resulted in anger, violence and riots.

Third, inter-ethnic hostilities have recently emerged as a new and dangerous urban trend. Many large U.S. cities in the 1980s experienced high growth rates in both Hispanic and Asian immigrant groups, while black population stagnated as the black middle class moved to better neighborhoods, and whites were migrating to the suburbs (see Abbott, 1993; Frey, 1993a, 1993b, 1993c; Frey and Farley, 1993; Portes and Stepick, 1993). Cities with the largest increases in minority population in the 1980s were Los Angeles, New York, San Francisco and Miami (Frey, 1993a). Their minority populations now include not only blacks, but also large numbers of Asians and Hispanics.

Inter-ethnic hostilities in inner-city areas emerged as the poor urban blacks found themselves surrounded, and in some instances displaced, by large numbers of newly arrived foreign immigrants. Hispanics, many of whom were poor and undereducated, were now competing with blacks for scarce job opportunities, shopping in black stores, and living in black neighborhoods. Asians, many of whom had arrived with capital, higher education and entrepreneurial skills found their American Dream limited to operating inner city businesses and convenience stores with poor blacks and poor Hispanics as their customers and employees.

In sum, disadvantaged blacks were joined in their inner city neighborhoods by Hispanic immigrants, who were also experiencing prejudice and discrimination. Asian immigrants replaced the whites as business and store owners in economically depressed neighborhoods. The economic restructuring of cities led to job losses, adding to the competitions and tensions. The results were growing inter-ethnic hostilities taking the form of local conflicts and disputes between blacks and Hispanics, blacks and Asians, and Asians and Hispanics.

Examples of inter-ethnic hostilities have become all too common in Los Angeles (see Light, 1988). Before the riot, a Korean merchant shot and killed a young, unarmed black girl who was thought to be stealing. Blacks then staged a boycott of Korean grocery stores. A white judge later ruled that the Korean grocer would not have to serve jail time for the killing. During the riot, Korean stores and businesses were targeted for burning and looting by blacks and Hispanics. Korean merchants responded by mounting an armed defense of their property, having assumed that the local police were not going to protect them. The perceptions that whites are indifferent toward the plight of inner city minorities, and that the police and courts do not provide safety and justice, serve to heighten the prospects of inter-ethnic tensions escalating into personal violence and property destruction.

Summary of Chapters

There are nine chapters in this book concerning the causes of the Los Angeles riots, an analysis of the event, and the consequences of the unrest for the future of U.S. cities. Specifically, the chapters analyze the demographic setting, politics, racial attitudes, the justice system, the profile of riot arrests, the incidence of property damages, inter-ethnic conflicts, multicultural associations and the distinctions between the Watts rebellion and the 1992 riots. Each chapter provides insight into the role of the underclass, black-white tensions and inter-ethnic hostilities in explaining the Los Angeles riots.

The chapter by Peter Morrison and Ira Lowry identifies some of the demographic "preconditions" for the Los Angeles riots. They argue that ethnic and racial change in the South Central area resulted in escalating tensions. In South Central, many of the affluent blacks departed and were replaced by Hispanic immigrants. In addition, Asian immigrants moved into surrounding neighborhoods. There were episodes of ethnic and racial conflicts in the South Central area, for instance, between Korean merchants and black and Hispanic residents. The authors argue that the racial and ethnic patterns of arrests and property damage in the Los Angeles riots provide evidence for the hypothesis that the riot was an outgrowth of demographic change.

Another precondition was the large numbers of young males with time on their hands who were available to participate in the unrest. The authors estimate that the South Central area had about 50,000 men between 16 and 34 who were neither employed nor in school. The economic circumstances of these young men fit the classic demographic profile of the underclass. They provided the critical mass of individuals who were available, willing and capable of committing crimes, property damage and looting after the trial verdict.

Morrison and Lowry argue that one of the painful lessons from the Los Angeles riot is that immigration and chronic unemployment leave numerous other central city areas in the nation with a potentially explosive situation. Multiracial tensions in poor inner-city neighborhoods are to be expected. Black unemployed youths will continue to be available and motivated to engage in riots. While riots may not be avoidable, the authors argue that damage and destruction can be minimized in future outbursts through better mobilization of local law enforcement agencies.

Raphael Sonenshein's chapter describes the "Bradley coalition" of white liberals and blacks ruling Los Angeles politics for two decades prior to the April 1992 riot. This biracial alliance allowed the city to reduce black-white tensions after the 1965 Watts riots and avoid the racially polarized politics faced by many large U.S. cities. After the Los Angeles riot, this coalition achieved another stunning victory by passing a police reform measure by a two-to-one margin. The June 1992 ballot measure, a response to the King beating, placed the police under more civilian control.

A year after the riot occurred, the political winds in Los Angeles appeared to change dramatically. City voters elected Richard Riordan, a white conservative Republican as their mayor over Michael Woo, a Democratic liberal city councilman who could not mobilize the Bradley coalition of white liberals and blacks. Daryl Gates, the white police chief, was replaced by Willie Williams, a black police official from Philadelphia.

Yet even these signs of major shifts reflect the fact that Los Angeles politics still revolve around white liberals, white conservatives and blacks. At a time when half of the city's population is Latino or Asian, biracial politics are still defining change. Sonenshein argues that inter-ethnic hostilities between blacks, Latinos and Asians brought about by conflict and economic competition increases the difficulty of achieving a majority-minority "rainbow" coalition in local politics. The low voter registration of Latinos, and their relative absence in the political process, is another limiting factor (see also de la Garza, 1987). The challenge today is for Los Angeles and other inter-ethnic U.S. cities to broaden the profile of political participation in voting and elected offices or risk the increasing prospects of inter-ethnic hostilities.

The chapter by Fukurai, Krooth and Butler reviews the actions by the criminal justice system surrounding the Rodney King beating and the trial verdict. Their findings indicate several crucial sources of black-white tensions in the police and court system.

The authors point out that the issue of police brutality has continued to be a source of anger and criticism toward the Los Angeles Police Department among minorities (see also Davis, 1992). A quarter of the 8,274 public complaints against the police in the late 1980s were for excessive use of force, and many of these complaints came from minority neighborhoods. In 1991, the Christopher Commission appointed by Mayor Bradley concluded that an inordinate number of use of force complaints involving a small number of police officers went unpunished. The beating of Rodney King, then, was perceived by many blacks as a validation of their worse fears about police misconduct.

Next, the author's point out that the trial jury system does not always result in a representative jury and a fair trial for nonwhites. In the case of the Rodney King beating, the trial was changed from racially and ethnically diverse Los Angeles County to predominantly white Ventura County, on the basis of the claim that publicity prevented the police officers from receiving a fair trial in Los Angeles. Further, jury selection processes tend to under-represent minorities by selecting jurors from lists, such as voter registration, which favors the choice of whites. A "not guilty" verdict for white police officers accused of excessively beating a black man, tried in a mostly white county by a mostly white jury, served to underscore for blacks, once again, the racial biases they can face when trying to receive just and fair trials.

Fukurai et al. offer several suggestions for increasing the racial representativeness of juries. These include the use of multiple source lists for selecting jurors, that is, more than voter lists, and requiring that new trial sites have race and ethnic makeups of the jury pool similar to the original trial site. Given the role that court decisions have had in sparking outbursts of violence, such as in Los Angeles and Miami, reducing racial bias in juries is obviously a critical step toward improving black-white relations.

The Chapter by Lawrence Bobo and his colleagues examines racial attitudes in Los Angeles County. The researchers present a unique study of public attitudes across ethnic and racial groups immediately before and after the trial verdict and unrest. Their findings indicate that the Los Angeles riot had no effect on public opinion toward racial attitudes, including the causes of economic inequality between blacks and whites. Blacks also continued to receive more negative stereotyping than other racial and ethnic groups.

One of the unfortunate outcomes of the riots was that blacks became more pessimistic about their problems of discrimination and their likelihood of being treated fairly.

The UCLA researchers also conducted a series of focus group interviews to learn about attitudes and perceptions across the Latino and Asian communities. For several reasons, it is difficult to assess the opinions of Asians and Hispanics in opinion surveys, such as small sample sizes for respondents from these specific minority groups, language barriers to telephone interviewing, and cultural barriers toward responding to questions on race and ethnicity. Their indepth qualitative studies found a disturbing pattern of inter-ethnic hostilities, including negative stereotyping and prejudices between Koreans and Latino residents. The sources of these impressions appear to be Latino experiences in the workplace and in retail stores. The negative feelings of Latinos toward Koreans help to explain their participation, along with blacks, in the riot activities against Koreans.

Bobo et al argue that black-white tensions are still strong, and that the outburst of anger, violence and destruction by blacks in Los Angeles must be understood in the context of the racial hostility that blacks continue to face. They point to the need to develop new mechanisms for inter-ethnic dialogues and dispute resolution. The authors conclude that alternatives to joblessness and low-wage work experienced by inner-city poor blacks for decades should also be a high priority.

The chapter by Joan Petersilia and Allan Abrahamse provides a detailed look at the arrests made during the Los Angeles riot. Most arrestees, as would be expected, were men who were under the age of 34. The surprising finding in their study is that half of all the arrests were of Latinos, while one in three were black residents.

The Latino arrest rates are noteworthy because this is a riot that was sparked by a mostly white jury's decision not to punish white police officers for the beating of a black man. The Latino arrests are also significant because they are in sharp contrast with the mostly black arrests in the 1965 Watts riot.

Clearly, the high proportion of Hispanics among the riot arrests is a reflection of the new ethnic composition of the South Central area. However, other explanations cannot be ignored. There are possibilities of police biases in the arrests. For instance, the police may have used the riots as an excuse to arrest those who they perceived as illegal immigrants. Perhaps the arrests of Hispanics were also attempts by the police to show force without inflaming the situation by arresting blacks. The most disturbing lesson from the riot arrests, whether or not they reflect the actual distribution of riot participants, is that alienation and frustration is evident in the new immigrant groups in the inner city, as well as among blacks. Thus, the potential for future riots would seem to be high.

Kathleen Tierney's chapter reviews the property damage and violence in Los Angeles, using a collective behavior analysis to look for signs of similarities and differences with previous urban riots. The factors in common with other outbursts include black outrage against actions perceived as racist by the police and the courts, followed by the looting and burning of local stores. The riot was similar in these respects to episodes in the 1960s, and also to Miami in the 1980s.

In two respects, however, the Los Angeles riots seemed to signal a new form of urban civil disturbance. First, there was the targeting of Korean businesses for looting and burning by blacks and Hispanics living in the area. There was also the participation of Hispanics in the arrests for looting and rioting. These patterns indicate that inter-ethnic hostilities, and not only black-white tensions, are now a part of urban unrest.

Tierney concludes that future urban disturbances may follow the new pattern found in the Los Angeles riots. That is, civil unrest could also include several racial and ethnic groups striking out at each other. Broad structural changes underway in urban societies that limit job prospects, such as foreign immigration, deindustrialization, the emergence of global cities and an international economy and the loss of high wage manufacturing jobs could all serve to increase tensions between blacks and other inner-city minority groups.

Regina Freer's chapter examines in detail the inter-ethnic hostilities between blacks and Koreans in the South Central area. Freer argues that there are lessons to be learned from the Los Angeles experience, given that inter-ethnic conflicts have emerged in other cities. The troubled relationship between blacks and Koreans over the past few years is highlighted by incidents such as a Korean grocer shooting and killing a black customer, a black boycott of Korean stores and, of course, the burning and looting of Korean businesses during the Los Angeles riots. Clearly, the financial frustrations and economic difficulties facing these groups have contributed to the escalating tensions.

Freer points out that the limited job opportunities available to these groups, and competition for increasingly scarce economic resources, are actually at the root of the black-Korean conflict. Korean immigrants often find that the professional jobs they trained for are not available when they arrive in America. To survive economically, many are thus forced to invest the capital they brought with them into risky and marginally profitable small retail establishments. Blacks with little cash and bleak employment prospects are the frequent customers in Korean-owned stores. Consumers in poor neighborhoods are often faced with high prices and a limited selection of goods in their local stores, and few nearby alternatives for better shopping.

Outside efforts to mediate the disputes between black residents and Korean merchants have centered on ways to improve communications. However, Freer argues that it is unlikely that the contacts will be positive so long as Koreans and blacks find themselves competing in a difficult economic environment. Freer suggests that a comprehensive economic development plan that would bring jobs and public services to inner-city areas is what is really needed. But too often, city priorities lean toward downtown interests, such as retaining and attracting large corporations, rather than improving conditions for the most needy residents. In the long run, Freer points out, a shift of city policies toward low-income areas would help overall economic development by reducing the incidence of conflicts and riots which have frightened many businesses away from America's central cities.

James Regalado's chapter reviews the status of multiracial coalition-building in Los Angeles. These efforts have an important role in reducing inter-ethnic hostilities. They are also critical as cities seek ways to transcend the past black-white political issues and include the voices of Asian and Latino populations.

The author points out that, in order to succeed, multiracial coalition-building must go beyond simple notions of "dialogue to ease tensions" which have been their focus in the past. These organizations must deal with the fundamental issues faced by ethnic and racial minorities, such as political representation, jobs and redevelopment, economic inequalities across racial and ethnic groups, and how to achieve a balance between racial and ethnic identity and multiethnic cooperation.

Regalado summarizes some of the current efforts in Los Angeles toward multiracial coalition-building. These include the black-Korean Alliance, the Black-Latino Roundtable, the Ethnic Coalition, the New Majority Task Force, and the Multicultural Collaborative. Some of their failures are explained by limited public funding, the involvement of mostly elites from the community, an emphasis on bicultural organizations, and too narrow a vision of their goals.

On a note of optimism, Regalado points out that there are some examples of grassroots organizations, with multiracial participation, that are dealing with the fundamental issues that can reduce inter-ethnic hostilities.

In the final chapter of the book, David Sears compares the 1965 Watts riot with the 1992 Los Angeles riots. The author is in an ideal position to provide us with some historical perspective, having conducted one of the most important studies of the 1965 Watts riot (Sears and McConahay, 1973). He points out several of the remarkable similarities in these riots, such as the critical role of a police confrontation with a black motorist, that the disturbances began in roughly the same mostly black area, and that the local police ultimately lost control of an angry and violent crowd.

The similarities across riots indicate to Sears that the conditions for many inner-city blacks have not improved and that black-white tensions still run very high. In fact, global economic trends have resulted in dwindling job opportunities for blacks living in the South Central area. Moreover, the issue of mistreatment by white police officers remains a real issue for blacks. Also, while racial discrimination has been outlawed, the persistence of prejudice and an unsympathetic attitude of whites toward health and welfare funding, school integration and affirmative action programs leaves many blacks feeling uneasy about their relations with whites and society's institutions.

The 1992 riot is different, according to Sears, in the involvement of

Latino rioters and the specific targeting of Korean businesses. These new trends reflect changing demographics in South Central Los Angeles and the fact that the economic decline of the area is placing ethnic and racial groups in conflict and competition.

Sears concludes by stating that the 1992 riots underscore the economic difficulties faced by U.S. cities. High-paying job opportunities continue to decline, and state and federal assistance is severely limited. Sears notes that an important lesson to be learned is, once again, the serious problems facing blacks in American society, such as the presence of a large underclass and continuing black-white tensions.

Lessons for the Urban Future

Clearly, there are lessons to be learned from the Los Angeles riots. The findings reported in this book have future relevance, since Los Angeles and other U.S. cities are now struggling with the factors that led to the outbreak of violence. That is, the presence of an underclass, black-white tensions and a rise in inter-ethnic hostilities are realities of modern urban life. City leaders face difficult odds in addressing these problems, as they see job opportunities dwindle through economic restructuring, the flight of the middle class to the suburbs, and limited assistance from state and federal governments facing budget deficits. In this section, I will briefly summarize what we have learned about the riot's causes, what actually took place and the consequences of the riots. Then, I will offer suggestions for avoiding future riots, and point to long-term solutions for U.S. cities and race relations.

Several causes were found for the Los Angeles riots. There was the presence of a large number of inner-city black youths living in a state of chronic unemployment, violence and despair. There were highly visible instances of white injustices toward blacks, involving dramatic actions by the police and court system. Last, demographic changes occurred in the South central area, in the form of a decline in high-wage job opportunities and an increase in Asian and Hispanic immigrants. As a result of demographic changes, there were repeated episodes of inter-ethnic conflict.

The Los Angeles riots were a series of destructive outbursts. They began with black crowds expressing outrage over the trial verdicts, followed by black youth violence against the police and white motorists, and then escalating into the burning and looting of buildings. South Central rioters also targeted Korean-owned businesses, with whom they had unrelated but very serious grievances. Hispanic immigrants later joined with blacks in the riots, and their large numbers and poverty made them major participants in the looting.

All of consequences of the Los Angeles riots are not yet known. The coalition of white liberals and blacks that has dominated Los Angeles politics has lost some power. In the mayor's office, a white Republican conservative replaced a black Democratic liberal. But the biracial coalition has also had some victories. Voters approved a police reform measure that increased civilian control. Moreover, in the Los Angeles Police Department, a black official from Philadelphia replaced the white police chief. As for the court system, the jury's verdict in the Rodney King beating trial seems to have had a noticeable impact. Recent trials involving the Rodney King beating and related incidents in Los Angeles seem to have paid more attention to the representation of racial and ethnic minority groups in the selection of jury members.

As for the economic impacts, soon after the riots ended, elected officials and corporate leaders launched the "Rebuild LA" effort. This was an attempt to attract the private sector to invest in the South Central area devastated by fires and looting, and to bring economic vitality back to a community that is facing a long-term economic decline. It was also a painful admission that the state and federal government, in today's fiscal climate, could not afford the financial commitments that are essential. Thus far, the much-needed progress toward short-term rebuilding and long-term recovery in the South Central area has been painfully slow.

It is impossible to measure the indirect economic effects of the Los Angeles riots. This is a region that has been hard hit with several difficulties at once, including a decline in military and defense employment, corporate downsizing, relocations, traffic congestion, air pollution, fires and, most recently, earthquakes. However, it is obvious that Southern California has had enormous job losses in the 1990s and has lagged behind the rest of the nation in the recent economic recovery. Tourism has slowed and foreign investors seem to have cooled to the idea of owning property in the Los Angeles area. The image of Los Angeles as a futuristic "global city" seems to have been placed in jeopardy.

In my opinion, there are other consequences, as voters and politicians have been applying the lessons they thought they learned from the Los Angeles riots.

In public opinion polls taken after the riots, most Los Angeles, Orange County and San Francisco Bay Area residents admitted that they were jittery about race relations and worried about future riots. Crime and illegal immigration have moved toward the top of the list of voter concerns. Politicians have responded to voters by proposing tougher sentences for criminals, such as "Three Strikes" legislation for serious repeat offenders. There were also calls for increased patrols of the U.S.-Mexico border, immigration policy reforms, and a "Save Our State" ballot initiative which would deprive illegal immigrants of government services.

Given what we have learned from the Los Angeles riots, I would like to offer suggestions for avoiding future episodes. A most important lesson is that we should not be surprised, as many were in Los Angeles in 1992, by the recurrence of riots. Civil unrest could be a part of the urban future, and cities where riots have taken place in the 1960s are not immune. The necessary ingredients for unrest in the 1990s are present in many U.S. cities, including a minority underclass, black-white tensions and inter-ethnic hostilities.

As for limiting the possibilities of future riots, there are three important and challenging tasks. First, we must move the inner-city underclass out of its poverty. Second, white injustices towards blacks need to be reduced. Third, positive relations between the inner-city minority groups should be encouraged.

I next offer some policy recommendations for the long-term issues facing U.S. cities and race relations. These proposals seek to go beyond the recent discussion of solutions, such as tougher criminal sentencing and stricter immigration controls, which fall short of addressing the root causes of urban problems.

First, a major public investment is needed to change the conditions of the inner-city underclass. This involves education, job training, redevelopment, housing, health and welfare. It could also mean that some inner city minority residents will need to be relocated to housing adjacent to suburban employment. Efforts such as "Rebuild LA" will not suffice. Real change will require substantial financial resources over a long period from federal and state governments.

Second, many institutions should work to reduce black-white tensions. Diversity training by schools and employers would help to discourage prejudice. Policies to increase the racial representation of trial juries would increase trust in the courts. Community policing in minority neighborhoods and citizen input in police policies would help to build better race relations.

Finally, comprehensive efforts are needed to reduce inter-ethnic hostilities. Community dialogues are a critical first step to understanding. However, these efforts should be followed by programs to increase voter participation, political representation, employment opportunities and business development. Public investment in efforts which will encourage better inter-ethnic relations will go a long way toward improving the future of U.S. cities.

References

Abbott, Carl. 1993. *The Metropolitan Frontier.* Tucson: University of Arizona Press.

Baldassare, Mark. 1986. *Trouble in Paradise: The Suburban Transformation of America.* New York: Columbia University Press.

Baldassare, Mark. 1992. "Suburban communities." *Annual Review of Sociology* 18:475-94.

Baldassare, Mark. 1994. *Suburban Communities: Change and Policy Responses.* Greenwich, CT: JAI Press.

Blalock, Hubert M., Jr. 1979. *Black-White Relations in the 1980s: Toward a Long-Term Policy.* New York: Praeger.

Blauner, Robert. 1989. *Black Lives, White Lives: Three Decades of Race Relations in America.* Berkeley: University of California Press.

Cohen, Nathan. 1970. *The Los Angeles Riots: A Socio-Psychological Study.* New York: Praeger.

Cohen, Jerry and William Murphy, 1966. *Burn, Baby, Burn.* New York: Dutton.

Crump, Spencer. 1966. *Black Riot in Los Angeles.* Los Angeles: Trans-Anglo Books.

Davis, Mike. 1992. *City of Quartz: Excavating the Future of Los Angeles.* New York: Vintage Books.

De La Garza, Rodolfo O. 1987. *Ignored Voices: Public Opinion Polls and the Latino Community.* Austin, Tx.: University of Texas Press.

Farley, Reynolds and William H. Frey. 1994. "Changes in the segregation of whites from Blacks." *American Sociological Review* 59: 23-45.

Feagin, Joe R. 1991. "The continuing significance of race: Antiblack discrimination in public places. *American Sociological Review* 56: 101-116.

Fogelson, Robert. 1969. *Mass Violence in America: the Los Angeles Riots.* New York: Arno Press.

Frey, William H. 1993a. "The new urban revival in the United States." *Urban Studies* 30: 741-74.

Frey, William H. 1993b. "Race, class and poverty polarization across metro areas: Population shifts and migration dynamics." Population Studies Center Research Reports No. 93-293. University of Michigan: Ann Arbor, Mich.

Frey, William H. 1993c. "Interstate migration and immigration for whites and minorities, 1985-1990: The emergence of multi-ethnic states." Population Studies Center Research Reports No. 93-297. University of Michigan: Ann Arbor, Mich.

Frey, William H. and Reynolds Farley. 1993. "Latino, Asian and Black segregation in multi-ethnic metro areas: Findings from the 1990 census." Population Studies Center Research Reports No. 93-278. University of Michigan: Ann Arbor, Mich.

Galster, George C. and Edward W. Hill. 1992. *The Metropolis in Black and White: Place, Power and Polarization.* New Brunswick, N.J.: Center for Urban Policy Research.

Gooding-Williams, Robert. 1993. *Reading Rodney King, Reading Urban Uprising.* New York: Routledge.

Hazen, Dan. 1992. *Inside the L.A. Riots*. New York: Institute for Alternative Journalism.

Jaynes, Gerald David and Robin M. Williams, Jr. 1989. *A Common Destiny: Blacks and American Society*. National Academy Press: Washington, D.C.

Kasarda, John D. 1988. "Economic restructuring and America's urban dilemma." Pp. 56-84 in Mattei Dogan and John D. Kasarda (editors). *The Metropolis Era, Volume I: A World of Giant Cities*. Beverly Hills, Ca.: Sage Publications.

Kasarda, John D. 1993. "Inner-city poverty and economic access. Pp. 4-1 to 4-60 in Jack Sommer and Donald A. Hicks (Editors). *Rediscovering Urban America: Perspectives on the 1980s*. Washington D.C.: U.S. Department of Housing and Urban Development.

Kelly, Barbara. 1989. *Suburbia Re-examined*. New York: Greenwood Press.

Kluegel, James R. 1990. "Trends in whites' explanations of the Black-White gap in SES." *American Sociological Review* 55: 512-525.

Light, I. 1988. "Los Angeles." Pp. 56-96 in Mattei Dogan and John D. Kasarda (Editors). *The Metropolis Era, Volume II: Mega-Cities*. Beverly Hills, Ca.: Sage Publications.

Los Angeles Times. 1992. *Understanding the Riots*. Los Angeles: Times Mirror.

Massey, Douglas S. and Nancy A. Denton. 1987. "Trends in the residential segregation of Blacks, Hispanics and Asians: 1970-1980." *American Sociological Review* 52:802-825.

Massey, Douglas S. and Nancy A. Denton. 1989. "Hypersegregation in U.S. metropolitan areas: Black and Hispanic segregation along five dimensions." *Demography* 26:373-91.

Massey, Douglas S. and Nancy A. Denton. 1993. *American Apartheid: Segregation and the Making of the Underclass*. Cambridge, Mass.: Harvard University Press.

Oberschall, Anthony. 1968. "The Los Angeles riot of August 1965." *Social Problems* 15: 322-341.

Pettigrew, Thomas. 1971. *Racially Separate or Racially Together?* New York: McGraw-Hill.

Pettigrew, Thomas. 1980. *The Sociology of Race Relations: Reflection and Reform*. New York: Free Press.

Pettigrew, Thomas. 1985. "New Black-White Patterns: How to best conceptualize them?" *Annual Review of Sociology* 11: 329-346.

Portes, Alejandro and Alex Stepick. 1993. *City on the Edge: The Transformation of Miami*. Berkeley, Ca.: University of California Press.

Sassen, Saskia. 1990. "Economic restructuring and the American city." *Annual Review of Sociology* 16:465-90.

Sassen, Saskia. 1991. *The Global City: New York, London, Tokyo*. Princeton, N.J.: Princeton University Press.

Sassen, Saskia. 1994. *Cities in a World Economy*. Thousand Oaks, Ca.: Pine Forge Press.

Schuman, Howard, Charlotte Steeh and Lawrence Bobo. 1985. *Racial Attitudes in America: Trends and Interpretations*. Cambridge, Mass.: Harvard University Press.

Scott, Allen J. 1988. *Metropolis: From the Division of Labor to Urban Form*. Berkeley, Ca.: University of California Press.

Sears, David and John McConahay, 1973. *The Politics of Violence: The New Urban Blacks and the Watts Riot*. Boston: Houghton Mifflin.

Sigelman, Lee and Susan Welch. 1991. *Black Americans' Views of Racial Inequality*. New York: Cambridge University Press.

Sonenshein, Raphael J. 1993. *Politics in Black and White: Race and Power in Los Angeles*. Princeton, N.J.: Princeton University Press.

Wilson, William J. 1978. *The Declining Significance of Race: Blacks and Changing American Institutions*. Chicago: University of Chicago Press.

Wilson, William J. 1987. *The Truly Disadvantaged: The Inner City, The Underclass and Public Policy*. Chicago: University of Chicago Press.

2

A Riot of Color:
The Demographic Setting

Peter A. Morrison and Ira S. Lowry

When the police officers who beat Rodney King were exonerated by a predominantly white suburban jury on April 29, 1992, street corner disturbances immediately erupted in two black neighborhoods of South Central Los Angeles. Within a few hours, these disturbances escalated into a three-day riot that damaged people and property over an area of almost 60 square miles. Since then, these three days of mob violence, arson, and looting in Los Angeles have usually been represented in the press and other public forums as a political protest by blacks against manifest injustice to a fellow black, brutally mistreated by white police officers. However, a careful look at the sequence of events and the actual participants in terms of race and ethnicity suggests that this view greatly oversimplifies and misrepresents the civil tensions that erupted on April 29, 1992. Although whites who happened to be in the wrong place at the wrong time were harassed and beaten, the truly systematic targets of violence were retail establishments, ranging from neighborhood convenience stores to discount houses and supermarkets; Korean shopkeepers were especially at risk. And over half of those arrested by the Los Angeles police during six days of civil disturbance were Hispanic, not black.

In this chapter we adopt a demographic perspective on this "riot of color" that engulfed selected parts of metropolitan Los Angeles while leaving most of the area unscathed. Although demographic factors cannot "explain" riots, they are one salient, quantifiable facet of the tensions and processes that fuel them. An understanding of the demographic setting can sharpen social science interpretations of civil unrest in cities and how it propagates.

Our analysis suggests that the local demographic setting in this

19

instance was ripe for unrest. Ethnic tensions existed, and a large percentage of youthful men in the area were at liberty to participate. In the following pages, we consider how (1) disparate rates of population growth and the succession of ethnic groups within neighborhoods set the stage for competition and conflict, and (2) the population's distinctive economic and family circumstances augmented the supply of potential participants, whose involvement sustained the anarchy for several days.

Chronology of the Riot

For readers unfamiliar with the three-day civil disturbance that is the subject of this book, we provide a brief chronology. It draws heavily on a story in the *Los Angeles Times* for July 5, 1992, and from the *Times's* subsequent book, *Understanding the Riots* (*Los Angeles Times* Staff, 1992). Evans (1993) presents related information.

The first two recorded incidents took place in South Central Los Angeles on Wednesday afternoon, April 29, shortly after the King verdict was announced by the media. Both occurred in neighborhoods that are solidly black and generally prosperous: Hyde Park (near Crenshaw Boulevard and Florence Avenue in Figure 2.1) and the intersection of Florence and Normandie Avenue. Hyde Park especially stands out as a prosperous and stable black neighborhood: 85 percent of its residents in 1990 were black, median household income was $24,886, nearly 64 percent of the dwellings were owner-occupied homes, the unemployment rate was only 6.4 percent, and the crime rate was 86 per thousand residents as compared with 127 for South Central as a whole.

At 3:43 p.m., the police received a report that a young man at the corner of West 67th Street and 11th Avenue in Hyde Park had thrown a brick at a passing pickup truck. Others joined the attack on moving vehicles, then went on to beat a white pedestrian and throw him in a dumpster. A crowd soon assembled and moved toward shops and markets a few blocks away, where the looting began.

The second disturbance was reported at 4:17 at Normandie and Florence. Here also, blacks pelted passing vehicles with stones and broken concrete, dragged light-skinned motorists from their vehicles, then robbed and beat them. Police responding to emergency calls retreated under a fusillade of rocks and bottles. At 6:30, an 18-wheel truck hauling 27 tons of sand blundered into the intersection. Its white driver, Reginald Denny, was pulled from his cab and beaten nearly to death while TV cameras recorded the scene. Denny was finally rescued by several black men and women who got him back into the cab of his truck and drove it to Freeman Memorial Hospital.

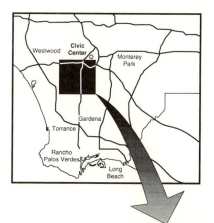

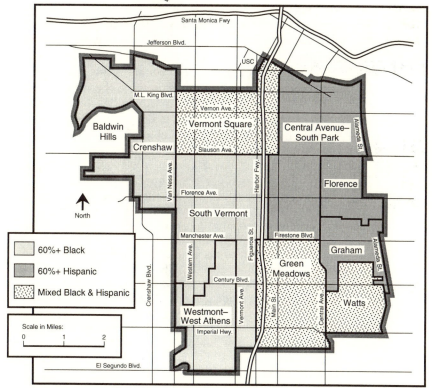

FIGURE 2.1 Neighborhoods of South Central Los Angeles (*Source:* RAND #414-03-0593)

The only focused political protest of the day occurred in front of police headquarters (Parker Center), demanding Chief Darryl Gates's resignation. About 6 p.m., several hundred demonstrators carrying signs gathered at Parker Center, over four miles northeast of the disturbances in South Central. Many of the demonstrators were white; signs identified representatives of the Progressive Labor Party and the Revolutionary Community Party. When the crowd began to break the windows of Parker Center, a police cordon forced the demonstrators back; the crowd turned down 1st Street, smashing automobiles and storefronts.

By 10 p.m., emergency calls were reaching the Los Angeles Police Department from all over South Central, and the violence had spread north to mixed black-and-Hispanic neighborhoods between the Santa Monica Freeway and Pico Boulevard. The Highway Patrol closed exit ramps on the major roadway through the riot area, the Harbor Freeway, hoping to prevent motorists from blundering into the chaos of the surface streets. Mayor Tom Bradley declared a local state of emergency and Governor Pete Wilson ordered the National Guard to activate 2,000 reserves.

In South Central, crowds roamed the streets, smashing, burning, and looting throughout the night. Hispanic residents of the area joined in, and people of all ages picked over the merchandise of burned-out stores. On Thursday, a particularly senseless orgy of violence occurred in Watts; as reported by the *Los Angeles Times*,

> About 200 blacks and Latinos smashed through the gates of the Watts Labor Community Action Committee, an anti-poverty organization that had brought jobs and social services to Watts after the 1965 riots. Inside, armed staff members held off the rioters—for maybe five minutes. Then looters chased them down Central Avenue, shooting, and set the complex on fire.
>
> Sixteen vehicles used to ferry Watts residents to shopping centers and medical offices were burned or vandalized. The offices were reduced to a pile of charcoal between roofless walls. Also destroyed were the contents of the commercial center—including a coin laundry, toy store, youth enterprise project, furniture and appliance shop, and food stamp office. Earnings from the commercial center helped pay for a homeless shelter, job training center and a senior citizens' housing project.[1]

Also on Thursday, the rioters literally mobilized. Carloads of young men from South Central sped up Western and Vermont avenues into Koreatown, the area between Pico and Santa Monica boulevards where most of the county's Koreans live. During the night, Korean vigilantes had organized to protect their shops and warehouses, erecting barricades and mounting armed guards. Though they were able to repel some assaults, by nightfall minimalls as far north as Santa Monica Boulevard and as far west as Fairfax Avenue were burned and looted. According to newspaper accounts, the looters came from all over Los Angeles once the word had spread that merchandise was available without payment; but Hispanic residents of Koreatown and Pico-Union (just east of Koreatown), being already on the scene, carried off most of the goods. Over the weekend, some looters had second thoughts, whether of conscience or of possible police inquiries. They moved the looted furniture and television sets from their dwellings to some anonymous alley or curb, or to depots established by civic groups for this purpose.

By Friday morning, the National Guard was in place and the worst violence was contained, though looting continued throughout the day. There were also minor disturbances in other areas of the county where blacks and Hispanics were locally concentrated, but the tide of violence receded. The riot was over.

Spatial Patterns of Ethnic Succession in Los Angeles

Territorially based ethnic tension is endemic in California, especially metropolitan Los Angeles. The region's ethnic and racial diversity has been fueled by a substantial influx of immigrants, and the area known as South Central Los Angeles underwent a rapid succession of ethnic groups during the 1980s. By 1990, residential settlement patterns presented a complex mixture of intermingling and separation along racial and ethnic lines, as depicted in the series of maps shown in Figs. 2.2 and 2.3. (These maps were prepared by Professor William Bowen, Department of Geography, California State University, Northridge, and are used with his permission.)

Residential patterns have transformed economic relationships among various groups in the population. Groups once the majority of inhabitants in certain areas were by 1990 just one of several minorities there. In Los Angeles County as a whole, ethnically non-Hispanic whites ("Anglos"), previously the majority of the population, had become a numerical "minority" by 1990. Their waning presence resulted mostly from Hispanic and Asian immigration, furthered to a degree by an exodus of whites from the area (see Table 2.1). During the 1980s, the county's Anglo population decreased by 8.5 percent; the Hispanic population increased by 62 percent and the Asian population by 110 percent. The non-Hispanic black population increased by less than 1 percent. (Census data distinguish "black" as a racial classification and "Hispanic" as an ethnic one. About 6 percent of persons who

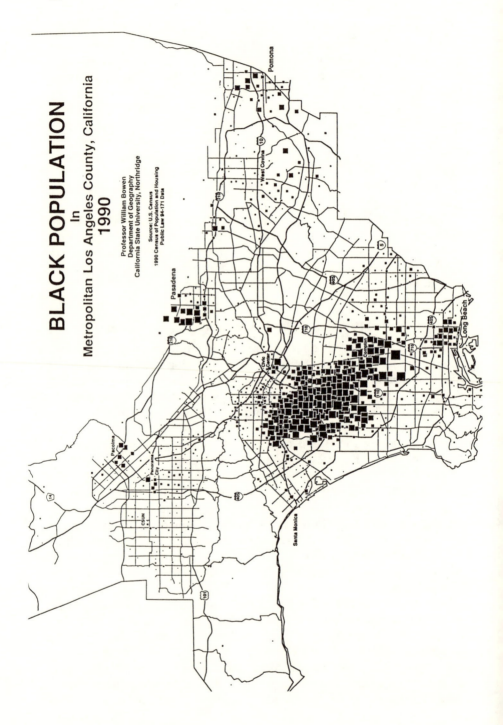

BLACK POPULATION
In
Metropolitan Los Angeles County, California
1990

Professor William Bowen
Department of Geography
California State University, Northridge

Source: U.S. Census
1990 Census of Population and Housing
Public Law 94-171 Data

25

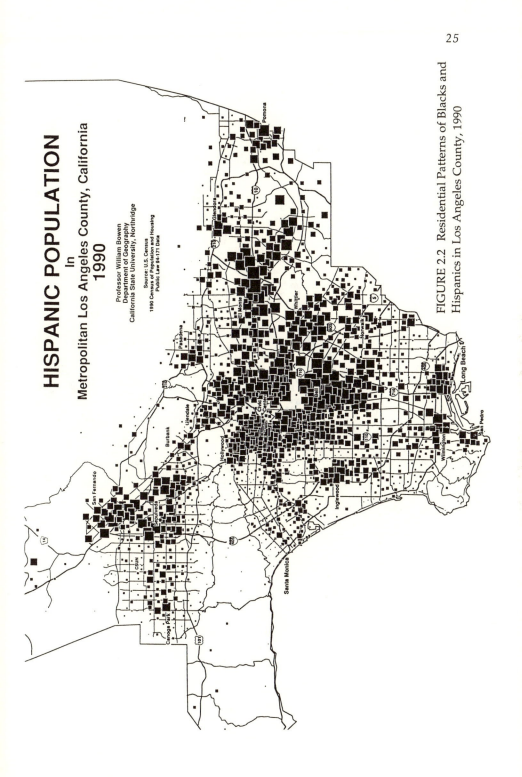

FIGURE 2.2 Residential Patterns of Blacks and Hispanics in Los Angeles County, 1990

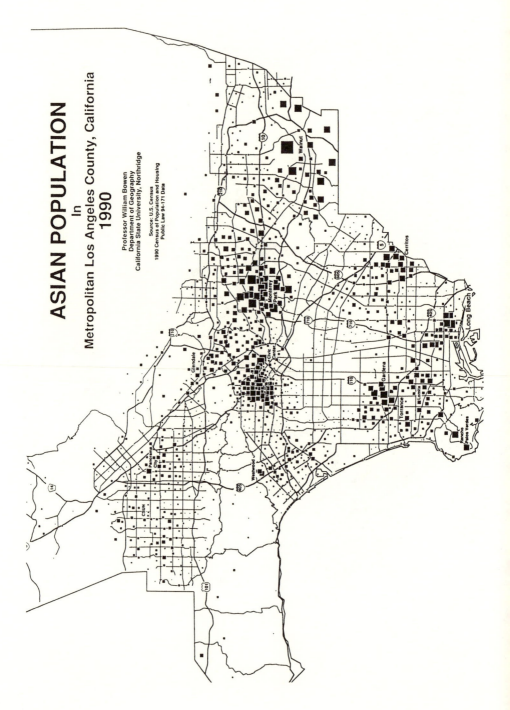

ASIAN POPULATION
In
Metropolitan Los Angeles County, California
1990

Professor William Bowen
Department of Geography
California State University, Northridge

Source: U.S. Census
1990 Census of Population and Housing
Public Law 94-171 Data

27

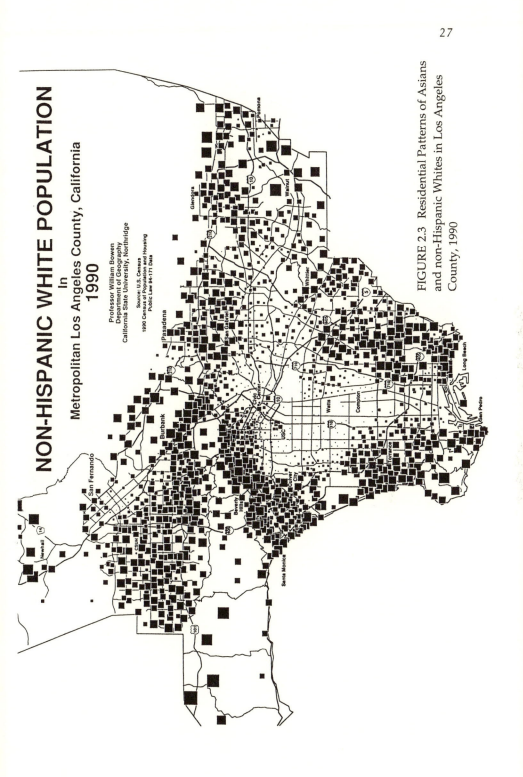

FIGURE 2.3 Residential Patterns of Asians and non-Hispanic Whites in Los Angeles County, 1990

TABLE 2.1   Ethnic Succession in Los Angeles County, 1980–1990

Racial or Ethnic Classification	Number of Inhabitants		Percent Change	Percent of All Inhabitants	
	1980	1990		1980	1990
Los Angeles County					
Non-Hispanic White	3,953,603	3,618,850	(8.47)	52.9	40.8
Black	943,968	992,974	5.19	12.6	11.2
Non-Hispanic Black	926,360	934,776	0.91	12.4	10.5
American Indian, Eskimo, and Aleut	48,120	45,508	(5.43)	0.6	0.5
Asian and Pacific Islander	455,415	954,485	109.59	6.1	10.8
Chinese	93,747	245,033	161.38	1.3	2.8
Filipino	99,043	219,653	121.78	1.3	2.5
Japanese	116,543	129,736	11.32	1.6	1.5
Korean	60,618	145,431	139.91	0.8	1.6
Other	85,464	214,632	151.14	1.1	2.4
Hispanic origin	2,066,103	3,351,242	62.20	27.6	37.8
Total Inhabitants[a]	7,477,517	8,863,164	18.53	100.0	100.0

[a]Detail does not add exactly to total because some Asians and Pacific Islanders and some American Indians are counted as Hispanic and some Hispanics identified their race only as "Other." The discrepancy is less than 1 percent of the total population.
Source: Tables prepared by Eugene Turner and James P. Allen, Department of Geography, California State University, Northridge. Their tables are based primarily in STF-1 (complete count) records of the 1980 and 1990 Censuses of Population.

reported themselves as "black" also reported themselves as "Hispanic." Most are Spanish-speaking immigrants from Caribbean countries.)

Black Residential Diffusion

Like many other urban areas outside the South, Los Angeles acquired a sizable black population during and after World War II (see DeGraaf, 1962). During the 1940s and 50s, Southern blacks left impoverished rural origins for industrial employment opportunities; later, the decline of industrial employment in the metropolitan Midwest prompted urban blacks to pursue their fortunes in the West. From 1940 to 1990, the black population of Los Angeles

County quintupled to about 993,000 persons, concentrated in an area about 6.5 miles wide and 18 miles long. The earliest area of black settlement (and still its focus) is South Central Los Angeles, shown in Figure 2.1.

By 1990, a further transformation was apparent. Statewide, black population growth had moderated relative to past decades, and increasing numbers of blacks were leaving Los Angeles County. The magnitude of black net outmigration from the county was so substantial that it offset much of the black population's natural increase there. During the 1980s, black population increased a mere 5 percent countywide, less than a third as fast as the nonblack population.

Within Los Angeles County, the pattern of black settlement also changed. During the 1980s, blacks moved away from South Central neighborhoods, settling in Inglewood and Hawthorne to the west and in Downey, Paramount, and Long Beach to the southeast. These residential shifts reflect upward social mobility, for the most part, as those blacks who prospered moved to better housing and better neighborhoods. Still, South Central remained home to some 278,000 non-Hispanic black residents in 1990, 53 percent of the area's population (see Table 2.2).

Hispanic Residential Succession

As blacks moved out, Hispanics moved in. During the 1980s, immigration from Mexico and Central America combined with high rates of natural increase to swell the county's already large Hispanic population by 60 percent. By 1990, Hispanics had become the dominant ethnic group in the northeastern half of South Central Los Angeles (see Figure 2.1). Just west of downtown, the Pico-Union district also became a Hispanic enclave, populated mostly by Salvadoran immigrants as shown in Figure 2.4.

Enlargement of Asian Enclaves

The Asian population of Los Angeles County more than doubled during the 1980s, but from a much smaller base than the groups discussed above. Most of this growth derived from immigration and infused the county with linguistic, cultural, and religious diversity. The newcomers came mostly from China, the Philippines, Korea, and Japan; they ranged from destitute "boat people" to wealthy business people.

The scattered communities where these Asian immigrants have settled form a mosaic whose pieces reflect commonalities of cultural and ethnic origin. These enclaves nearly encircle the black/Hispanic

TABLE 2.2 Ethnic Composition of Neighborhoods in South Central Los Angeles, 1990

| | | | | Racial and Ethnic Status | | | |
| | | | | | Other Non-Hispanic | | |
Neighborhood	Non-Hispanic Black	Hispanic Black	Other Hispanic	White	Asian-Pacific Islander	Other[a]	All Persons
Number of persons:							
Crenshaw	54,683	1,761	9,095	1,794	2,041	532	69,956
Vermont Square	33,986	1,899	32,926	526	717	391	70,445
South Vermont	62,530	2,062	28,683	1,379	593	561	95,808
Westmont-W. Athens	27,641	544	10,728	494	372	124	39,903
Central Ave.-S. Park	38,102	3,435	63,592	852	944	477	107,402
Watts	18,260	579	13,101	98	13	107	32,158
Green Meadows	30,153	1,319	18,237	429	97	155	50,390
Florence	4,502	547	29,057	367	87	112	34,672
Graham	8,356	217	13,522	208	25	147	22,475
Total, South Central	278,213	12,363	218,941	6,147	4,889	2,656	523,209
Percent of all persons:							
Crenshaw	78.2	2.5	13.0	2.6	2.9	0.8	100.0
Vermont Square	48.2	2.7	46.7	0.7	1.0	0.6	100.0
South Vermont	65.3	2.2	29.9	1.4	0.6	0.6	100.0
Westmont-W. Athens	69.3	1.4	26.9	1.2	0.9	0.3	100.0
Central Ave.-S. Park	35.5	3.2	59.2	0.8	0.9	0.4	100.0
Watts	56.8	1.8	40.7	0.3	0.0	0.3	100.0
Green Meadows	59.8	2.6	36.2	0.9	0.2	0.3	100.0
Florence	13.0	1.6	83.8	1.1	0.3	0.3	100.0
Graham	37.2	1.0	60.2	0.9	0.1	0.7	100.0
Total, South Central	53.2	2.4	41.8	1.2	0.9	0.5	100.0

[a]Includes American Indian, Eskimo, Aleut, and other.

Source: Tabulation prepared by A. F. Abrahamse (RAND) from Census of Population, 1990, STF-3.

Note: According to the Bureau of the Census, "black" is a racial classification and "Hispanic" is an ethnic classificaiton. About 4.3 percent of South Central residents who reported themselves as "black" also reported themselves as "Hispanic." Most are Spanish-speaking immigrants from Carribean countries. Most Hispanics report their race as either "white" or "other."

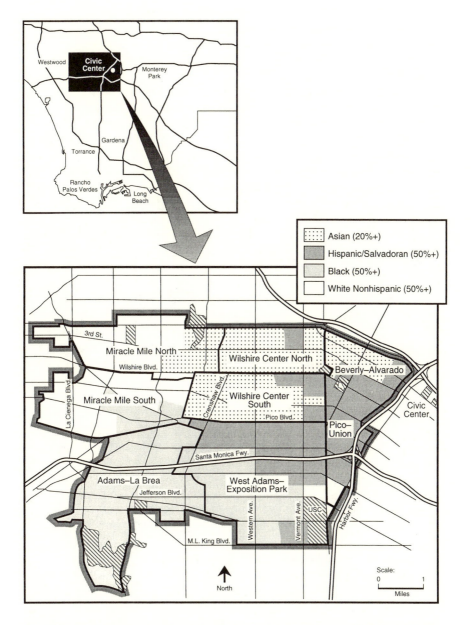

FIGURE 2.4 Neighborhoods of the Wilshire District (*Source:* RAND #414-05-0593)

core of Los Angeles County, but do not overlap that core (see Figure 2.3). Indeed, only 1 percent of South Central's population is Asian. Elsewhere in the county, Asians collectively constitute only a minority of all residents. (Less than 1 percent of the 1,600 census tracts in Los Angeles County had Asian majorities in 1990.)

Koreatown, in the Wilshire District about three miles north of South Central, is of special interest because it was a major target for arson and looting during the 1992 riot. Koreatown's identity derives less from its numbers of Korean residents than from the heavy investment Koreans have made there in commercial enterprises along Wilshire Boulevard and Western and Vermont avenues. The Wilshire District, shown in Figure 2.4, has about 74,000 Asian residents, mostly in the eastern part: Beverly-Alvarado, Wilshire Center North, and Wilshire Center South (see Table 2.3). In the area we have designated Koreatown, about 60 percent of the Asian population is Korean and 28 percent Filipino; most of the rest is Chinese or Japanese.

Just east of Koreatown is the county's principal community of Salvadorans, centered on Pico-Union. Here, virtually all the census tracts populated by substantial numbers of Asians actually have larger numbers of Hispanics.

The western part of the Wilshire District also suffered riot damage. It consists of a non-Hispanic white neighborhood, Miracle Mile North; a mixed black-and-white neighborhood, Miracle Mile South; and a heavily black neighborhood, Adams-La Brea. The area between Koreatown and South Central is West Adams-Exposition Park, a mixed black and Hispanic neighborhood.

Ethnic Tension

The pattern of ethnic succession in this part of Los Angeles County reveals territorial competition and potential underlying tensions between groups (see Oliver and Johnson, 1984). The black community of South Central Los Angeles may regard the incursion of Hispanics as "threatening" (since the latter now form a demographic majority in nearly half of the traditional black ghetto). During the past decade, black-Hispanic rivalry for political power and patronage jobs in Los Angeles County has often been reported by the press; ethnic tension in residential neighborhoods has been less apparent.

The relationship between blacks and Asians is very different. Asians are the most rapidly increasing racial group in Los Angeles County, but they have entered South Central Los Angeles economically only, not as residents. That is, Asians entered this territory as shopkeepers—Korean and Filipino owners of the multitude of

TABLE 2.3 Ethnic Composition of Neighborhoods in Wilshire District of Los Angeles, 1990

| | | | | Racial and Ethnic Status | | | |
| | | | | Other Non-Hispanic | | | |
Neighborhood	Non-Hispanic Black	Hispanic Black	Other Hispanic	White	Asian-Pacific Islander	Other[a]	All Persons
Number of Persons:							
Adams-La Brea	32,385	1,293	16,739	2,140	3,031	455	56,043
W. Adams-Exposition Pk	45,428	3,876	60,338	6,747	7,285	1,103	124,777
Beverly-Alvarado[b]	1,948	70	27,478	3,790	9,479	279	43,044
Pico-Union[b]	1,872	226	62,687	6,632	3,745	608	75,770
Miracle Mile North	1,570	116	2,368	32,726	2,575	80	39,435
Miracle Mile South	16,542	446	5,293	19,878	3,319	344	45,822
Wilshire Center North	5,341	368	26,774	12,191	21,895	403	66,972
Wilshire Center South	6,545	691	49,106	6,651	22,972	446	86,411
Total, Wilshire District	111,631	7,086	250,783	90,755	74,301	3,718	538,274
Percent of All Persons:							
Adams-LaBrea	57.8	2.3	29.9	3.8	5.4	0.8	100.0
W. Adams-Exposition Pk	36.4	3.1	48.4	5.4	5.8	0.9	100.0
Beverly-Alvarado[b]	4.5	0.2	63.8	8.8	22.0	0.6	100.0
Pico-Union[b]	2.5	0.3	82.7	8.8	4.9	0.8	100.0
Miracle Mile North	4.0	0.3	6.0	83.0	6.5	0.2	100.0
Miracle Mile South	36.1	1.0	11.6	43.4	7.2	0.8	100.0
Wilshire Center North	8.0	0.5	40.0	18.2	32.7	0.6	100.0
Wilshire Center South	7.6	0.8	56.8	7.7	26.6	0.5	100.0
Total, Wilshire District	20.7	1.3	46.6	16.9	13.8	0.7	100.0

[a]Includes American Indian, Eskimo, Aleut, and other.
[b]Parts of LACDRP Statistical Area 9.11 (Westlake-Downtown). Beverly-Alvarado contains Census Tract Nos. 2126, 2127, 2128, 2129, and 2131.

Source: Tabulation prepared by A. F. Abrahamse (RAND) from Census of Population, 1990, STF-3.
Note: According to the Bureau of the Census, "black" is a racial classification and "Hispanic" is an ethnic classification. About 4.3 percent of South Central resident who reported themselves as "black" also reported themselves as "Hispanic." Most are Spanish-speaking immigrants from Caribbean countries. Most Hispanics report their race as either "white" or "other."

convenience stores who work on the premises stocking shelves and ringing up sales—but made their homes outside South Central's traditional boundaries. Some Japanese, Chinese, and Koreans live inside the northern boundary of South Central, but their numbers are not increasing. However, a colony of 750 Cambodians recently settled in the Central Avenue-South Park neighborhood.

The Korean community in Los Angeles has emerged as an ethnic community engaged in small businesses (Lee, 1989; 1992). During the riots, blacks and Hispanics of South Central and Pico-Union jointly looted and burned retail establishments thought to be owned by Asians (especially Koreans) or non-Hispanic whites. Black and Latino shopkeepers hastened to label their storefronts (e.g., "BLACK-OWNED") or personally stood by to deflect rioters; most such establishments were spared, but some were heedlessly or accidentally torched. Manifestly, the Korean shopkeepers had nothing to do with the injustice of the jury's verdict in the King case, or with the harassment of blacks by white police. However, relations between blacks and Koreans had been especially tense ever since a Korean grocer in South Central killed a black teenager in 1991 during an argument about payment for merchandise. In both individual and crowd behavior, one grievance often revives another.

Who Rioted?

However widespread were the grievances of South Central's residents, it should be noted that the active participants in the riot were mostly adolescent and young adult males. The only available statistical descriptions of active participants are based on arrests. In Chapter 6, Petersilia and Abrahamse analyze riot-related arrest data they obtained. A year later, the *Los Angeles Times* reported the results of its analysis of 694 people convicted of riot-related felonies (more than 90 percent of them looters).

Many rioters were not arrested, of course, and we do not know how accurately arrestees reflect the composition of all participants. The statistics analyzed by Petersilia and Abrahamse exclude all juveniles and also adults processed through the courts of East Los Angeles, Downey, Culver City, Inglewood, and Compton. No arrest statistics were reported for April 29, the day the riots began—apparently because few arrests were made until the next day.

Petersilia and Abrahamse's data indicate that 88 percent of persons arrested for riot-related activity were male and 80 percent were between 18 and 34 years of age. They defined riot-related arrests to include charges of civil disturbance (curfew violation, disorderly conduct, false alarm, vandalism, trespassing, disturbing the peace, arson), traffic violations (driving under the influence, hit-and-run, etc.), drug possession or sale, and crimes against property (burglary, receiving stolen property, theft, auto theft, forgery, looting). Some of these crimes (e.g., driving under the influence) are quite common in ordinary times, but arrest rates for all were higher during the riot period.

The *Los Angeles Times* based its study on 694 probation reports sampled from nine courthouses across Los Angeles County. (See "Most Looters Endured Lives of Crime, Poverty," *Los Angeles Times*, May 2, 1993, pp. 1, 34-35.) It covers 43 percent of the riot-related felony cases concluded as of late April 1993. The *Times* cautions that its study "does not cover the thousands of rioters who were not arrested, nor those arrested on misdemeanor charges, usually curfew violations." The *Times* further notes that the participation of Latinos may be underrepresented because some were turned over to immigration authorities and not processed through the courts, and that the sample does not include juveniles, whose cases are not public. According to the *Times* data, 89 percent of the convicted felons were male and 50 percent were 25 or younger.

This concentration of young men will focus our further inquiry. Why were so many participants "available" here but not elsewhere in the county? How do young males in South Central differ from their counterparts elsewhere in the county? More generally, what demographic clues might inform a social science interpretation of how the riot propagated spatially?

Availability of Young Males

A first noteworthy feature of South Central Los Angeles is the abundance of young men at liberty to participate in civil disturbances. The 1990 census recorded nearly 90,000 male residents between the ages of 16 and 34, over 17 percent of South Central's total population and 59 percent of all working-age males (16 to 64 years of age). Although these fractions are similar for Los Angeles County as a whole, what distinguishes the young men in South Central is the large proportion who are neither in school nor employed.

The 1990 census data released so far do not enable us to focus exactly on the *young* males of interest here, but for males 16 and older, 42 percent were either unemployed or not in the labor force (see Table 2.4). (For the 16-34 age group, this proportion surely is higher, given what else we know.) In round numbers, then, we estimate that close to 50,000 men aged 16-34 were "available" to participate. That is, they were not obliged to show up at school or for work on the first

TABLE 2.4   Employment Status of Persons 16 Years and Older: Comparison of
Black and Hispanic Populations of South Central Los Angeles, 1990

Employment Status	Black		Hispanic	
	Male	Female	Male	Female
Number of Persons				
In labor force:				
In Armed Forces	118	24	59	0
Civilian:				
Employed	42,877	50,964	53,200	27,280
Unemployed	10,493	7,559	7,596	5,879
Not in labor force	37,335	62,670	14,531	34,741
Total	90,823	121,217	75,386	67,900
Percent of Total				
In labor force:				
In Armed Forces	0.1	0.0	0.1	0.0
Civilian:				
Employed	47.2	42.0	70.6	40.2
Unemployed	11.6	6.2	10.1	8.7
Not in labor force	41.1	51.7	19.3	51.2
Total	100.0	100.0	100.0	100.0

Source: Tabulated by A. F. Abrahamse (RAND) from Census of Population, 1990,
STF-3.
Note: Entries in this table include persons 65 years and older, few of whom are in
the labor force; however, the available data do not identify them separately by
sex and race or ethnicity.

full day (Thursday) following the initial evening of widespread
rioting. Consistent with this observation, the *Times* reports that
among the convicted felons it sampled, 66 percent were not employed
and 60 percent were high school dropouts.

Demographically, South Central Los Angeles was ripe for civil
disturbance: It contained a critical mass of young males who had no
regular occupation, little reason to feel bound by social rules, and the
physical energy needed to stone, loot, burn, and run from the police.
The jury's exoneration of the police who beat Rodney King triggered
the action, but the resulting explosion of human energy lacked
political focus. Both the recorded events and observers' descriptions
indicate that most participants were rioting for fun or profit, not as the
vanguard of a "rebellion" or "insurrection." Among the 694 convicted
felons, 60 percent had a prior arrest record, and half of these repeat

offenders had prior felony convictions; two of every five convicted felons had lived at their present address one year or less; another 11 percent were homeless or transients.

Socialization of Young Males

This relatively large pool of young males at liberty to assemble reflects both the lack of employment opportunities and individual choices. The former condition depends largely on the economy; the latter reflect behavioral norms, which can be reinforced or undermined by local economic conditions. Insofar as families instill those norms, our present interest centers on the types of family situations that prevail in South Central Los Angeles and among the *Times* sample of convicted felons.

The 1990 census describes the family situations only of the contemporary children from whom South Central's future population of youthful males will derive, but the data are revealing. Many of these children apparently lack adult supervision and persuasive adult role models. South Central is home to nearly 182,000 children under 18 years of age (see Table 2.5). The census shows about 44 percent living with both parents, 46 percent with one parent, and 10 percent with neither parent. Most single parents are mothers (82 percent), and more than half of all single parents work outside the home. Although children might have other adult male role models, only 52 percent actually live with their own fathers. Specifically:

- 38 percent of South Central's children aged 12-17 live in families where their mother is the only parent present (compared with 22 percent countywide);
- In families with children aged 18 and older present, 50 percent of those in South Central are headed by women with no husband present (compared with 31 percent countywide);
- South Central's children more often start out life in a one-parent family because they are born to women who have never been married. Fully 37 percent of the children born to women under age 35 have mothers who have never married (compared with 20 percent countywide).

The *Times* data on people convicted of riot-related felonies demonstrate a link to this demographic context. These data reveal that few of those who were arrested for felonies were members of two-parent families. Only 11 percent were themselves married; and of those still at home, twice as many lived with one parent as with both.

TABLE 2.5   Presence and Age of Children by Employment Status of Parents: South Central Los Angeles, 1990

Age of Child and Status of Parents	South Central L.A.		Los Angeles County	
	Number	Percent	Number	Percent
Under 18 years:				
Living with two parents:				
Both parents in labor force	37,771	20.8	827,805	35.6
Father only in labor force	33,407	18.4	610,735	26.3
Mother only in labor force	3,609	2.0	36,723	1.6
Neither parent in labor force	5,207	2.9	60,113	2.6
Total	79,994	44.1	1,535,376	66.0
Living with one parent:				
Living with father:				
In labor force	12,192	6.7	123,905	5.3
Not in labor force	2,916	1.6	17,282	0.7
Subtotal	15,108	8.3	141,187	6.1
Living with mother:				
In labor force	31,625	17.4	296,384	12.7
Not in labor force	37,019	20.4	198,329	8.5
Subtotal	68,644	37.8	494,713	21.3
Living with neither parent	17,817	9.8	154,834	6.7
All children under 18 years	181,563	100.0	2,326,110	100.0

Source: Tabulation prepared by A. F. Abrahamse (RAND) from Census of Population, 1990, STF-3.

Hispanic Participation

As the riot spread from its origins in black neighborhoods of South Central, it picked up new recruits—specifically, Hispanics who did not particularly share the black grievances but may have lacked allegiance to the established order. During six days of rioting, 51 percent of those arrested for riot-related crime were classified as Hispanic on their arrest records; 43 percent of the 694 convicted felons were classified as Latino. (Latinos may be underrepresented in the *Times* sample of convicted felons, since some were turned over to immigration authorities and not processed through the courts.) In every category of crime except illegal possession of firearms, Hispanic arrests exceeded black arrests. Nearly all arrestees, both Hispanic and black, were male, but the Hispanics were younger. About 60 percent of the Hispanic arrestees (but only 30 percent of the black arrestees) were between 18 and 24 years of age. (These arrest statistics exclude persons under 18 years of age.)

Although rigorous comparisons between arrest rates and populations at risk are not feasible, it appears to us that riot participation rates for young males (18 to 24 years) were about the same for blacks and Hispanics; the Hispanic population of South Central Los Angeles and nearby areas is heavily weighted with young adult males and has few males over 45. On the other hand, riot participation by older males seems to have been much more common among blacks than among Hispanics, given the populations at risk (see Table 2.6).

We are not sure of the reason for the different age pattern of black and Hispanic rioters, but we suspect that it is connected to family structure. Hispanics tend to marry young and have children soon after; domestic commitments may well limit the "availability" of all but the youngest Hispanic males for riot participation. Consistent with this hypothesis, over 60 percent of all Hispanic households in South Central are married couples; just 7 percent are composed entirely of unrelated individuals (usually single persons living alone). By comparison, only 28 percent of black households in South Central are married couples, and nearly a third are composed entirely of unrelated individuals (see Table 2.7). The latter group includes single males 25 to 34 years of age, whose participation in the riots was not constrained by family responsibilities. The 1990 census data available for this analysis did not include tabulations of household size by race, ethnicity, or sex, so we cannot confirm this hypothesis. Comparing the proportions of family and nonfamily households by age of head for a heavily black and a heavily Hispanic neighborhood lends some support to our interpretation.

Conclusions

In our view, the salient *preconditions* for South Central's riot were (1) territorially based ethnic tensions and (2) an abundance of young men with time on their hands. The *occasion* for the riot was an event of deep emotional significance to many inhabitants of South Central: the acquittal of white police who beat a black arrestee. The announcement of the verdict triggered several street-corner disturbances that under other circumstances might have been self-limiting or easily contained by competently organized police action. But on April 29, 1992, the disturbances flared into three days of arson, looting, and random violence.

Although some observers insist on describing the riot as a political statement—a "rebellion" against the white power structure —we find such a description misleading. Half of those participating in the riot were Latinos, not ethnically linked to Rodney King. The rioters' primary targets were not the property of or institutions

TABLE 2.6   Relative Incidence of Riot Arrests by Age and Ethnicity: Black and Hispanic Males, South Central Los Angeles, 1990–1992

| | Number of Persons | | Percent of Total | | Percent of Arrestees | | Relative Incidence | |
Age Interval	Black Male	Hispanic Male	Black Male	Hispanic Male	Black Male	Hispanic Male	Black Male	Hispanic Male
18 to 24 years	13,809	20,876	15.9	29.5	28.8	56.9	1.82	1.93
25 to 34 years	21,070	25,845	24.2	36.6	42.5	30.6	1.76	0.84
35 to 44 years	15,130	13,949	17.4	19.7	22.8	9.9	1.31	0.50
45+ years	36,987	9,989	42.5	14.1	5.9	2.6	0.14	0.18
Total	86,996	70,659	100.0	100.0	100.0	100.0	1.00	1.00

Source: Population counts are from the Census of Population, 1990, STF-3, for South Central Los Angeles. Arrests for riot-related crimes are based on records of the Los Angeles Municipal Court for 30 April through 5 May 1992.
Note: "Relative Incidence" is the ratio of arrestees to population, each measured as a percentage of the relevant total. It is the clearest indicator of riot participation rates by age, given the uncertainty of absolute values for both numerator and denominator.

TABLE 2.7 Comparison of Black and Hispanic Populations of South Central Los Angeles, 1990

	Percent of Households	
Item	Black	Hispanic
Household and Family Composition		
Family with own children:		
Married couple	11.2	51.5
Male head, no wife present	2.1	8.3
Female head, no husb present	18.7	14.8
Family without own children:		
Married couple	16.8	8.8
Male head, no wife present	3.4	5.2
Female head, no husb present	15.2	4.3
Nonfamily household[a]:	32.5	7.1
All households	100.0	100.0
Mean household size (persons)	2.78	5.28

[a]Consists of unrelated individuals or a person living alone—mostly the latter.
Source: Tabulations prepared by A. F. Abrahamse (RAND) from Census of Population, 1990, STF-3.
Note: About 6 percent of those who reported themselves as "black" also reported themselves as "Hispanic." Most are Spanish-speaking immigrants from Carribean countries.

controlled by the white power structure, but retail shops owned by Koreans. A number of establishments owned by blacks and Latinos were also trashed and looted. Probation reports on those convicted of riot-related felonies clearly indicate that looting was the primary motivation for most rioters who were caught; few were consciously "political."

Ethnically charged events, especially interethnic violence, defamatory speech, and commercial fraud, are common and perhaps inevitable features of a multiethnic society. But they seldom result in anything more than graffiti, a shouting match, or one-on-one violence. What made South Central ready for conflagration, we think, was a long accumulation of grievances against ethnically different neighbors who were accessible for reprisal, combined with the availability of a large pool of idle young men who had little stake in civil order.

Territorially Based Ethnic Tension

Territorially based ethnic tension is endemic in California and a number of other multiethnic states. In California, one of every four cities has no racial or ethnic majority; its population is composed of three large ethnic groups ("Anglo," Latino, black) and perhaps a dozen small ones (Filipinos, Koreans, Vietnamese, Hmong, Armenians, Iranians, etc.), each clustered residentially but in adjoining neighborhoods. The tides of immigration and assimilation continuously wash against the conventional boundaries of these neighborhoods, so that one's ethnic territory and ethnic identity are never entirely secure.

The salient aspects of ethnic difference include race, national origin, language, social customs, recency of arrival, and civil status (citizens, legally resident noncitizens, illegal residents). Though nearly all such groups are quick to adopt some of the values and lifestyles of the prevailing popular culture (as revealed by television) and to learn the prevailing language, most cling fiercely to their ethnic identities—that is, to their sense of a shared history and shared future that makes them responsible for each other's welfare. Ethnic identity has its roots in some historical community of people who inhabited a specific territory, developed a common language and culture, and practiced endogamy. The surprising feature of ethnic identity is its persistence for generations among those who left their homelands to mingle with other populations, as has been the case of immigrants to America (Lowry, 1982).

According to an idea articulated as early as 1782 and gaining currency throughout the 19th and early 20th centuries, America was destined to be a melting pot of immigrant ethnic groups, each losing its separate identity in a new blend that drew the best genetic and cultural qualities from its components (see Gordon, 1964, Chapter 5; Glazer and Moynihan, 1963; Yancey, Erickson, and Julian, 1976). The idea was so appealing to both the popular and scientific mind that contrary evidence was rarely noted. Yet, throughout our history, conspicuous divisions have persisted between blacks, Anglos, Asians, and Latinos; between Protestants, Catholics, and Jews; and between Irish, Italians, English, and other national-origin groups. The divisions are reflected in ethnic endogamy, voluntary associations, and exclusionary practices in employment, education, and housing.

Ethnic cohesion and residential clustering go together; but they are most likely to cause interethnic trouble when some ethnic populations are growing locally and others are shrinking—whether because of differential vital rates, in- and out-migration, or assimilation and upward social mobility. We have pointed out how the black ghetto of South Central has been reshaped by the numerical growth and territorial expansion of Los Angeles' Latino population, and nearly surrounded by a growing population of Asians who enter the ghetto as shopkeepers but live outside the area. This pattern of ethnic pressure on residential neighborhoods, less familiar than the black-on-white pressure that prompted the "white flight" to the suburbs in the 1960s, is a source of tension in other California cities as well as in Los Angeles.

Young Males with Time on Their Hands

South Central's large pool of young males, neither steadily employed nor in school, is a pattern repeated within other California cities. The daily lives of these youths include drug and alcohol abuse and frequent criminal enterprises. Among those convicted of riot-related felonies in Los Angeles County, 60 percent had criminal records and only a third were employed. Three-fifths were high school dropouts.

Young males of all ethnic groups have abundant physical energy and a taste for risky enterprises. An important function of the traditional family is to restrain this energy and channel it into socially useful activities. An important function of the economic system is to provide rewarding opportunities for socially useful activities. In South Central and elsewhere, families and the economy have jointly failed in these functions, leaving young males largely unprepared for adult life and responsibilities and for serious engagement in the world of work.

Regrettably, the failures of socialization and employment opportunities reinforce each other. South Central's family structure is weakened by the inability of adults to find jobs that will support an intact family; poorly socialized young men are generally the last and most reluctantly hired, and only when labor is scarce. Most reformers pin their hopes on education and job-training by public institutions, expecting them to take over the traditional family's now-abdicated responsibilities. But even this is probably too late.

Prognosis for More Riots

If, as we contend, territorially based ethnic tension is endemic in multiethnic states such as California and most cities contain a large pool of young idle males instantly available for vandalism and looting, we ought to expect more riots. We do, but only one per city.

We think that the Los Angeles riot of April 1992 could have been prevented by competently organized police action between the time of the initial disturbances and the general conflagration. To be sure, it is easy to criticize failed police tactics from the comfort of an academic armchair, but in this case it seems clear that the police command structure simply evaporated, leaving the troops in the field without guidance. The chief of police was attending a fund-raising party in Beverly Hills during the crucial hours, and none of his subordinates seemed willing to commit manpower to the trouble spots even though officers were assembled and ready for action.

Such a conspicuous breakdown usually has civic consequences. In this case, Los Angeles acquired a new police chief, and he meticulously prepared for the next likely riot flashpoint—the verdicts in the federal court trial of the police who beat Rodney King. Because two officers were found guilty of violating King's civil rights, black leaders declared a victory and there was no riot. But it was also clear that the police would respond quickly and much more effectively to street-corner disturbances this time around.

After a riot, many who participated have second thoughts. It is generally agreed that the damage inflicted by rioters to their own turf was a heavy blow to economic enterprise in South Central Los Angeles, and that it deprived the residents of access to convenient retail and financial services. Residents of South Central who did *not* riot—a clear majority—are unlikely to welcome a replay.

Incidents of interethnic violence or injustice will surely occur in the next few years, and some will result in street-corner disturbances. We doubt that these disturbances will flare again into a major riot. Before that can happen, Los Angeles must first forget what it learned this time.

Lessons from the L.A. Riot

If history carries any lessons here, they pertain to the two preconditions—ethnic tensions over territory and a critical mass of idle young men—that make areas like South Central ripe for conflagration. They are preconditions that all Californians must confront and address in the future, as the State's changing demographic complexion heightens ethnic identification with territory.

Today Los Angeles is one of only two among California's 58 counties where no single racial or ethnic group is the "majority" population. This ethnic mosaic consists of four large groups—Anglos, Hispanics, blacks, and Asians—or numerous small ones, since people actually identify themselves as Salvadorans, Filipinos, Koreans, Vietnamese, Hmong, Armenians, Iranians, and others. Typically, each group clusters residentially, often in neighborhoods that adjoin ethnically different territory.

Variants of this ethnic mosaic structure will emerge in ever more California counties during the 1990s. We estimate that 15 counties will have acquired this demographic complexion by 2010. On a statewide basis, California will have become a collection of "minorities," thereby outmoding that term. But vocabulary trails reality where local tides of immigration and assimilation wash against old neighborhood boundaries, challenging the established ethnic territory and identity. So long as ethnicity corresponds to geography, every "us" implies a "them."

Tension over turf will be a persistent feature of California's multi-ethnic society, but the tension could be peacefully managed under favorable circumstances. An important unfavorable circumstance is the presence, especially in low-income neighborhoods, of a large number of idle young males, neither steadily employed nor in school. Young males, whatever their ethnic identities, have energy and a taste for risky enterprises. Traditionally, their families have joined with schools and workplaces to restrain adventures and channel energy into gainful employment and subsequently into a recognized stake in a peaceful and safe community. All three of these institutions are visibly failing those functions, not just in South Central, but in low-income urban areas throughout the state. For those Californians who value both social justice and civil order, the prospects are bleak.

Notes

For a more extensive discussion, see the author's companion paper, "A Riot of Color: The Demographic Setting of Civil Disturbance in Los Angeles," RAND P-7819, presented at the session on "Racial Economic Inequality and Race Relations" which was presented at the annual Population Association of America meetings, Cincinnati, April 2, 1993. Views expressed here are the authors', not those of RAND or sponsors of its research.

1. *Understanding the Riots*, p. 81.

References

DeGraaf, Lawrence B., 1962. *Negro Migration to Los Angeles, 1930 to 1950*, doctoral dissertation, University of California, Los Angeles.

Evans, Caswell A., Jr., 1993. "Public Health Impact of the 1992 Los Angeles Civil Unrest," *Public Health Reports*, Vol. 108, No. 3, pp. 265–272.

Glazer, Nathan, and Daniel Patrick Moynihan,1963. *Beyond the Melting Pot*, The MIT Press and Harvard University Press, Cambridge, MA.

Gordon, Milton M., 1964. *Assimilation in American Life*, Oxford University Press, New York.

Lee, Dong Ok, 1989. *The Socio-Spatial Incorporation of New Immigrants in the Post-Industrial City: Korean Immigrant Enterpreneurs in Los Angeles*, doctoral dissertation, Department of Geography, University of Kentucky.

Lee, Dong Ok, 1992. "Commodification of Ethnicity: The Sociospatial Reproduction of Immigrant Entrepreneurs," *Urban Affairs Quarterly*, Vol. 28, No. 2, December pp. 258–275.

Levitan, Sar A., Richard S. Belous, and Frank Gallo, 1988. *What's Happening to the American Family?* rev. ed., Johns Hopkins University Press, Baltimore and London.

Los Angeles Times Staff, 1992. *Understanding the Riots, Los Angeles Times*, Los Angeles.

Lowry, Ira S., 1982. "The Science and Politics of Ethnic Enumeration," in Winston A. Van Horne (ed.), *Ethnicity and Public Policy*, University of Wisconsin System, Milwaukee, pp. 42–61.

Oliver, Melvin L. and James H. Johnson, Jr., 1984. "Inter-ethnic Conflict in an Urban Ghetto: The Case of Blacks and Latinos in Los Angeles," *Research in Social Movements, Conflict and Change*, Vol. 6, pp. 57–94.

Petersilia, Joan, and Allan Abrahamse, 1993. "The Los Angeles Riot of Spring, 1992: A Profile of Those Arrested," *Police Forum*, Vol. 3, No. 4, October pp. 1–12.

Turner, Eugene, and James P. Allen, 1990. *An Atlas of Population Patterns in Metropolitan Los Angeles and Orange Counties*, California State University, Northridge.

Yancey, William L., Eugene P. Erickson, and Richard N. Julian, 1976. "Emergent Ethnicity: A Review and Reformulation," *American Sociological Review*, Vol. 41, No. 3, June pp. 391–403.

3

Los Angeles Coalition Politics

Raphael J. Sonenshein

When an amateur cameraman captured Los Angeles police officers beating black motorist Rodney King on March 3, 1991, remarkable events unfolded within Los Angeles politics. The seemingly unassailable police department faced mounting calls to reform its practices. Within two years, a large group of the city's political leaders had left office, to be replaced by very different people. The most dramatic changes were the election of a new Republican mayor after twenty years of Democrat Tom Bradley's dominance, and the selection of an outside police chief to lead the previously closed LAPD. These surprising political developments were all influenced by the beating of Rodney King and the civil unrest of 1992.

The *politics* of the Rodney King case and of the urban violence that grew out of it provide an extraordinary window into the evolving coalition politics of Los Angeles. My research uncovered the historical evolution of an extraordinary biracial coalition led by black mayor Tom Bradley, linking African-Americans and liberal whites, particularly Jews (Sonenshein 1989; 1993a). The development of a strong biracial coalition in Los Angeles challenged the dominant pessimism on interracial politics and required an expansion of models based on midwestern and eastern cities (Sonenshein 1989). Indeed, the rise of the Bradley coalition and its later difficulties helped explain the failure of biracial politics in New York City (Sonenshein 1990).

In New York City, there was a conflict of interest between blacks and white liberals and interracial leadership networks were poorly developed. The situation was quite the opposite in Los Angeles. Before the rise of the liberal coalition, blacks and white liberals were both political outsiders and their shared political interests complemented

47

their ideological alliance. Strong interracial leadership facilitated coalition. Community activists and politicians, both black and white, developed mutual trust working together in civil rights and local politics (Sonenshein 1990).

The police have been at the heart of the struggle for minority incorporation in Los Angeles, and controversies over police accountability have sustained durable coalition patterns. Even before the disturbances of 1992, the King case breathed new life into conflicts and alliances among the city's major groups.

In this chapter, I will examine coalition patterns at the elite and mass levels that arose during the controversy. This study is based on a detailed analysis of public documents, council minutes and videotapes, *Los Angeles Times* polls and private polls, newspaper articles, and an analysis of the 1993 Los Angeles mayoral election.

Los Angeles Coalition Politics Before the Rodney King Case

In 1973, Los Angeles made history when city councilman and former police officer Tom Bradley defeated Mayor Sam Yorty. In a city with a population less than 18% African-American, Bradley's election marked a milestone of crossover politics. His coalition was based on overwhelming black support, the votes of the great majority of Jews and white liberals, and majority backing from Latinos. He had a strong base of allies in the city council, and proceeded to construct a durable coalition.

Between 1973 and 1985, the Bradley coalition displayed extraordinary unity and breadth, holding a majority of the city council and dominating the city government. A network of black and Jewish leaders provided internal cohesion, consistently defusing interracial conflicts. Increased support came from Latinos and Asian-Americans. With its hold on city politics, the biracial coalition increased minority representation at city hall, augmented city hiring of minorities, obtained federal aid for inner city programs, redeveloped downtown and began to challenge the autonomy of the Los Angeles Police Department. After Bradley's landslide re-election in 1985, however, the coalition began to show signs of aging and internal division. It steadily lost its hegemony over city politics.

A series of economic changes and a number of specific decisions propelled the coalition's decline. Downtown redevelopment had been a cornerstone of Bradley's regime. A pro-business development program fostered a huge edge in campaign funds for liberal politicians, and thereby set the coalition apart from neighborhood grass-roots politics. With the loss of federal and state aid after the passage of Proposition

13 in 1978 and Reagan's election in 1980, the city government lacked a strategy or the resources to attack poverty.

When in the 1980's development began to spread to the largely white liberal westside, it set off a powerful slow-growth movement. Bradley's 1985 decision to allow oil drilling in the Pacific Palisades made him the target of the environmental movement—which had once been a pillar of his support. When Minister Louis Farrakhan came to town in 1985, Bradley's African-American and Jewish supporters quarreled bitterly—placing the Mayor uncomfortably in the middle.

As the 1989 mayoral election came onto the horizon, Bradley was buffeted by criticism from former allies on the city council. Councilman Zev Yaroslavsky of the white liberal Fifth district seemed certain to run against Bradley. The Fifth had been the pillar of Bradley's white liberal support, and Yaroslavsky's opposition implied a real danger to the coalition.

Although Yaroslavsky eventually backed away from taking on Bradley for the mayoralty, community opposition led the mayor to revise his economic policies. Bradley brought environmentalists into his administration, and began to push for the sort of "linkage" of development to community services that other cities had begun earlier. Even without strong challengers, Bradley was nearly forced into a runoff in the 1989 mayoral primary. Two relatively unknown candidates held Bradley to 52% of the vote, his poorest showing since his 1969 defeat by Mayor Sam Yorty.

Near the end of the campaign Bradley became enmeshed in a serious financial scandal. He had long been employed as a consultant to several local banks, and was accused of steering city deposits to one of his employers. The charge was devastating and for a time it seemed that Bradley might be forced from office. When a city attorney's report cleared Bradley of criminal wrongdoing, he had survived the scandal—although with a tarnished reputation. By 1991 he had regained some share of his former power.

This chapter will show that the Rodney King case had a lot to do with restoring the coalition lines that had been fraying as the city grappled with the growth issue. Growth issues divided minority and white middle-class communities. While minority communities were desperate for growth, middle-class white neighborhoods felt choked by buildings, traffic and people. By contrast, the search for police accountability brought liberal whites and minority groups closer together. Reforming the LAPD had been one of the central goals of the liberal biracial coalition. While Bradley was often characterized as terminally cautious, he challenged the police even at severe cost in moderate and conservative white support. His long struggle with the

LAPD certainly hurt him in his unsuccessful 1982 gubernatorial race against Republican George Deukmejian.

When the Rodney King beating took place, Los Angeles coalition politics was already in a state of flux. Bradley had few allies and many challengers within the city council. The media were often critical. The 1989 financial scandal had devastated Bradley, leaving him "just another politician" to many voters and to many in the city's elite. While his standing among the voters had risen to higher levels, his image of probity had not recovered. There was no longer a united progressive coalition leading the city, combining the separated governmental powers. Many politicians were looking ahead to the 1993 mayoral election and anticipating Bradley's retirement.

One wonders what might have happened had camcorders been in wide use during the period of coalition hegemony—when the mayor and the council majority constituted a strong alliance. But what is truly remarkable is that the King case haltingly and inconsistently rebuilt some of the coalition lines that had become frayed, and ultimately led to an astonishing coalition victory—a popularly supported reassertion of civilian control over the police.

Long before the April violence and even before the beating of Rodney King, much rethinking had been underway about the Los Angeles biracial coalition. On the left, Bradley's liberal coalition politics were never particularly appealing—especially the coalition's ties to business. Among progressive African-Americans, Bradley's style of coalition leadership often seemed to fall short. Latinos and Asian-Americans, noting their increased numbers, chafed at the city's focus on black and white politics. Together, Latinos and Asian-Americans comprised about one-half the city's population in 1990 (see Table 3.1).

Much of the new thinking involved "rainbow coalitions" of color and class. The rainbow ideal derives from Jesse Jackson's 1984 and 1988 presidential campaigns, but can be traced back even earlier to Stokely

TABLE 3.1   Population of the City of Los Angeles, 1990

	Percent	Number
White	37.3	1,299.604
Black	14.0	487,674
Latino	39.9	1,391,411
Asian	9.8	341,807
Total		3,485,398

Percentages total more than 100 due to rounding
Source: United States Census.

Carmichael and Charles V. Hamilton's classic *Black Power* (1967). In Carmichael and Hamilton's theory, interracial coalitions based on ideology (ties with white liberals) will fail to advance the black community. The best coalitions form on the grounds of self-interest. Color and class are elements of self-interest and, in this view, provide a solid basis for coalition politics.

Rainbow politics has obvious appeal for Los Angeles progressives. With Latinos and Asian-Americans increasing in numbers, a black-Latino-Asian alliance would represent a clear majority of the city. As class issues become more salient in Los Angeles politics, economics could provide a common way to overcome racial animosities. Superficially, the rainbow coalition should be a perfect fit for the new era of multiracial politics.

The problem is that on closer examination Los Angeles rainbow coalitions look less promising than advertised. As Erie, Brackman and Ingram (1992:89) have noted: "The rainbow model . . . is an ideological gloss that obscures as much as it illuminates the realities of ethnic power in Los Angeles." Ethnic conflict and economic competition significantly undermine the potential of such alliances. Further, ideological differences will not be easy to overcome. In a survey of California blacks, Latinos, Asians and whites, Cain, Kiewiet and Uhlaner (1986:29) found that:

> Whether there will be a political coalition of minorities depends on which issues prove to be most salient in the future. On many issues that separate lower and higher income groups, Latinos and blacks will coalesce in opposition to most Whites and Asian-Americans.

Uhlaner (1991) argued that while there are no insurmountable obstacles to black-Latino-Asian alliances, the participation of Asians would likely be limited to immigrant-generations. Her data also showed strong affinities between blacks and Latinos, as compared to whites. These studies provide an invaluable taste of reality for those who hypothesize the easy formation of coalitions of minorities. Well before the violence, inter-minority street conflicts had been increasing in the city (Oliver and Johnson 1984; Johnson and Oliver 1989). These conflicts were unlikely to be assuaged by the violence, and in some cases were severely exacerbated. The violence itself was marked by open warfare between rioters and Korean-American storeowners. Not long after the disturbances, African-Americans and Latinos began competing for jobs in the reconstruction effort in South Central Los Angeles (*Los Angeles Times* 13 June 1992).

The available research seems to indicate that the most likely rainbow coalition is between blacks and Latinos. Ideological compatibility seems to be much higher between these two groups than it is with either Asian-Americans or whites. While alliance with Asian-Americans is not ruled out in any of these studies, their higher economic status, and relatively conservative partisan and ideological positions mean that alliance will require substantial cultivation.

In his study of Los Angeles, Jackson (1988:26) found that "the voting data presented here clearly demonstrate the prospect for a coalition forming between the black and Hispanic communities of Los Angeles." In general, Jackson found "extreme polarization between the black and white communities of Los Angeles", and argued that "we would find blacks at the liberal end of the spectrum and Anglos at the conservative end. Hispanic voters would fall in between."

Mike Davis (*Los Angeles Times*, 1 June 1991) dramatically expressed this picture of a city divided in which the only choices are between a minority coalition and white dominance -and a city in which there are no longer relevant differences between white liberals and white conservatives:

> In the first case . . . minority white rule in the city is re-established by the continuing collusion of neo- liberal and conservative council members. The Hollywood Hills cease to be an important ideological divide. . . . In the second scenario . . . a new generation of activists . . . start to lay the foundation for a durable rainbow coalition whose fulcrum is a black-Latino alliance.

The vision of a city divided between resentful minorities and comfortable, conservative whites (the "Bladerunner" scenario) is dramatic, but both misleading and self-fulfilling. The reality is that color is likely to be a shaky ground for minority alliances, and that whites are much more politically diverse than expected. Urban violence generally leads people to presume the extinction of cross-racial alliances. This belief was widespread after the Watts uprising. Yet well after Watts, ideological differences among whites were crucial elements of the minority struggle for political power (Browning, Marshall and Tabb 1984).

An underlying and unspoken assumption of the rainbow model has been the marginalization of white liberals. That indeed has been part of its appeal to those unhappy with liberal biracial coalitions. The rainbow approach is based on "rational choice" coalition theories in which coalition members maximize their advantages and can create coalitions anew from common interest (Riker 1961).

The "Bladerunner" assumption even indirectly influences research;

testing the rainbow model does not require scholars to search for ideological differences among whites. Whites instead become a politically monolithic comparison group. Where white divisions are considered relevant, they are often examined by social class (Hahn and Almy 1971; Jackson 1988). But ideological division among whites will not only emerge from a class analysis; indeed the strongest ideological divisions among whites are among whites of comparably high social status (Shingles 1989).

Experience suggests that coalitions *for* minority equality may not only be coalitions *of* minorities. Coalitions *for* economic equality may not only be coalitions *of* the dispossessed. The missing piece, and a critical key to the puzzle of Los Angeles's future, is the potential role of liberal whites in minority coalitions.

A critique of coalition theory advanced by Hinckley (1981) may provide a more realistic way to explore future coalitions in Los Angeles. Hinckley drew attention to the role of historical memory and elite trust in coalitions. While acknowledging the importance of rational self-interest, Hinckley argued that new coalitions do not arise out of thin air; they incorporate the previous experiences of potential coalition partners. In short, the most likely coalition to form may be the coalition that already exists.

My research indicates that over a span of nearly three decades— from 1964 up to the present—there has been a consistent and politically important gap between white liberals and white conservatives in Los Angeles. I have examined two council districts, the liberal 5th on the westside and the conservative 12th in the northwest Valley, in a wide range of elections. Both are overwhelmingly white, highly educated, and highly mobilized. The westside 5th, however, is the most Jewish of the city's districts and the most liberal. The northwest valley 12th is the most Republican and conservative.

In election after election, an ideology gap appears between the white liberal Fifth and the white conservative Twelfth—a difference of as much as 25 percentage points. It appears in party registration, presidential and gubernatorial voting, voting on ballot propositions, and in local elections. Theories of the future of Los Angeles politics that ignore this crucial division among the most highly mobilized and powerful whites will miss a central feature of minority politics.

The King Case

The film of the King beating first aired on the evening of March 5. The emotional impact of the video was unprecedented. A *Los Angeles Times* poll found that a huge percentage of the city had seen it (Poll

Report #245, March 7-8, 1991). Civil liberties organizations noted that the beating itself was hardly uncommon, but the visual images made all the difference. Soon pressure began to build on Police Chief Gates to accept responsibility, and indeed to resign.

The dramatic events that comprised the King controversy piled one atop the other. They began with the airing of the film, continued through Bradley's call for Gates's resignation in early April, the police commission's decision to place Gates on leave—a move immediately overturned by the city council—city council elections in April and May, and the release of the Christopher Commission report in July. And of course all of these events were ultimately overshadowed by the massive violence that broke out in April 1992 when a jury acquitted the officers on most of the counts.

The initial period of the controversy seemed to support the notion that liberal coalition politics had died in Los Angeles. Bradley's council base was virtually non-existent. Two of the three black council seats were in effect vacant. Gilbert Lindsay (9th district) had died and the retiring Robert Farrell (8th district) was a lame duck. The third seat was held by Nate Holden (10th district), a bitter enemy of the mayor, and a Gates supporter. Liberal politicians were nervous about challenging the police. Many felt that the case would mark the long-predicted end of the black-liberal coalition (Meyerson 1991).

In a poll taken shortly after the controversy began, the *Los Angeles Times* found that, as after the Watts riot, blacks differed from whites and Latinos in evaluating the chief of police (Table 3.2). For example, blacks were far less likely to approve of Gates than either whites or Latinos. But the difference was far smaller than in 1965, when they were almost totally polarized (Sears and McConahay 1973).

The most dramatic elite development in the first period was the public statement by the council's only Asian-American member Michael Woo that he favored Gates's resignation. While Bradley and his staff worked behind the scenes to remove Gates, Woo's public stance placed him alone out front. Woo had taken an extraordinary gamble.

For those who favor the "coalition of color" theory, Woo's move could be seen as reflecting rainbow politics. But Woo cannot only be understood as an Asian-American. He was also the representative of a district, the 13th, with a large constituency of white liberals. His position on Gates, along with Congressman Howard Berman's similar stance (Meyerson 1991), provided the first signs of liberal support for the black position.

Bradley was being pressed within the African-American community to take a stronger stand and at the same time his "hidden hand"

TABLE 3.2   Approval and Disapproval of Bradley and Gates Job Performance, 1991–1992

	(1)	(2)	(3)	(4)	(5)
Bradley					
Total	61-28	57-30	53-39	48-41	38-55
Whites	56-34	49-41	41-48	NA	27-70
Blacks	66-27	54-34	64-31	NA	47-41
Latinos	66-22	66-18	63-32	NA	49-42
Gates					
Total	33-55	31-61	35-57	28-64	16-81
Whites	36-55	42-52	45-46	NA	18-79
Blacks	23-75	12-81	13-82	NA	5-93
Latinos	32-49	20-70	29-62	NA	16-79

Sources: Based on *Los Angeles Times* Poll reports: 1) After King beating, #245, March 7-8, 1991; 2) Before Bradley called on Gates to resign, #247, March 20-21, 1991; After Bradley called on Gates to resign, #249, April 3-4, 1991; After the release of the Christopher Commission Report, #254, July 11-14, 1991; After the riots, #281, May 9-12, 1992.

program to remove Gates was sparking criticism from the city council and resentment from the public. In the black community, the atmosphere was tense. When County Supervisor Kenneth Hahn backed Gates, he faced significant opposition. To the black-owned *Los Angeles Sentinel*, Hahn "may have uttered words that could forever taint his longstanding popularity with L.A.'s black community" (4-10 April 1991). Bradley faced strong pressure to call for Gates's resignation. Black voters reported strong interest in 6th district council member Ruth Galanter's position on Gates as a factor in their vote in her upcoming re-election bid (*Los Angeles Times*, 10 April 1991).

The pages of the *Sentinel* bear witness to the high voltage of the King case in the black community. It was the headline story virtually every week that it was in the news. Each week there were a half-dozen or more stories, editorials, cartoons and columns. On several front pages, the *Sentinel* showed extremely graphic color photos of victims of police beatings.

When black councilman Nate Holden, a strong Gates supporter, attended a public meeting on the issue, the *Sentinel* reported: "Then in walked Holden, to an onslaught of jeers and profane verbal fireballs ... Just why Holden attended the rally ... is a mystery ... All he did was walk into a boiling cauldron of malcontent—malcontent for him." (April 17).

A *Los Angeles Times* poll two weeks later revealed that Bradley was being hurt by the controversy among whites and blacks but not at all with Latinos (Table 3.2). Gates himself was losing minority backing and gaining white support as the controversy continued. The police issue was reconfiguring public opinion.

The controversy took a dramatic turn on April 2nd when Bradley publicly called on Chief Gates to resign. The next day, Bradley's police commission placed Gates on indefinite suspension for the period of the investigation. An outraged city council overruled the commission in a stormy April 5th meeting, and reached an agreement with Gates to preempt his threatened lawsuit against the city by restoring him to office.

The city council had gone to war against the mayor. The vote to override the police commission was 10-3. Even liberal councilmembers were nervous about confronting Gates, and their conflicts with Bradley led them to feel no obligation to support him. Joining Woo in opposition were only black councilmember Farrell and Ruth Galanter, who was facing re-election under tremendous pressure to oppose Gates in her biracial 6th district. At the same meeting, another less publicized vote was held to appropriate $150,000 for a police commission investigation of the LAPD. The voting lines were much closer on that vote to "normal" coalitions. The motion by Yaroslavsky and the 4th district's John Ferraro passed 9-4, with all four valley councilmembers opposed (city council proceedings, April 5, 1991).

These days were the climax of the controversy, and seemed to show a city government in chaos. The *Times* editorialized, business leaders called on the mayor and council to get together, and the public was confused. The establishment pressure on Bradley took its toll; soon he was meeting with Gates and council president John Ferraro to make a tentative peace.

The three day climactic controversy in early April placed Bradley in a highly risky position. He took on the Los Angeles city council and Gates, and the council stuck with the chief. At the same time, he reoriented his base of support. While his overall popularity fell, his minority base solidified. This was well within the pattern of coalition politics—despite the image of Bradley as a nonracial mayor. The biracial coalition was first built in the black community before it expanded into a citywide coalition—and without its black base, it was lost.

Like Woo, the cautious Bradley had taken an extraordinary gamble. A *Times* poll taken during and shortly after these events showed that his public support had again shifted dramatically (Table 3.2). Clearly, the Gates issue was an electoral loser for Bradley among whites, whether he vacillated or acted. But Bradley had salvaged a deteriorating situation among blacks and neither position seemed to affect his standing among Latinos. In a hypothetical mayoral race between Bradley and Gates, Bradley now won easily among minorities but only narrowly among whites *(Los Angeles Times* Poll report #249, April 3-4, 1991).

On the Tuesday after the three days in April, the city held a primary election. The primary led to May runoffs in the 6th, 8th, 9th and 12th districts. Two were vacant seats in the black community (#8 and #9), one was a biracial liberal district (#6) and the last (#12) was the white conservative district.

The Gates issue was a part of each race. In the biracial 6th, Galanter had to justify her balancing act on the issue. In the 12th, Bernson used Gates's strong support to combat liberal slow-growth challenger Julie Korenstein. In the 8th and 9th, black candidates competed to stand out against Gates. The black community was about to shift its representation, with the retirement of Farrell and the death of Lindsay. With Nate Holden's election in the 10th in 1987 there would be a new generation of black representation in the council.

For some time, a new factional division had been growing in the black community. The Bradley coalition itself had arisen as a progressive alternative to the moderate, machine politics of the Jesse Unruh-Mervyn Dymally group. That division, the basis for the early biracial coalition, was along class lines and placed the Bradley forces on the "left" of the moderate Dymally regulars tied to Jesse Unruh (Sonenshein 1993). Bradley's organizational base was in upwardly-mobile black communities while Dymally's home ground was poorer and working class.

In the 1980's and beyond, Bradley's new black competitors came from the left. He himself had long ago moved to the moderate center. Jesse Jackson's 1984 and 1988 presidential campaigns challenged Bradley to reconnect himself to the black community as Jackson explicitly pushed black and progressive themes. Jackson's ally Maxine Waters emerged as a rival of Bradley in the African-American community.

Waters had been Bradley's close ally in the 1970's and was the key organizer of Bradley's factional challenge to Dymally. A dynamic activist, Waters soon carved out her own base. She established a strong low-income and working-class constituency in her 48th assembly district. Her political strength was such that she was soon independent of Bradley. Although she was seen as part of his organization, the mayor failed to formally endorse Waters in her 1976 assembly campaign. She won anyway. In Sacramento, Waters became a close ally of Speaker Willie Brown, and soon amassed considerable legislative power—all independent of Bradley. In 1978, a split in the Bradley camp led to the election of a Dymally ally in the 49th assembly district as Waters endorsed Marguerite Archie and Bradley backed Willis Edwards. Waters's candidate did far better than Bradley's.

By 1984, Waters was becoming well known as a progressive leader, and formed a close alliance with Jesse Jackson. In 1988, she was one of Jackson's national chairpersons and a member of his inner circle. In 1990, Waters left her 48th assembly seat to run for Congress and endorsed Archie (now Archie-Hudson) for her seat. Bradley endorsed Robert Farrell. Again Waters's candidate easily defeated Bradley's.

The Waters-Bradley rivalry had its roots not in class conflict, but rather in ideology and style. Waters, like Jackson, is issue-oriented and a passionate advocate for minority and low-income communities. She is much more black-oriented than Bradley and is also a national feminist leader. When she selects candidates in the city council races, her endorsement carries clout.

Bradley had never been an issue leader, and had always been a problem solver. As a big city, coalition-oriented mayor, he had become a symbol of the status quo and a figure of the establishment. Waters's issue-based approach and her own experience as a local problem solver challenged Bradley's style in his home base in a way that Jesse Jackson could not. Her constituency also allowed Waters a political freedom that the African-American mayor of a multiracial, moderate city could not possibly possess.

The King case highlighted their differences. Waters was the dominant figure in the black movement against Gates, leading rallies and demanding Gates's resignation. When Supervisor Hahn backed Gates, Waters led a protest by black leaders. She maintained steady pressure on Bradley to call for Gates's resignation. Waters backed Robert Gay in the 9th to succeed Lindsay, while Bradley supported Rita Walters. Waters endorsed Roderick Wright in the 8th against Bradley's choice Mark Ridley-Thomas.

Another runoff election far to the northwest would also be influenced by the King story. Councilman Hal Bernson was facing a strong challenge from liberal Julie Korenstein in the city's most conservative district. The issue was development—in particular Bernson's support for a large Porter Ranch project. To widespread surprise, Korenstein was making serious inroads into Bernson's base. While the black council races tested Bradley's strength in the African-American community, the 12th district race tested Gates's electoral power. He strongly backed Bernson, who made massive use of Gates's endorsement in the conservative 12th.

Bradley headed off Maxine Waters's group as both his candidates won. Walters defeated Gay by fewer than 100 votes, and Ridley-

Thomas narrowly defeated Wright. These victories enhanced Bradley's power reputation among elites, aided by Gay's tearful, televised concession: "The mayor is an extraordinarily influential individual in this city" (*Los Angeles Times*, 6 June 1991). Now Bradley had two black allies on the council—both assertive opponents of Gates.

In the 12th, Bernson barely beat Korenstein, and his victory confirmed Gates's conservative drawing power. As Gates's political reach demonstrated, there was still a strong conservative constituency in the city. The message would not be lost on vulnerable city council incumbents.

Bradley suffered a major citywide defeat with the passage of a charter amendment to increase the power of the city council (amendment #5). The measure was placed on the ballot after Bradley inadvertently signed it and became an indirect test of public support for Bradley's executive power during the King controversy. The measure passed with over 59% of the vote.

There were some divisions along racial lines on amendment #5. The only districts in which Proposition 5 did not receive a majority were four black or biracial areas—6,8, 9 and 10. There was a considerable gap between the black 8th and the other key districts. It was close to identical in percentage in the other areas. The biggest gap in *margin* (nearly 8,000 votes) was between the black 8th and the white conservative 12th.

The vote on Amendment #5 indicated that in the precarious post-hegemony world, Bradley's coalition had become much narrower. Indeed, the city council was making important inroads into his governmental power. With proposition 5 in place, the new council was likely to further challenge Bradley. But with Bradley's success in the black council races and Gates's win in the 12th for Bernson, there would also be a revival of ideological and racial politics. On the police issue, where would the city's other constituencies and leaders jump?

Now that minority support had realigned on the Gates issue, and was set in the city council, Bradley's only strategy for a citywide victory on police reform was to reframe the issue. With his reputation injured by the financial scandal and the rise of conflict with the council, Bradley would have failed if he had made the King issue a referendum on himself. Ironically, the progressive position was able to win only because its chief historical symbol stayed in the background.

In July the Christopher Commission that Bradley had appointed in the spring made its report—and it was a shocker. Unexpectedly, the commission headed by attorney Warren Christopher issued a stinging report that highlighted the failure of the LAPD and other city officials to rein in police brutality. Most dramatically, the commission released transcripts of police conversations on car computers. The transcripts contained numerous examples of racist and sexist phrases. The most famous was the reference to "gorillas in the mist" (Independent Commission 1991: 71-74).

Almost immediately, the Commission report overrode the conflicts between the mayor and the city council. It drew strong elite support, including the *Los Angeles Times*—which gave little credit to Bradley for the creation of the commission. Minority spokespeople expressed surprise and satisfaction that the report was so hard-hitting. Most remarkably, the lineup in the city council shifted rapidly. For a short time, the city leadership looked as it had during the era of coalition hegemony. As long as they weren't discussing Tom Bradley, but only the commission Bradley had appointed, they were lavish in their praise.

In the face of Bradley's political liabilities, the commission ended the black isolation on the issue and built a majority constituency. A *Los Angeles Times* poll showed very strong support for the Commission's recommendations (report #254; July 11-14, 1991); private polls showed that backing for the report crossed racial and many ideological lines (Fairbank, Maullin and Associates).

With the release of the Christopher Commission report, the elite breakdown in the coalition began to temporarily repair itself, as members rallied to the recommendations. The anti-reform group was predictable—white valley councilmembers—and liberal council members joined the anti-Gates majority. By now, Bradley had two new allies on the council; Gates's strongest base was in the 12th. In September, the council's ad hoc committee recommended a series of 21 provisions, mostly in line with the Christopher Commission.

A dithering city council, which in April had scuttled a Police Commission proposal to place Gates on leave, pulled together and placed a charter amendment on the June 1992 ballot to implement its recommendations. Proposition F amended the city charter to set term limits for the Police Commission and the Chief of Police; create an independent staff for the Commission; change the method of choosing and removing the Chief; and revise the process of disciplining police officers, including adding a civilian member to officer misconduct panels. The Chief would be limited to two consecutive five-year terms.

Even with the centrist appeal of the Christopher Commission, the police issue still generated coalition divisions. We can examine coalition lines through a private citywide poll conducted by Fairbank, Maullin and Associates in September 1991 (Table 3.3). On the question of Daryl Gates, the city divided along familiar racial and ideological lines. Overall, 41% of the voters approved of Gates. But on party, religion and race (pillars of coalition politics in Los Angeles) the lines are clear.

Democrats were twice as likely as Republicans to view Gates unfavorably. Blacks and Latinos were close together, with under a third of each viewing Gates favorably. Of all groups, Jews had the least favorable view of Gates, and were only one-fourth as likely as white Protestants to view him very favorably. From the very start of the controversy, private polling showed these group lines to be quite consistent on a wide range of police-related questions (Fairbank, Maullin and Associates).

Evolutionary perspectives are necessary to understand coalitions. At each stage of coalition development in Los Angeles, an initial period of polarization of key groups was followed by vacillation and movement of others. Blacks start out on the left, white conservatives on the right, with white liberals and Latinos in the middle. This process, at both the elite and mass levels, operated once again in the King case.

The black community represented the firmest base for the progressive position. At the start, this was more at the mass level than the elite level because of Bradley's cautious response and the turnover of black council members. After the events of April and May, the black community was strongly unified around opposition to Gates, with the exception of maverick Nate Holden. (Holden had been endorsed by the police union and former chief Ed Davis in his 1989 campaign against Bradley.)

As the Rodney King issue evolved well before the violence of 1992, fragmented coalition lines shifted and reformed into a pattern closely resembling the long-term coalition patterns of the city's politics.

The Latino leadership did not provide strong support for the black position in the early phases of the controversy. Such office holders as

TABLE 3.3   Evaluation of Gates by City Voters, 1991

	Dems	Reps	Whites	Blacks	Latinos	Jews	W.Protests.
1	16	36	29	8	10	9	37
2	17	23	20	18	7	27	25
3	24	17	15	39	34	18	12
4	31	16	28	29	24	36	16

1=very favorable; 2= somewhat favorable; 3=somewhat unfavorable; 4=very unfavorable
Source: Fairbank, Maullin and Associates, September 1991.

Councilman Richard Alatorre and County Supervisor Gloria Molina were close to invisible. On the surface, this looked like the post-Watts atmosphere of 1965, when Latinos lined up with whites. But there are important differences. By 1991 Latinos were registering very strong support for Bradley in the *Los Angeles Times* poll and in private polls. During the period of Bradley's toughening stance, this support hardly changed. By contrast, blacks started out positive, then became less favorable as Bradley seemed to vacillate; when he toughened on Gates, their support grew.

As the issue evolved, the Latino position shifted at the mass level, and then with the election of Mike Hernandez to succeed Molina in the 1st district, at the elite level as well. Latino anger at Los Angeles County sheriffs for violence against Latinos began to shape a common effort, and there was a steady shift toward the black position.

The Rodney King case restored and strengthened the long-term coalition conflict in Los Angeles by turning the city's attention from economic policy toward the racial and ideological issues that had divided and energized city politics since 1964.

As the Ventura County jury went into its deliberations in late April 1992, Bradley's coalition had come to a position of strength—although surely not the hegemony of earlier years. Liberal opponents like Yaroslavsky were drawn into the confrontation with Gates and Asian-American councilman Michael Woo had directly called for Gates's resignation.

There was every reason to believe that the June measure, backed by Bradley's elite allies in the business community, the *Los Angeles Times*, African-Americans, Latinos and white liberals, would pass in a low turnout election. That prediction assumed what nearly everybody assumed—that the jury would bring in a guilty verdict on some or all of the charges against the LAPD officers.

The political context of the 1992 violence, then, was the survival of a wounded, aging political coalition dominated by African-Americans, white liberals, and downtown business. Latinos, though restive with the shape of city politics, were still supportive of Bradley. Conservatives were on the defensive because of the King videotape. There was no vital insurgency either from the left or the right to challenge the regime, but there was also little enthusiasm behind it. Against all odds and predictions, the coalition still held power.

Conclusions

The "not guilty" verdicts in Simi Valley set off major civil violence in Los Angeles. The uprising in 1992 was complex and varied. Some have called it a "class riot"; others have called it the first "multiracial riot." While some have found major political content in the violence, others disagree. There will be a tendency to attach a single definition to the 1992 violence, but that search for simplicity may be misplaced. Perhaps the most accurate assessment would be that it was several different, overlapping riots.

Black anger against the innocent verdicts in the Rodney King case was obviously at the heart of the uprising. While most people were shocked by the jury's decision, the rage in the African-American community went much deeper and was about much more than the individual verdict. To African-Americans more than any other group, the verdict was the straw that broke the camel's back, rather than an exception to the rule of justice. A long stream of police misconduct toward Blacks of all social classes built a wave of resentment; the jury decision seemed to endorse all the times that police officers stopped, insulted or injured African-Americans. And beyond the police issue was the economic decline of South Central Los Angeles. Abandoned by industries, banks, and insurance companies, bereft of stores and shops, and feeling cut off from city hall, many in the area felt a powerful alienation from the system.

The scope of the violence in 1992 was much greater than in the 1965 Watts riot. The death toll reached 58; there were 2,383 injuries, over 17,000 arrests, and an estimated $785 million in property damage (*LAT* 11 May 1992; special issue). The South Central riot was, paradoxically, both more frightening and more widely understandable than the Watts conflagration. It spread outside the black community to threaten Hollywood, Koreatown, and even Beverly Hills. There was no sense of safety anywhere—and that universal dread can have important political consequences. But unlike 1965, the precipitating moment of the violence was clearly visible outside the African-American community. Millions of Americans had seen the Rodney King beating on videotape, and the great majority of those who heard the verdict found it unjust. But who had seen the arrest of Marquette Frye in 1965, the event that had set off the Watts riot?

Potentially, the 1992 violence could have played the same role for the conservative leader, Chief Gates, that the Watts riot had done for Mayor Yorty and Chief Parker in 1965. A strong and effective response to the violence might have strengthened Gates's hand and doomed the June police measure. Of course, this did not occur. Gates's dereliction of leadership—symbolized by his attendance at a fundraiser against the June measure while the city burned—brought a storm of criticism. While rioters were indeed villified in 1992, that negative perception shared space with Gates as the instigator of a monumental government fiasco.

The logical inference that the unrest would be politically advantageous for local conservatives was therefore muddied by the massive decline in Gates's professional reputation. Weeks after the violence, Gates's disapproval rating reached an astonishing 81% (*Los Angeles Times* 15 May 1992). By contrast, in the wake of the Watts violence, 79% of whites and 74% of Mexican-Americans viewed Chief Parker favorably; blacks, with a 10% approval rating of Parker, were far from the other groups (Sears and McConahay, 1973: 59, 165).

But the violence hurt Bradley as well. His reputation as a peacemaker had been one of his greatest political assets. Yorty could treat civil disorder as a vindication of his hard-line policies; Bradley had no such way out. Bradley began to receive blame for the economic problems of South Central Los Angeles. The riot made it more difficult to bridge the racial gap—a difficulty already apparent in the struggle with Gates. Bradley's conflict with Gates may have helped him with minority communities, but it hurt him citywide. Even though Gates seemed to be the real loser in the riot, continuing evidence of Bradley's conflict with the Chief reduced the mayor's support. Post-riot polls confirmed that decline, as Bradley's overall support fell to 38% (*Los Angeles Times* 15 May 1992).

Within the black community, the violence may have shifted the ground under the earlier Bradley-Waters rivalry. After the disturbance, Bradley could not easily speak for the African-American community—and of course he had rarely been a racial spokesman before. There he was pre-empted by Congresswoman Maxine Waters, whose eloquent and militant statements of the black position captured great public attention. Where there is no middle ground, the center is a tough place to occupy.

While the 1965 violence generated much federal aid, few expected massive federal help to flow to Los Angeles in 1992. Then it was Los Angeles that was reluctant to participate; in 1992 it was Washington. Federal money and the redirecting of city resources allowed progressive leaders in the 1970's to initiate new programs without raising city taxes. Los Angeles was now forced to come up with local solutions, and local money to pay for them. While this crisis gave Bradley an opportunity to make his business links work for South-Central Los Angeles and to influence local banks to invest more heavily in the inner city, it also left the local coalition vulnerable to blame if positive change did not occur.

The 1992 riots revealed just how difficult rainbow politics could be. The Los Angeles eastside, a strongly Mexican-American community, remained largely uninvolved in the violence. To the extent that there was Latino participation, it came primarily from recent immigrants, many Central American, in South-Central Los Angeles (*Los Angeles Times* 8 May 1992).

Most powerfully, the assault on Korean-owned businesses was one of the most violent inter-minority confrontations in memory. The images of a shooting war in the streets will remain vivid long after the unrest settles. The closest analogy is the role of Jewish shopkeepers in black New York City neighborhoods decades ago, but even those brittle relations never escalated to heavily armed and violent confrontation. The bond of "common color" is likely to be a thin reed indeed.

Almost unnoticed in the cascade of violence and public debate was the ballot measure to reform the Los Angeles Police Department, scheduled for the June 2nd election.

The campaign for police reform had brought much of the old liberal biracial coalition together one more time. It received substantial support from minority and white liberal organizations (although a number of white liberal elected officials delayed supporting the measure until later in the campaign). Max Palevsky, one of Bradley's earliest Jewish financial backers, provided $25,000 toward the reform campaign fund (*Los Angeles Times*, 24 March 1992). Downtown business, drawn in part by their association with attorney Warren Christopher, provided major funding for the Proposition F campaign (*Ibid.*)

Reporter Frank Clifford noted that "the campaign has a familiar ring, combining downtown financial muscle with an ethnically diverse campaign committee made up of civil rights and religious leaders from all over the city. It is much the same mix of corporate money and ethnic variety that has provided Mayor Tom Bradley with a winning edge over the past two decades" (*Ibid.*). The conservative opposition, led by Gates and former Mayor Sam Yorty, was just as familiar.

Disorder in the city seemed likely to jeopardize Proposition F, perhaps galvanizing conservatives in opposition. But public and private polling indicated that police reform had developed a solid base of support. Between February and May 1992, the measure retained majority support even among whites. A strong majority favored its passage before and after the Simi Valley verdict. Blacks, Latinos, and Jews—the pillars of police reform—were the backbone of Proposition F, but whites were also generally in support (Fairbank, Maullin, and Associates; *Los Angeles Times* Poll report, #281).

On June 2, 1992, the city's voters passed Proposition F by a 2-1 margin. This extraordinary event marked the first time since the rise of Chief Parker more than forty years before that the city government had restored civilian control of the police. The coalition lines in the vote showed the durability of the patterns underlying the biracial coalition. The base for Proposition F was in the African-American community. In the three council districts with the largest black populations, 92%, 90%, and 86% approved. The lowest level of support lay in the Valley. In the three white Valley districts, 52%, 54%, and 46% approved. Only in the conservative 12th, did more oppose than approve (54-46).

In white liberal districts, Proposition F won easily. The Fifth offered 71% approval, twenty-five points more liberal than the white conservative 12th. And the Fifth cast the most ballots in the city, maximizing its impact. The measure passed easily in the two Latino districts, 70% and 65%, but with a smaller number of ballots cast.

The crucial importance of biracial alliance on police reform is shown by the margin of victory in the black Eighth district (24,024) and the white liberal/Jewish Fifth district (22,645). They were very close together, and both provided key contributions to Proposition F's passage.

The dramatic events of 1991 and 1992 took the Bradley regime and the people of Los Angeles to peaks and valleys of discord, confrontation, and change. In the end, Bradley managed to obtain an extraordinarily valuable and costly victory—the beginning of reform of the LAPD. But his own support suffered serious erosion, and the city passed through a massive civil trauma.

The winning campaign to implement police reform must be considered one of the greatest victories of the biracial coalition that took power in 1973. Few had the inclination to stop and applaud, however, in a city still digging itself out from the shells of hundreds of burned buildings, and the raw taste of injustice and violence. The future remained unsettled and uncertain for the Los Angeles community; only later might people look back and see what had been accomplished.

The long-term impact of the violence of 1992, and the Rodney King case that led up to it, was demonstrated in the mayoral election of 1993. (For more detailed analyses of that election, see Sonenshein 1993b and Kaufman 1994.) While the King case restored some of the coalition lines of modern Los Angeles politics, the liberal coalition suffered a clear defeat in the mayoral race. Conservative Republican financier Richard Riordan easily defeated liberal councilmember Michael Woo in the June runoff, marking the end of the twenty-year reign of the Tom Bradley coalition.

The mayoral runoff provided a clear test of the electoral appeal, in the post-riot era, of the rainbow and the conservative models of urban leadership. Woo sought to hold the left and build a coalition of color, but found that while his base could win him a place in the two-person runoff, he could not possibly construct a majority in a nervous, white-dominated electorate. He had none of Tom Bradley's ability to appeal to moderate white voters. Riordan's slogan, "Tough enough to turn L.A. around" captured the concerns of white moderate voters—precisely the people who voted solidly for Bill Clinton's presidential campaign in 1992. In the area of leadership, as well as on the key issues of crime and the economy, the voters rated Riordan far ahead of Woo (Sonenshein 1993b).

Most strikingly, Riordan won a majority of the historically liberal 5th district—the first time in memory that the Fifth had voted against the liberal mayoral candidate. In a city with a two-thirds minority population, the registered voters were two-thirds white, and they had their say in June. The San Fernando Valley, reduced in influence by the Bradley regime, turned out at the highest levels, and returned to center stage at city hall.

Riordan's victory showed that the political consequences of the Rodney King beating and the violence that followed the acquittal of the four police officers would continue to be felt for some time to come. This should not be surprising. The Watts uprising took place in 1965, and when black councilman Tom Bradley challenged Mayor Sam Yorty in 1969, the violence was still fresh enough to encourage moderate white voters to shy away from the black progressive candidate and to re-elect Yorty. Riordan's election showed that the restoration of order commanded a majority of the voters. But this should not be mistaken for a wholesale shift to the right in Los Angeles, or the permanent end of biracial coalition politics. In that sense, the city's politics have not returned full circle to the days of Sam Yorty and Chief William Parker.

With the exception of the election of Riordan—a most significant exception—the voters of Los Angeles continued to endorse a path of moderate liberalism. They backed a remarkable police reform package and the election of Bill Clinton by similarly wide margins in 1992. They registered huge support for Willie Williams, the African-American police chief recruited from Philadelphia to turn the LAPD around. In 1993, they elected the city's first openly gay council member, as well as the Valley's first Latino representative. Had a moderate Democrat made it into the mayoral runoff, he or she might well have defeated Riordan.

Riordan's mayoralty itself showed the durability of the city's shift away from Yorty-style conservatism. In his first months in office, Riordan attended the annual Gay Rights Parade, appointed some reformers to the Police Commission, built close ties to the Clinton administration, and in general was less threatening to progressive goals than had been anticipated. Riordan formed a close alliance with Willie Williams, the popular police chief. By contrast, his fellow Republican Rudolph Guiliani of New York City, also elected mayor in 1993, alienated gay rights groups, kept a wary distance from the Clinton administration, and declared the police sacrosanct in budget discussions.

The dramatic struggle over the police department, radically transformed by the Rodney King case, revived the historical coalition lines of Los Angeles. But that development obscures the great need for new politics and new policies in the city. While much has stayed the same, much has irrevocably changed in Los Angeles. The model of downtown redevelopment trickling down to the inner city is no longer viable as Los Angeles's sole economic policy. New ways must be found to generate resources and apply them directly to the areas that need help. Without federal aid, local leaders will have to take on the awesome task of enlisting private financial interests and taxpayers in the reconstruction.

The city must also deal creatively with the rise of Latinos and Asian-Americans. The Latino assertion highlights the growing gap between voters and residents of the city. Business as usual will be to represent voters. But Latinos will have to contest that approach; otherwise, the long lag between turning residents into voters will set the community back even more. For a time, Latinos (and on occasion Asian-Americans) may find that they need to challenge existing coalitions in order to carve out a senior role in coalitions yet to form. Latinos will likely pursue labor organizing in low-wage industries as a way to bypass local political immobilism and win concrete victories for communities.

The biracial coalition itself will likely continue in some form even with a conservative mayor. Liberals and moderates still dominate the city council, and in most elections the city majority is still moderately liberal and strongly Democratic. The passage of Proposition F in the ashes of civil violence showed the durability of progressive strength. The relationship between blacks and white liberals has been longstanding, not just in Los Angeles but in less polished forms in other cities and in national politics. It has a deep base, as well as deep conflicts.

When the biracial coalition took power in 1973, it defeated a long-dominant conservative coalition. The conservative base did not disappear; it only became weaker. It lodged in the chief of police and in areas like the Northwest Valley's 12th council district. It fought rear-guard actions, and sometimes won; it exercised a substantial veto over city policy through bloc votes against city tax increases.

Although weakened by Gates's inactions in the city's crisis, that coalition survived to win back control of the mayor's office in 1993.

One possibility is that the future of Los Angeles coalition politics will be a type of *overlay*, in which the biracial coalition continues to exist, but in a more fragile state. The city develops far more pluralistic politics, but not like the party politics of the east and midwest. Rather it will be a Los Angeles version. Politics will change as groups low in voter registration, or even citizenship, mobilize in the workplace and begin to challenge the rules of local politics. In time, the long-anticipated assertion of the Latino community will emerge as thousands become citizens, and as many of those new citizens become voters.

The political system of Los Angeles faces a challenge both of leadership and participation. Those who have been most oriented toward participation—the progressives—must once again study how to build citywide majorities in support of their leadership. Anticipating that demographics would change politics, they have failed to maintain the trust of the majority of the existing electorate. In the search for rainbow coalitions, progressives have neglected the search for interracial alliances essential to majority coalitions.

Those who in the aftermath of the civil disorder were most trusted to provide leadership in the search for order—the moderates or conservatives—need to learn the importance of incorporating new and unfamiliar groups into the city's governance. Winning and holding power principally with the support of whites may represent a useful temporary expedient; but in time, the city must be governed on a multiracial, multiethnic basis.

In a city with bewildering demographic and social diversity, leaders must become expert in the art of coalition building and conflict reduction. Indeed, they must learn to seek both justice *and* peace. The path to a more democratic city must be eased through the recognition that Los Angeles is now two cities: one of political eligibles and the other made up of political ineligibles, non-citizens living outside the political community. One-third of the city's adults are not citizens (Pactech 1992). The political system must become more relevant to the economic life of the majority of the people who live in Los Angeles.

In the face of the great problems Los Angeles faces in rebuilding its community, the political system also needs to be more effective. The civil unrest generated a fairly undemocratic response from city hall. Mayor Bradley appointed Rebuild LA (now RLA) to bring corporate money into South Central Los Angeles; it soon appeared that this was to be the extent of political leadership on rebuilding the inner city.

Mayor Riordan has also favored the insider, top-down approach of corporate leadership. Like Mayor Bradley, his close ties with the city council have allowed him to carry out some of his policies in the face of a weak mayor—strong council charter.

It is time for Los Angeles city hall to open up to new ideas and to new participants, by experimenting with new formats for public involvement. While politics has always held a relatively low salience in Los Angeles, the series of massive dislocations faced by the city in recent years may shake the community into a higher level of political interest—if the institutions exist to nurture and sustain it. Even if the charter is never changed to increase the power of the mayor, a greater level of public involvement, drawing on the great breadth of local media, could re-energize the search for community solutions. Partisan politics will never return to nonpartisan Los Angeles, but even without parties, the community can seek to create a lively and engaging politics.

The city is becoming more complex, more international, more politically attuned. New groups coming in will now not only have to deal with the earlier, and now revived conservative stratum, but also with the remaining power of the minority and white liberal alliance. Alternative paths may have to be carved out to open the paths of participations to new groups and new approaches. Out of that mixture of old groups and new, old ideas and new, will arise the halting and hopefully creative political responses that will shape Los Angeles in the years to come.

References

Browning, Rufus, Dale Rogers Marshall and David Tabb. 1984. *Protest Is Not Enough: The Struggle of Blacks and Hispanics for Equality in City Politics.* Berkeley, CA: University of California Press.

Cain, Bruce E., D. Roderick Kiewiet, and Carole Uhlaner. 1986. "The Political Impact of California's Minorities." Paper presented at the annual meeting of the Western Political Science Association.

Carmichael, Stokely and Charles V. Hamilton. 1967. *Black Power: The Politics of Liberation in America.* New York: Random House.

Erie, Steven P., Harold Brackman and James Warren Ingram III. 1992. "Paths to Political Incorporation for California's Newer Minorities." California Policy Seminar Research Report, University of California.

Fairbank, Maullin and Associates. Various polls.

Hahn, Harlan and Timothy Almy. 1971. "Ethnic Politics and Racial Issues: Voting in Los Angeles." *Western Political Quarterly* 24:719-30.

Hinckley, Barbara. 1981. *Coalitions and Politics.* New York: Harcourt Brace Jovanovich.

Independent Commission on the Los Angeles Police Department (the Christopher Commission). 1991. *Report.*

Jackson, Byran O. 1988. "Ethnic Cleavages and Voting Patterns in U.S. Cities: An Analysis of the Asian, Black and Hispanic Communities of Los Angeles." Paper presented at the Conference on Comparative Ethnicity, University of California, Los Angeles.

Johnson, James, Jr. and Melvin Oliver. 1989. "Interethnic Minority Conflict in Urban America: the Effects of Economic and Social Dislocations." *Urban Geography* 10:449-463.

Kaufman, Karen. 1994. "Us Versus Them: A Group Conflict Analysis of the 1993 Los Angeles Mayoral Election." Paper presented at the annual meeting of the Western Political Science Association.

Krikorian, Greg. 1983. "Caution: Spies At Work." *California Journal* 14:415-417.

Los Angeles Times.

Los Angeles Times Poll. Various Reports.

Meyerson, Harold. 1991. "The End of Liberal L.A." *LA Weekly,* April 12-18.

Oliver, Melvin L. and James H. Johnson, Jr. 1984. "Inter-ethnic Conflict in an Urban Ghetto: The Case of Blacks and Latinos in Los Angeles." *Research in Social Movements, Conflict and Change* 6:57-94. JAI Press.

Pactech Consultants. 1992. Report to the Los Angeles City Council for the Redistricting Process.

Riker, William. 1961. *The Theory of Political Coalitions.* New Haven: Yale University Press.

Sears, David O. and John B. McConahay. 1973. *The Politics of Violence: The New Urban Blacks and the Watts Riot.* Boston: Houghlin Mifflin Company.

Shingles, Richard D. 1989. "Class, Status and Support for Governmental Aid to Disadvantaged Groups." *Journal of Politics* 51:933-964.

Sonenshein, Raphael J. 1989. "The Dynamics of Biracial Coalitions: Crossover Politics in Los Angeles." *Western Political Quarterly* 42:333-353.

———. 1990. "Biracial Coalitions in Big Cities: Why They Succeed, Why They Fail." Pp. 193-211 in *Racial Politics in American Cities,* edited by Rufus Browning, Dale Rogers Marshall, and David Tabb. New York and London: Longman Press.

———. 1993a. *Politics in Black and White: Race and Power in Los Angeles.* Princeton, NJ: Princeton University Press.

———. 1993b. "Is This the End? Biracial Coalition in the 1993 Los Angeles Mayoral Election." Paper presented at the annual meeting of the American Political Science Association.

Uhlaner, Carole. 1991. "Perceived Prejudice and the Coalition Prospects of Blacks, Latinos and Asian-Americans." Pp. 339-372 in *Racial and Ethnic Politics in California,* edited by Byran O. Jackson and Michael B. Preston. Berkeley, CA: Institute for Governmental Studies.

4

The Rodney King Beating Verdicts

Hiroshi Fukurai, Richard Krooth, and Edgar W. Butler

As a landmark in the recent history of law enforcement and jury trials, the Rodney King beating trials are historically comparable to the 1931 Scottsboro case (*Norris v. Alabama,* 294 U.S. 587, 1935) or the 1968 Huey Newton case (*Newton v. California,* 8 Cal App 3d 359, 87 Cal Rptr 394, 1970). The King beating cases are also similar to Florida trials that led to three urban riots and rebellion during 1980s in Miami, Florida in which police officers were acquitted of criminal charges in the death of three blacks: Arthur McDuffie in 1980, Nevell Johnson in 1982, and Clement Anthony Lloyd in 1989. The 1980 McDuffie riots, for instance, resulted in eighteen deaths and eighty million dollars in property damage (*Barry v. Garcia,* 573 So.2d 932 933, 1991). An all white jury acquitted police officers of all criminal charges in the face of compelling evidence against them, including the testimony of the chief medical officer who said that McDuffie's head injuries were the worst he had seen in 3,600 autopsies (Crewdson, 1980). The verdict triggered violence because it symbolized the continuation of racial inequities in the criminal justice and court system.

Similarly, in the King beating trial and jury verdict which was rightly called "sickening" by then-President Bush and condemned by all segments of society, the King embroglio also provides an opportunity for evaluation and reform of police procedures, law enforcement structures, and jury trials.

In the first state trial, on April 29, 1992, a predominantly white jury had tried and exonerated four Los Angeles white police officers on assault charges for the beating of a black motorist. This was both despite and due to visual court evidence of the continuous beating of King by police officers, images that had been captured on videotape by a resident of a nearby apartment. The acquittal by the predominantly

73

white jury stunned and angered many people who had regarded the videotape of the incident as incontrovertible evidence of police brutality, racism, and a police force out of control. It also highlighted the racial tensions imploding just below the surface in Los Angeles, the nation's second-largest city. It brought into focus the anger of racial minorities who had long criticized the Los Angeles Police Department (LAPD) for its use of excessive force against members of racial and ethnic minorities.

In the period between January 1986 and December 1990, for instance, there were 8,274 total allegations in complaints by public made against LAPD officers and 24.7% of them were allegations of LAPD officers' excessive force, the largest complaints during that time. As a result, there have been a variety of lawsuits alleging improper use of force by LAPD officers. Many of those complaints came from the neighborhoods with the largest concentration of racial and ethnic minorities (Report of the Independent Commission, 1991, p.55).

The 1992 acquittal of four white police officers thus immediately set off angry reactions and protests by racial minorities in Los Angeles. Mayor Tom Bradley dismayed that "today the system failed us. The jury's verdict will never blind us to what we saw on that videotape" (Mydans, 1992a). Los Angeles District Attorney Ira Reiner added: "We disagree with the jury, but are obliged to accept the integrity of that verdict." President Bush reacted to the verdict differently, hedging: "The court system has worked. What's needed now is calm, respect for the law" (Mydans, 1992b). And then-Democratic presidential candidate Bill Clinton hammered President Bush for not being more "personally involved in healing the racial divisions in this country" (Abramson et al., 1992).

The underlying issue of the beating incident and subsequent urban riot in 1992 has addressed the question of whether justice within the criminal court system was served in the state trial of the four white police officers for beating of a black motorist. Yet, though the public and media largely focused on the police brutality and racial conflicts with law enforcement agencies in inner-cities, one area of the criminal court system has gone largely unchallenged: *The Jury*. Scrutiny of the jury system suggests that the 1992 acquittal of the four white officers was not an anomaly but an inevitable consequence of the jury system in which the position of racial and ethnic minorities in the social system in general and the court system in particular has been molded by socio-historical factors of subordination (Fukurai et al., 1991a, 1991b, 1993).

Jury Trials and Racial Disenfranchisement

The right to a trial by jury is deeply embedded in the American democratic principle. The Fifth, Sixth, and Seventh Amendments to the U.S. Constitution guarantee the right to a jury for all criminal cases and in all civil suits exceeding twenty dollars. Similarly, the constitution of each state guarantees a trial by jury. Consequently approximately eighty percent of jury trials in the world take place in the United States (Hans and Vidmar, 1986).

The United States is known for its democratic ideal. A jury speaking for the community represents an essential ingredient of a democratic government that derives its power from the people. The jury shows that harmony is possible if we listen to each other and seek a unified judgment from a diversity of viewpoints. But these benefits of democracy can be only attained if the assembled jury is representative of a cross-section of the community so that the persons deliberating can legitimately claim to speak on behalf of the community. Any bias in jury selection and representative participation by various segments of society undermines the legitimacy of jury trials in the eyes of citizens.

Recent studies of the jury system and jury selection, however, challenged the ideal of a representative jury and a fair trial by one's peers. While the jury is required to be composed of a fair cross-section of the community, racial and ethnic minorities are consistently underrepresented in the vast majority of both federal and state courts (Fukurai and Butler, 1991, 1994a, 1994b; Fukurai et al., 1993; Butler et al., 1994). Historically the jury in America has been dominated by white males. The persistent underrepresentation of racial minorities has contributed to public distrust and lack of faith in the legal system (Van Dyke, 1973; Fukurai et al., 1993). Many racially motivated jury trials, such as 1980 and 1984 Greensboro trials in Greensboro, North Carolina, 1980 McDuffie trials in Miami, Florida, and 1992 Rodney King beating trials in Los Angeles, provided an example of structural biases in the jury selection process that systematically eliminated potential black and other minority jurors from serving on juries (Levine, 1991). As a result, the defendants were tried by the predominantly white juries and received the verdicts not perceived to reflect the shared collective sentiments of the general community.

In the first state jury trial of four Los Angles white police officers, for example, the jury's acquittal prompted angry demonstrations by students and black and minority organizations across the country. Many minority groups considered the videotape of incident as evidence of police brutality and racism and felt that justice had failed to prevail in the trial of four white police officers. Federal officials then reopened the criminal case as a civil rights matter. In February, 1993, the second federal trial began for the same four LAPD officers for the violation of King's civil rights. While the federal trial ended with the conviction of two officers, research indicates that, despite the conviction of the officers by the federal jury, there are even greater biases built into the federal jury selection process than the state jury which acquitted the defendants. Biases such as source lists used for jury selection and the request for potential lengthy sequestration for final jurors had effectively eliminated large numbers of eligible racial and ethnic minorities, the poor, and women from serving on federal juries. Thus, even greater representative disparity was found in the federal jury whose compositions did not reflect a fair cross-section of the community in the Los Angeles federal court jurisdiction.

This paper, then, examines the following substantive issues: (1) underlying factors that led to the beating incident and racism within the police department and the criminal justice system; (2) biases in jury selection procedures at the California state court; (3) selection biases at the second federal jury trial and further evidence of greater discriminatory mechanisms in the selection of federal juries; (4) questions on the legitimacy of the jury verdict; and (5) the aftermath following the verdict of the accused police officers and eroding public confidence concerning jury trials and jury verdicts.

The Beating Incident

For a deeper understanding of the impact of the jury verdict in the beating trial, a brief synopsis of the incident is essential. The incident began at approximately 12:40 a.m. on Sunday morning, March 3, 1991, when California Highway Patrol Officers (CHP) Melanie Singer and Timothy Singer first observed that the white Hyundai driven by Rodney King was speeding in the Pacoima area of the northeastern San Fernando Valley in Los Angeles. The CHP officers reported that King's Hyundai "was traveling at 110 to 115 m.p.h." (Report of the Independent Commission, 1991, p.4). King was driving, accompanied by two black male passengers, Bryant Allen and Freddie Helms who later died in an unrelated auto accident. After King's car was signaled to stop by the police car, King failed to stop. LAPD patrol car, assigned to Officers Lawrence M. Powell and Timothy Wind, then joined the pursuit as the LAPD's primary pursuit car. A Los Angeles Unified School District police squad car which was in the area also jointed the pursuit. King finally pulled through the intersection and came to a stop.

When police cars pulled over to the side of the street, George

Holliday, a resident of a nearby apartment, began to videotape the incident. King was on the ground. He rose and moved toward Powell. Taser wires were seen coming from King's body. Sergeant Stacy Koon acknowledged that he ordered the baton blows directing Powell and Wind to hit King with power strokes. He ordered to "hit his joints, hit his wrists, hit his elbows, hit his knees, hit his ankles" (Report of the Independent Commission, 1991, p.7). Passenger Allen and Helms both heard screams from King but could not see any of the beating. They were ordered not to look and to keep their heads on the ground. When Helms tried to raise his head to get it out of the dirt, he was kicked in the side and hit in the head with a baton, drawing blood. Helms was treated at Huntington Memorial Hospital the next morning. King was booked for evading arrest and held for three days. He was released on Wednesday, March 6, after prosecutors determined that there was insufficient evidence to prosecute him.

The initial report of the beating came at 12:56 a.m. when Koon's unit reported to the Watch Commander's desk at Foothill Station, "You just have bit time use of force, and beat the suspect of CHP pursuit, Big Time." The station responded at 12:57 a.m., "Oh well, I'm sure the lizard didn't deserve it, HAHA, I'll let them know, OK" (Report of the Independent Commission, 1991, p.14). Powell's and Wind's unit also exchanged the following messages with patrol officers working in the Sunland Tujunga area of Foothill Division, who were not at the scene of the beating.

> [From Powell/Wind] "I haven't beaten anyone this bad in a long time."
> [From Foothill Division]"Oh not again, why for you do that, I thought you agreed to chill out for a while."
> [From Powell/Wind] "I think he was dusted, many broken bones later after the pursuit." (Report of the Independent Commission, 1991, p.15).

At Pacifica Hospital where King was taken for initial treatment, nurses reported that the officers who accompanied King openly joked and bragged about the number of times King had been hit (Report of the Independent Commission, 1991, p.15).

George Holliday and Paul King, Rodney King's brother, tried to report what they felt was the apparent police abuse. The same day that the beating took place, Paul King first went to the Foothill Station to complain about the treatment of his brother; however, the police officer in the department failed to generate complaint reports. George Holliday also called the Foothill Station on Monday, March 4 to report the incident and offer his videotape to the police. The desk officer, however, made no attempt to learn any details of the event

Holliday witnessed. No personnel complaint was generated as a result
of his call. Confronted with what he viewed as disinterest on the part
of the LAPD, he made arrangements with Los Angeles television
station KTLA to broadcast the videotape on Monday evening. The
following day, the tape received national exposure on the Cable News
Network (CNN), and thereafter was reported widely in the media all
over the world.

Investigations and the Path to the Jury Trial

After the beating incident was televised on March 4, the public
reaction was immediate and overwhelming. By March 6, the Federal
Bureau of Investigation, the Los Angeles District Attorney's Office,
and the Los Angeles Police Department's Internal Affairs Division
began investigations. The Police Commission, the civilian panel that
oversee the operation of the Police Department, also began an inquiry.
On April 1, the Independent Commission was created by Los Angeles
Mayor Tom Bradley and soon merged with the Commission created by
Los Angeles Chief of Police Daryl Gates. Such efforts to investigate
the possible police assault charges against police officers were
also endorsed by City Council President John Ferraro, District Attorney
Ira Reiner, City Attorney James Hahn, and many other public
officials.

Four officers were indicted by the District Attorney's Office for
criminal charges including assault with a deadly weapon. Those
officers were: Sergeant Stacy Koon and Officers Lawrence Powell,
Timothy Wind, and Theodore Briseno. Both Koon and Powell were
also charged with submission of a false police report. The District
Attorney's Office, however, did not seek indictments against the other
19 LAPD officers who were at the scene and did not attempt to prevent
the beating or report it to their superiors. Ages of those bystanders at
the scene of the beating ranged from 23 to 48 years, including one black
male, one black female, and four Hispanic males (Report of the
Independent Commission, 1991, pp.11-13).

On March 14, the indicted officers pled not guilty. Concerned about
the police brutality by LAPD officers, United States Attorney General
Dick Thornburgh ordered a review of brutality complaints against the
LAPD. On May 1, in response to the beating, Mayor Tom Bradley
appointed a commission headed by former Deputy Secretary of State
Warren Christopher, to investigate the police department. On May 4,
the Police Commission, whose members were appointed by the mayor,
suspended Los Angeles Police Chief Daryl Gates. Rodney King and his
wife Crystal, filed a federal civil rights lawsuit against the city on

May 8. Two days later, the grand jury announced that it would not indict any of the 19 police officers who were bystanders at the beating.

The Christopher Commission released its report on July 9, 1991, including a recommendation of Chief Gates to retire from his office and a range of proposals for both procedural and structural changes in LAPD. The panel concluded that the department suffered from a siege mentality and that a relatively small number of officers accounted for an inordinate number of uses of force but went unpunished. In September 1991, the Los Angeles City Council later approved a ballot measure containing many of the Christopher Commission recommendations, including the greater civilian control of the police department. The initiative went before voters on June 2, 1992 and gained strong support from the voters.

On March 4, the state jury trial began and the opening statements were given before the jury. The jury comprised of 10 whites, 1 Hispanic, and 1 Asian. John Barnett, lawyer for accused officer Briseno, revealed that his client would implicate the other three defendants. Meanwhile, Mayor Tom Bradley announced the choice of Willie L. Williams, a black man who was Chief of Police in Philadelphia, to succeed Chief Daryl Gates. On April 29, 1992, the jury finally reached the verdict. The jury was hung on one count against Powell and announced not-guilty verdicts on all other charges.

Jury Selection and the Trial Jury of Twelve

The jury for the trial of four police officers emerged through a network of screening processes known as jury selection. The California Code of Civil Procedures specifically provides the guideline for the selection of jurors. While jury selection is an important screening process to empanel a group of citizens selected from a cross-section of the community, the shortcoming of the jury selection process and its impact on racial and ethnic representation are known. For instance, the jury selection process has its own biases and filtering mechanisms that prevent full community participation by members of racial and ethnic minorities. Past research has substantiated that the current jury and jury selection system has continued to underrepresent prospective minority jurors in the jury box (Butler and Fukurai, 1991, 1992; Fukurai et al., 1991a, 1991b).

There are eight stages of jury selection in both California and federal courts. (1) First, a given population in a specified geographical area is defined as eligible for jury service. (2) Then, source lists are obtained and/or generated so as to enable the selection of potential jurors. (3) Next, a master file (or wheel) is constructed, which contains a list of names compiled randomly from the source lists. (4) Jury qualification questionnaires are sent to randomly selected candidates; from the returned questionnaires, a qualified jurors file is constructed, which contains names of those who have met various requirements for jury service, such as residency, citizenship, and English language proficiency. (5) From this juror list, potential jurors are assigned to impanelment lists and to various courts. (6) Jury panels are now brought together, composed of those potential jurors who actually show up at the courthouse. (7) After assignment to a courtroom and a trial, the *voir dire* screening process begins. It is designed to eliminate potential jurors who may be biased and unacceptable to prosecuting and defense attorneys. (8) This culminates in a selection of specific jurors for the jury box and the alternates.

The logic of the entire selection process is based on screening, from the target population to those who finally enter the jury box. According to the law, the purpose of the selection procedure is to choose a jury that reflects a fair cross-section of the community. The chosen jurors are then viewed as being impartial and qualified to represent the community.

Some of the shortcomings and problems of the selection process are known. How closely juries reflect a community's cross-sectional segments depends on the success of the procedures by which jurors are chosen. For instance, at the first stage of jury selection, the change of venue plays an important role in deciding the trial site and the kind of jury pools available for the trial. Additionally white, black and Hispanic representation on a master file and source list, as well as their qualifications for jury service, are considered to be important determinants of balanced racial participation on jury panels. The selection of a jury foreperson is also important because he/she tends to dominate and often dictate the conversation during deliberation processes, thereby exerting significant influence on the possible outcome of the trial (Fukurai et al., 1993, pp.39-80). Thus, in each of the selection stages, there are many other factors influencing jury participation, and these can have a *cumulative effect* on the racial and ethnic composition of jury panels. In the various stages of jury selection, moreover, there are a series of informal filtering techniques that shape and determine the racial, ethnic, and class balance of prospective jurors. In the state trial, three specific stages of jury selection played a key role in determining the jury composition and subsequently the outcome of the trial. Those are: (1) Stage 1 for the change of venue, (2) Stage 7 for voir dire in screening prospective jurors for the final jury, and (3) Stage 8 for the deliberation process by the twelve jurors who survived the rigorous screening process of jury selection. Those three stages of jury selection played an important role in screening out large eligible minority jurors from serving on the first Rodney King beating trial.

The Change of Venue

The jury selection begins with the declaration of the district where the trial is to take place. This feature defines the jurisdiction and geographic area served by the court. The law states that the trial is to take place where the alleged crime was committed. Since the beating took place in Los Angeles County, the jury trial should have taken place in the superior court in Los Angeles. However, the law in California also indicates that when the trial gains too much publicity and the court faces difficulties in selecting a group of "impartial peers," a change of venue may be granted so that the defendants have the chance of being tried before "unbiased" and impartial jurors. Because of the publicity on the beating incident and deep emotions expressed by the residents in Los Angeles, the state Second District Court of Appeal granted a change of venue on July 23, 1991.

Meanwhile, the Second District Court of Appeal removed black Judge Bernard Kamins from the beating case, citing improper private communications between the judge and prosecutors. He was later replaced by a white Los Angeles Superior Court Judge, Stanley M. Weisberg. Judge Weisberg, known to be the most efficient and competent judge in Los Angeles, also presided over the second trial of the famous McMartin preschool child molestation case in 1990 (Butler et al., 1994).

Four months later, on November 23, newly appointed Judge Weisberg selected Ventura County as the new venue for the beating case. The prosecution argued that if the trial was to be moved, it should go to Alameda County in the San Francisco Bay area, where racial makeup is similar to the original trial site of Los Angeles. Judge Weisberg, however, stated during a hearing in Los Angeles that he selected Ventura County over Alameda County on the basis of such factors as convenience for the parties, expense, and the availability of a courtroom in Simi Valley whose proximity would allow residents of Los Angeles to attend the trial (Reinhold, 1992a). He also eliminated a second proposed site, south of Los Angeles in Orange County, because no courtrooms were available. He stated that he did not consider demographics in picking a new venue (Stevens, 1992). Judge Weisberg also rejected the change of venue to Riverside County, though he gave no reason for why he bypassed Riverside (Reinhold, 1992c).

Trying to find unbiased jurors for the beating trial was an exercise in futility. Practically, everyone with television sets had seen the beating. If the case had remained in Los Angeles County, the jury could have included the broader representation of racial and ethnic minorities. According to the 1990 U.S. Census, the population composition in 1990 Los Angeles was 40.8% white, 10.5% black, 37.8% Hispanic, 10.2% Asian, and 0.3% Native Americans. In the venue of Ventura County, on the other hand, blacks comprised only 2.2% of the population, Hispanics 26.1%, Asians 5.2%, Native Americans 0.5%. Whites, however, comprise 65.9% of the entire population. In Simi Valley City where the Superior Court of Ventura County is located, the racial distribution is even more skewed towards a greater proportion of white residents. For example, 79.9% of the county residents are white, compared to 1.5% black, 12.7% Hispanic, 5.3% Asians, and 0.5% Native Americans.

If the trial had taken place in the Central Superior Court District in Los Angeles, greater representation of members of racial minorities could have been ensured because the Superior Court is located in the City of Los Angeles where approximately 63% of city residents are members of racial and ethnic minorities. Specifically, minority residents comprise: 13.0% black, 39.9% Hispanic, and 9.2% Asian of the jurisdiction.

The California Second District Court of Appeal, however, granted the change of venue, citing the political turmoil over the Los Angeles Police Department, and thus overruled originally-appointed Judge Kamins who decided that the four officers be tried in Los Angeles. Further, the change of venue to Ventura County assured that the fate of four police officers on trial for beating the black motorist would be in the hands of jurors drawn from a community that was largely white, largely middle-class, and the residence of choice for many police officers (Stevens, 1992).

In Los Angeles County, only 48 percent of residents owned their own homes and more than 15% of the population had an annual income less than $10,000. By contrast, in the City of Simi Valley where the trial was held, people were mostly employed, attended one of the city's 47 churches, were involved in its 25 primary and secondary schools, were well off economically, and practiced a middle-class life style where three-quarters of the residents owned their own homes. In recent years, many members of the Los Angeles Police Department had fled for personal safety to Simi Valley. Los Angeles Loyola Law School Professor Laurie L. Levenson, for example, said that "The responsibility for this verdict falls on the jury. Frankly, the people in Simi Valley worship the police" (Gross, 1992). Thus, the jury selected from the residents in Simi Valley neighborhoods was expected to be politically conservative and pro-police (Smith, 1992).

After the verdict on April 29, the prosecution drew fire for not fighting the change of venue. Prosecutor Terry L. White who is black, however, did not object strenuously to the choice of Ventura County for the trial. He initially agreed that the trial should be moved from Los Angeles County to a different site for a fair trial, and showed satisfaction with Ventura County as an ultimate trial site for the four white officers (Smith, 1992).

Voir Dire

In January 1992 Judge Weisberg ordered the 2,000 member jury pool, the largest in the history of the state. The number of summoned jurors was much greater than the total summons for the high-profile McMartin Preschool molestation trial, which lasted 7 and half years, ending in August 1990 in Los Angeles (Butler et al., 1994). In the beginning of February, 1992 the selection process began with the mailing of a questionnaire to prospective jurors in the jurisdiction. It was followed by courtroom interviews with more than 260 prospective jurors in an effort to discover any biases about the highly publicized beating. The total of 205 jurors who appeared at the courthouse were assigned to King's beating trial.

On February 6, pre-voir dire questionnaires were distributed to every prospective juror assigned to the trial. The questionnaires, which listed 102 questions and names of 173 possible witnesses, asked the jurors a variety of questions on their attitudes toward law enforcement agencies, potential racism and prejudice against minorities, and their feelings and opinions about the videotape. The questionnaires were distributed to every prospective juror to evaluate whether they were biased in a way that might prevent them from examining the case impartially.

The questions, for example, included the following:

1. Do you think police officers treat people differently in low income neighborhoods than they do in middle to upper income neighborhoods?
2. What are your views towards the police in general or the role of the police officer?
3. Do you feel that a police officer's testimony will be more truthful or accurate than that of a civilian?
4. What are your views towards police officers as individuals?
5. Do you believe police officers can make mistakes?

6. Do you believe that a police officer should be the subject of criminal prosecution if he has committed what the law declares to be a crime while on duty?

7. Do you believe that the conduct of a police officer in the field should be the subject of criminal prosecution if he has committed what the law declares to be a crime while on duty?

The pre-voir dire questionnaire also asked questions about potential racism and biases towards racial and ethnic minorities. For example, one of the questions included:

Is there anything about such a scenario [possible beatings of the black motorist by white police officers] that causes you concern?

After the prospective jurors filled out the questionnaires, they were called in to the courtroom for the voir dire screening session. On the basis of their responses to the questionnaire, Judge Weisberg questioned prospective jurors about their opinions and possibly biases about the case. Judge Weisberg's discretion in dismissing and giving excuses to potential jurors from the jury pool played a significant role in selecting a predominantly white jury for the trial. For example, on February 20, despite the repeated objections by prosecutors, Judge Weisberg dismissed the first group of 10 prospective jurors who said that they were outraged by the videotape. Responding to a 102-item questionnaire, several prospective jurors vividly described their recollections of the videotape. The first juror, dismissed at the defense request, wrote that "the officers were obviously beating the man, which was unnecessary because [he] was on the ground in handcuffs." Another prospective juror said that the officers had acted "brutally and beyond reason." She was excused. Of the first 40 persons allowed to remain on the panel, only one was black. Two other blacks were called but excused, one for hardship reasons and one because he said that he had concluded the police officers used excessive force (Cannon, 1992)

In most states, attorneys on both sides conduct most of this voir dire questioning. But in California, Proposition 115, a massive rewrite of California criminal law that voters passed in June 1990, shifted that questioning of voir dire to the judge. Thus, attorneys in the trial could only submit questions, but they were in the nature of follow-up questions, and the judge was not obliged to use them. Proposition 115 supporters generally billed the measure as a way to speed up justice, but opponents said that it would mean the loss of essential safeguards in the criminal justice system. The problem of attorneys' inability to directly question prospective jurors was more evident in the beating trial because the prosecution obviously failed to evaluate and reveal potential jurors' biases and possible prejudice on the basis of jurors' prior occupations and associations with law enforcement agencies.

With the prosecution facing a jury pool like that in Simi Valley, a pro-police and conservative community, the defense clearly appeared to gain an advantage. The defense was seeking jurors who were independent-minded enough to look beyond the apparent ambiguity of the videotape, while at the same time being sympathetic to authority figures like law enforcement officers. For example, when the judge questioned each juror, his questions might not include in-depth questions that attorneys would have asked. The effect of the restrictive nature of the question sessions seemed to reflect on the kind of jurors selected for the jury box.

Thus, the final jurors selected by both the defense and prosecution attorneys reflected the lack of detailed information on the background of prospective jurors during voir dire which could have been discovered by the prosecutors. For example, the final jury included three persons who were relatives of police officers and three jurors who were members of the National Rifle Association. With close associations with law enforcement agencies, those potential jurors were more likely to share the life experience and morals that may have been underling factors in the crime in question. Thus, they may have been willing to impute to the defendants a weak intent to commit the violent act, assaulting a civilian with a deadly weapon. As a consequence of the inability to carefully and objectively examine each prospective juror through direct questionings, the prosecution failed to identify potential biases of jurors and eliminate them by the use of a peremptory challenge.

The Simi Valley jury of twelve did not include a single black juror. It was composed of six white men and four white women, one Hispanic woman and an Asian woman born in the Philippines. All jurors were married and had children. Their age ranged from 39 to 65; three were 65 or over; three between 50 and 59; three between 43 and 50; and three between 39 and 40. Eleven owned their own homes; and only the Hispanic juror, Virginia Bravo Loya, was a renter (Galloway and Griffith, 1992). Eight had either served in the armed forces or had spouses who have been in the military, going back as far as World War II. Five members of the panel said in the questionnaires that they owned or used guns while in the military or for hunting or recreational target shootings. Three jurors had relatives who have served on police departments, including a woman who said that her step-father was a police officer in Portland, Oregon, and another who said that his brother was a retired Los Angeles Police Department sergeant.

Five were registered Republicans: one a retired program manager for a government military contractor; one a retired real estate broker living in a house behind barbed wire with a pad locked chain-link front gate; another a retired teacher who served in the Navy as a shore patrolman, living in a large house behind a huge American flag on a tall pole; another with four small children; and the Filipino Amelia Pigeon living in a house assessed at $229,000. There were five Democrats in the jury that included one former military policeman with the Air Force; two relatively isolated individuals living in remote areas; and one divorced woman living alone in a modest home. (Reinhold, 1992b).

They were a secure, yet fearful, conservative-minded group. On the pre-voir dire questionnaires, all jurors stated that they had heard about the King beating. When jurors were asked whether they believed that police officers treated people in low-income neighborhoods differently from residents of middle- and upper-income areas, two jurors said that they believed that people in poor neighborhoods received different treatment, while nine said that the police treated citizens the same regardless of the area. One was undecided. Seven jurors said that they had been victims of crimes ranging from robbery to assault. On the questionnaires, all said that they had positive opinions of police in general and the role of police officers (Galloway and Griffith, 1992).

The Jury Box

Given the milieu from which the jurors emerged, all but the Hispanic juror were apparently convinced by this line of reasoning, and seemed to be looking to their own belief in security against the Rodney King, who for mere suspicion could be beaten by police officers acting under the color of authority. The large majority of eight jurors, however, were inclined to acquit almost from the beginning of their deliberations, overwhelming the four "dissidents" on not guilty verdicts for three officers. These four nonetheless "hung the jury" by holding out for at least one guilty verdict against defendant police officer Lawrence Powell.

One female juror told the press that she voted to acquit the officers because King had repeatedly resisted arrest and "was in full control" of the situation that resulted in his own beating. Another juror thought that King "was not being abused," but "was directing the action. He was the one that determined how long it took to put him in handcuffs because as long as he fought the patrolman, the policemen had to continue to try to maintain him, to keep from having more erratic felonious acts" (Daniels, 1992).

Another anonymous juror told the talk-show host Larry King that the videotape of the beating was "ludicrous," because Rodney King had "dictated all of the actions" (*Newsweek*, 1992a). Still another female juror said that she, another woman, and two men had pressed for guilty verdicts on the charges against the officers throughout jury deliberations, but were ultimately worn down by the 8-member majority. And though the jury forewoman said that "to me what I saw on the tape was excessive use of force," and that she "fought hard because I saw that justice was not being done," trying "to use the videotape as evidence," she surrendered to the consensus to acquit three officers and was left to hold on to her "own conviction" by siding for conviction of the fourth officer, thereby deadlocking the jury and raising the possibility that the D.A. could again charge him on this count (Daniels, 1992).

While the beating trial had two minority jurors, they might have looked at Rodney King's actions very differently from those who lived in Los Angeles County. John D. Gilleland, a psychologist from a jury consulting firm called Jury Analysts in Pennsylvania, stated that "[A] L.A. County jury, even if they had been 10 whites, one Hispanic and one Asian, would have had very different perceptions." Reasoning in a similar way, California legislators thus began considering proposals requiring that when cases are moved between jurisdictions they be transferred to areas of comparable ethnicity and density (Margolick, 1992).

Standing on the courthouse steps after the verdict, L.A. Councilwoman Patricia Moore called the result "a modern-day lynching." John Singleton, director of "Boyz N the Hood," said, "This is a time bomb. . . . It's going to blow up" (*Los Angeles Times*, 1992a; *Newsweek*, 1992b). "This was a jury well attuned to the defendants, while politically and demographically a world apart from the victim," declared African-American Judge LaDoris Cordell of the Santa Clara County Superior Court. "The Simi Valley 12 responded predictably—they sided with the protectors of justice against the bestial black man, even while witnessing daily a videotape exposing the relentless, inhuman assault of the four defendants. Such is the power of prejudice that this compelling evidence did nothing to dispel stereotypes" (Cordell, 1992).

Prosecution and Incompetence

The prosecution had done poorly. Despite what appeared as evidence of the uncontroverted videotaped police brutality, defense lawyers won the jurors over in defining the process that led up to the beating: that King could have avoided the beating in the first place by failing to resist; that King thus set the agenda for the beatings; and that the force justified by circumstances at the onset also justified whatever force flowed in subduing King. It was a fallacious argument because the police officers, not King, were on trial for the use of excessive force beyond subduing King.

The institutional court system may be to blame for black chief prosecutor Terry L. White's lack of aggressive prosecution. Yet Deputy District Attorney White saw no hope of obtaining a more favorable panel than those selected from the pool of over 200 potential jurors answering written questionnaires. With blacks making up only 2 percent of the population of Ventura County, nonetheless there were six blacks in the jury pool that Deputy D.A. White could have sought—though he did not use up all his arbitrary peremptory challenges to try to eliminate obviously unfavorable jurors. Nor did he try to move the venue to a place where black jurors might have been secured.

In California, in the interest of a fair trial, a single judge in a superior court may change venue from one jurisdiction to another, even where the demographics of the substituted locale may be dramatically different from the place where the alleged crime was committed. The appeals court had already ruled that the four officers could not receive a fair trial in Los Angeles County. And in the name of finding unbiased jurors—who undoubtedly were as familiar with the videotaped beating as those in Los Angeles—Judge Stanley Weisberg of the L.A. Superior Court had transferred the case from Los Angeles to Simi Valley that was an overwhelmingly white, conservative enclave and the home of the Ronald Reagan Presidential Library. Having represented many victims of police brutality, Los Alamitos lawyer Tom Barham thought that the facts of the King case "were so overwhelming that the court did backflips to give this trial every appearance of fairness." "Everyone from the president to the dogcatcher had their necks in a noose," said John Barnett, accused Officer Theodore Briseno's lawyer (*Newsweek*, 1992a).

John C. Burton , Co-chairman of the Police Misconduct Lawyers Referral Service in Los Angeles, asserted that L.A. County District Attorney Ira Riener was ambivalent about the case from the outset, that chief prosecutor Terry White took cues from his boss, that the lack of prosecutorial zeal stemmed from their role as "part of the same state apparatus as the police. They're used to prosecuting Rodney Kings, not defending them. To them, he's just another minority young man who's been chucked onto the junk pile" (Margolick, 1992).

The Federal Civil Rights Trial

The acquittal verdict by the first state jury prompted angry demonstrations by many political groups, students, and racial minorities across the country. The verdict and subsequent riots in many urban cities led federal officials to reopen the case as a civil rights matter.

After the 1992 verdict, there were a number of emerging structural and political factors that differentiated the federal trial from the state trial. For example, Bill Clinton was elected as the new president and he specifically stated that his administration would strive to improve the civil rights status of many minority groups. While both the Reagan and Bush administrations largely failed to improve the civil rights of minorities, the new administration showed stronger commitment to pay greater attention to issues of justice, and social and economic inequities. Thus, it seemed certain that the federal government would respond to the King case by sending two of their best federal prosecutors available: Barry F. Kowalski, Deputy Chief of the Justice Department, Civil Rights Division and Steven D. Clymer, working for the Los Angeles Bureau of the U.S. Attorney's Office and regarded as a rising star in bringing convictions in many difficult federal cases.

In February, 1993 the second trial for the civil rights violation of Rodney King began in the Central Federal District Court in Los Angeles, California, based on federal constitutional law defining criminal activity as intentionally depriving the victim of his civil rights.

The Federal Rodney King case was thus different than the first state trial where the charges were criminal assault under color and authority of law. For in the federal indictment three officers (Briseno, Powell, and Wind) were charged with depriving Rodney King of his civil rights to be free from the use of unreasonable force during an arrest under color of law, as well as aiding and abetting in a conspiracy to do so; and the supervising officer Sergeant Koon was charged with violating Rodney King's 14th Amendment right not to be deprived of liberty without due process of law when Koon failed to restrain the officers under his charge from repeatedly kicking and striking King. The federal criminal case thus had the element of the police officers' intentional infliction of on-the-scene punishment, without due process of law, depriving the victim of his civil rights to be secure in his person against arbitrary arrest, excessive force, and summary punishment by the police.

In the federal trial, similarly, three specific stages of jury selection played a key role in determining the jury composition and subsequently the outcome of the trial. These included: (1) Stage 2 for the source list from which federal jurors were selected, (2) Stage 4 for creating qualified jurors' lists by mailing jury qualification questionnaires to potential jurors who were randomly selected from the source list, and (3) Stage 7 for conducting voir dire in screening and selecting the final jury.

The Source List for Federal Juries

In many states including California, two source lists are used to compile the names of prospective jurors: (1) voter registration lists (ROV) and (2) motor vehicle registration lists (DMV). The American Bar Association (ABA, 1983, Section 3.7) provides the two criteria for the source lists: (1) inclusiveness and (2) representativeness. *Inclusiveness* refers to the proportion of the adult population on the source list; *representativeness* refers to the proportionate presence of cognizable groups on the list. The ABA suggests that voter lists supplemented by lists of licensed drivers will provide reasonable inclusiveness and representativeness.

In the federal system, however, voter registration lists are used as a source list because of the Jury Selection and Service Act of 1968 in which Congress was persuaded that voter rolls would meet the representativeness, or fair cross-section, test of random selection from the community, a requirement guaranteed by the Sixth Amendment to the U.S. Constitution (U.S. C., 1968, Section 1861).

The use of ROV lists alone, however, does not lead to a representative cross section of the community because of differential registrations by race and social class. Research estimates that voter lists automatically exclude approximately one third of the adult population, tipping prospective jury selection toward the elderly, the relatively affluent, the self-employed, and government workers, and away from minorities, including blacks, Hispanics, women, and the poor (Kairys 1972, pp. 777-780; Fukurai et al., 1993, pp. 43-47). Some observers of jury selection take the position that minority underrepresentation resulting from the exclusive use of the voter list is justified because it is the individual's responsibility to register to vote and those persons uninterested in voting probably will not make good jurors. As a result, the voter list can be viewed as a screening mechanism to eliminate those who are deemed undesirable (U.S.C. 1968, Sections 1792, 1796). Irvin Kaufman, chairman of the committee that drafted the 1968 Jury Selection Act, stated that the voter list "supplies an important built-in screening element. It automatically eliminates those individuals not interested enough in their government to vote or indeed not qualified to do" (U.S.C., 1967: 253). This position is clearly contradictory to the eligibility limitations specified in the Federal Jury Selection Act of 1968, which disqualifies only noncitizens; those under age 18; those who have not "resided for a period of one year within the judicial district"; those "unable to read, write, and understand the English language with a degree of proficiency sufficient to fill out satisfactorily the juror qualification form"; those "unable to speak the English language"; those with "mental or physical infirmity"; and those under indictment or convicted of an offense punishable by imprisonment of more than one year (U.S.C., 1968, Section 1985 (b)). While not a legally mandated criterion in the act, participation in the electoral process has become a *de facto* prerequisite to jury participation. This view has now taken on the status of *stare decisis*, the binding power of precedent.

Table 4.1 shows the reported voter registration by different racial groups in Los Angeles County, California. A lower voter registration rate is found among racial minority groups in both past and recent congressional and presidential elections. Research shows that Hispanic populations are most likely to be underrepresented in jury pools because of their lower registration rates. Hispanic electoral participation is even lower than that of the black population. For example, in the 1988 presidential election, 67.9% of whites registered but only 35.5% of the Hispanic-origin population registered. For the past fifteen years in California and Los Angeles, black adults had higher registration rates than whites. Nationally, however, although the registration rate of black voters was higher than that of Hispanics, it was consistently lower than the overall registration of white populations in both presidential and congressional elections between 1968 and 1992 (Fukurai et al., 1993, pp. 18-19). These data suggest that in Los Angeles, the use of ROV lists for federal juries had detrimental effects on Hispanic jury participation because more than 80% of Hispanics are systematically excluded from jury service at the outset.

It becomes no surprise that the racial composition of selected jurors for the federal civil rights trial was quite different from the racial composition of residents in the federal district court jurisdiction (see Table 4.2). For example, the jury in the federal trial of the officers consisted of nine whites, two blacks, and one Hispanic, which appears to be more representative than the state trial, which only included one

TABLE 4.1   Reported Registration in California and Los Angeles County by Race and Hispanic Origin in November 1980 and 1990 Election

Race	1990 California Percentage	1990 California Standard Error	1988 California Percentage	1988 California Standard Error	1980 Los Angeles Percentage	1980 Los Angeles Standard Error
Total Voting						
White	57.0	0.7	60.7	1.0	54.7	1.3
Black	62.4	2.7	69.5	4.2	65.1	4.0
Hispanic Origin*	25.7	1.2	24.4	2.1	18.8	3.4

*Persons of Hispanic origin may be of any race.
Source: U.S. Bureau of the Census, Current Population Reports, Series P-20, No. 370, 440, "Voting and Registration in the Election of November 1980," "Voting and Registration in the Election of November 1988," "Voting and Registration in the Election of November, 1990," U.S. Government Printing Office, Washington, D.C., 1981, 1989, 1991.

Hispanic and one Asian jurors. But the 1990 U.S. Census indicates that only 40% of Los Angeles County residents were white, and 60% were members of racial and ethnic minorities. Similarly, only half of the residents in the LA federal court jurisdiction which covers seven counties in southern California were white (50.6%). To truly reflect the community and claim to speak on behalf of the community, the member of white and minority jurors should have been almost equal.

TABLE 4.2   The Central Federal District Court Jurisdiction: Racial Compositions of Seven California Counties (Percentages)[1]

Places	White[2]	Black	Hispanic	Asian[3]	Native American[4]	Others
County						
Los Angeles	40.8	10.5	37.8	10.2	0.3	0.2
Orange	64.5	1.6	23.4	10.0	0.4	0.1
Riverside	64.4	5.1	26.4	3.3	0.7	0.2
San Bernardino	60.8	7.7	26.7	3.9	0.7	0.2
San Luis Obispo	81.2	2.0	13.3	2.7	0.8	0.1
Santa Barbara	66.1	2.5	26.6	4.1	0.6	0.1
Ventura	65.9	2.2	26.4	4.9	0.5	0.1
Federal Court Jurisdiction						
Seven Counties	50.6	7.7	32.5	8.6	0.4	0.2

[1]Figures are based on the 1990 U.S. Census.
[2]Calculated by subtracting the total nonwhite population from the total population (18 years or older) and divide it by the total population. Thus the variable can be named as non-Hispanic white populations.
[3]Asians included Pacific islanders.
[4]Native Americans include American Indians, Eskimos, and Aleuts.

The use of ROV thus systematically excludes racial minorities from jury selection and the federal jury in the King trial did not reflect the fair cross section of the community in Los Angeles County or the Federal Court District jurisdiction.

The Jury Qualification of Prospective Jurors

The fourth step in the federal jury selection procedure is to compile the name of qualified potential jurors, after the randomly selected jurors are screened by jury qualification questionnaires. Once the master file has been created, jury commissioners can take two discretionary steps in compiling the qualified-jurors file: (1) setting qualification standards and (2) designing the method for compiling the list of qualified jurors.

The 1968 Federal Jury Selection and Service Act specifies the qualifications for jury service in the federal court: (1) being "a citizen of the United States eighteen years old who has resided for a period of one year within the judicial district"; (2) having an ability "to read, write, and understand the English language with a degree of proficiency sufficient to fill out satisfactorily the jury qualification form"; (3) having an ability "to speak the English language"; (3) not being unable, "by reason of mental or physical infirmity, to render satisfactory jury service"; and (5) not having "been convicted in a State or Federal court of record of a crime punishable by imprisonment for more than one year," unless the person's civil rights have been restored by pardon or amnesty (U.S.C., 1968, Section 1965 (b), (5)).

In addition to the qualification, another important factor that is influential at the qualification stage of jury selection, particularly for trials like the federal King case, is jury sequestration. As few in Los Angeles were willing to serve in such a case out of fear and assuming responsibility, selecting a large jury pool and empaneling a jury of impartial peers to try the case was a critical factor in the ultimate outcome. Federal District Court Judge John G. Davies ordered that the jury would be sequestered and that the names of the jurors would remain confidential to prevent jury tampering and harassment—the first time in more than a decade that the Federal Court in Los Angeles had done so.

Fear of involvement and self-exclusion were immediate, major factors in selecting the jury for the second trial. For jurors from the first trial had been harassed and threatened after their names were published; hounded by the press and electronic media. To deal with public reluctance to get involved in a second trial, presiding Judge Davies stepped outside normal jury-selection procedures, sending out qualification questionnaires to prospective jurors based on their willingness to participate in a sequestered jury trial.

Technically speaking, the Federal District Court in Los Angeles was able to draw from a pool of more than 16 million residents spanning the seven-county central district of California. But rather than issuing summons, inquiries were sent out to an initial pool of 4,482 prospective jurors. Of these inquiries, 905 were not returned, some 3,347 respondents stated they could not serve on a sequestered jury for a trial, and only 230 (5.1% of mailed jurors) said that they would be willing to be sequestered in a trial that could last at least two months. Presiding Judge Davies then had 2,000 additional letters sent out to potential jurors, providing no information about the nature of the case, only asking preliminary questions intended to screen those who could not serve because of time conflicts with sequestration or other constraints.

Sequestration is a procedure to insulate jurors from publicity about the trial and information on the defendants that is not admissible in evidence. Because jury service is a hardship involving loss of personal time and provides inadequate pay, this personal burden is likely to result in a jury that is not representative of the community. Due to minimal compensation, prospective jurors who have less education and less income, and who are in secondary labor markets, tend to be underrepresented (Fukurai et al., 1993). Jurors with higher education and thus higher paying jobs are more able to sit on a sequestered jury (Fukurai and Butler, 1991). Thus, the resulting group of sequestered jurors is not likely to be representative of the community at large (Van Dyke, 1977, p.181; Fukurai et al., 1993, pp.159-160).

With $10 as their daily fee for jury service in Los Angeles, the lives of jurors were confined to a court-provided apartment for the entire duration of the trial. As the Mitchell-Stans trial in the early 1970's revealed, sequestered juries generally do not represent the fair cross-section of the community (Fukurai et al., 1993). Furthermore, the resulting verdicts by racially and economically demarcated juries do not have strong legitimacy in the eyes of citizens (Fukurai et al., 1993, pp.72-73).

Another important factor setting limits on minority participation at this stage of jury selection is the lack of follow-up of qualification questionnaires sent to prospective jurors. Because jury qualification questionnaires are generally sent by mail, highly mobile people have the least chance of receiving them and a permanent residence becomes essential if one is to participate in the process. One's labor market position as a migrant enhances the probability of being excluded from a jury pool, as those who move and fail to receive jury qualification questionnaires ("undeliverables") or to return them ("recalcitrants") cannot qualify for selection. In fact, such persons are systematically eliminated. Thus a potential juror who has just entered the job market, and/or who is placed in a less stable, secondary labor market, is likely to be eliminated long before being called into the courthouse. Even if he or she makes it into the courthouse, he or she is likely to be excused for reasons of economic hardship. Consequently, potential jurors from a less stable, secondary labor market have fewer chances of surviving the jury selection process, and in the world of job-structured benefits, those who failed to receive qualification questionnaires or who ask to be excused from jury duty are predominantly members of racial minorities (Fukurai et al., 1987; Fukurai and Butler, 1991, Fukurai et al., 1993, pp.21-22).

Voir Dire

Similar to the first state trial, voir dire - the seventh stage of jury selection - performed the important function in influencing the outcome of the federal trial. Like the state trial in Simi Valley, both prosecution and defense attorneys were prohibited from directly questioning prospective jurors. However, both lawyers in the federal trial were able to conduct in-depth analyses of bias in potential jurors who were assigned to the King trial. Before voir dire, all the assigned jurors were requested to fill out a 53-page, 125-item pre-voir dire jury questionnaire which information became the basis for the selection of final jurors in the trial.

While no black jurors did not serve on the first state jury, the voir dire in the second federal trial was conducted differently and two black jurors were finally selected to serve on the jury. During voir dire the defense had tried to exclude potential jurors who live in the riot area, particularly blacks, on grounds that they might find it difficult to vote for acquittals because that would lead to new disturbances in their residential areas. A black male the defense tried to remove was a Marine veteran who has lived in the Watts neighborhood for 25 years. The defense argued that he should be excused from the panel because the defense saw him as favoring the prosecution based on his experience in Watts and he probably has seen police abuse in his neighborhoods (Kramer, 1993). He also made the statement in the lengthy pre-voir dire questionnaire that he had been disappointed in the verdicts in Simi Valley. However, U.S. District Judge John G. Davies refused to allow the defense to exclude a long-time black resident of the Watts on the ground that jurors cannot be excluded on the basis of race (*Batson v. Kentucky*, 106 U.S. 1712 1986).

Similarly, the defense argued to exclude a black female postal worker from suburban Orange County. The defense challenged her credibility and sought to remove her from the panel. For example, one day before the trial was to begin the defense told Judge Davies that an excused juror, a white reserve policeman, had called to tell them that the postal worker "disdainfully" blamed defense lawyers about the absence of blacks on the previous jury in Simi Valley that virtually exonerated the officers of state criminal charges. Judge Davies, however, refused to allow the defense to remove the black female postal worker from the panel.

After the lengthy voir dire, it became evident that, for the first time in two years, black jurors were allowed to sit in the trial of four white police officers. In the state trial, almost all participants in the trial were members of the racial majority: all white defendants were represented by all white defense attorneys, the trial was presided over by a white judge, and white defendants were tried by a predominantly white jury which was selected from dominantly white residential areas. District Attorney Terry L. White in the state trial had been the only black person involved in the beating case. Originally appointed superior court judge, Bernard Kamins, was also black but he was later dismissed and replaced by a white judge Stanley Weisberg. While racial backgrounds of participants in the federal trial remained almost identical, the federal jury finally included jurors who shared the same racial and cultural background as the black motorist. For instance, the federal jurors had the following characteristics: (1) 9 white, 2 black, and 1 Hispanic and (2) 8 male and 4 female. The jurors also included: a former Marine, a Watts resident for 25 years, a worker in the real estate industry, a U.S. Postal Service worker, an insurance firm worker, a business dealer, a former security guard who has used a police baton on people twice but in one case then talked the man into giving up a potential weapon, a welder from Denmark who served on six juries, and a retail clerk.

During the trial the names of twelve federal jurors were not disclosed. They were only referred to by number in order to provide each juror greater protection and to try to insulate them from the public and media. However, close ethnographic observations in the courtroom indicated that the jurors were mostly in their 40s and 50s except Juror No. 7, who is a black women believed to be in her 20s who works for the U.S. Postal Service, Juror No. 10, a white man in his 20s, who once was convicted for driving under the influence, and Juror No. 12, a Hispanic man in his 20s or early 30s who said that he had never seen the videotape of King's beating and had no opinion about it.

On April 17, 1993 the jury finally deliberated approximately 60 hours and decided that two of four police officers, Sergeant Stacy Koon and Officer Laurence Powell, were guilty of violating Rodney King's civil rights. The other two officers, Timothy Wind and Theodore Briseno, were acquitted by the jury.

Conclusions

The jury serves as a reminder that we have a democratic government that derives its power from the people. However, recently mistrust of the jury system has been expressed by many observers and participants. Both accused and victims of crime sometimes doubt the fairness of verdicts, arguing that jurors acted out of emotion rather than reason, or that jurors are prejudiced to racially motivated cases. These criticism have serious consequences for the legitimacy of the judicial system because the jury plays such a unique and important role in our society.

The analysis of the King's beating trials suggested both legal and extra-legal factors that contributed to the acquittal of the white officers by the state jury and the subsequent urban riot. Those factors include: (1) the change of venue to a jurisdiction of a predominantly white community, (2) inherent biases in the jury selection system, ensuring the underrepresentation of minority jurors in the jury box, (3) elimination of a black judge on unsubstantiated information and overruling his decision that the trial be held in Los Angeles County where the alleged crime had taken place, and (4) racism within the Los Angeles Police Department, cojoined to a rising incidence of police abuse against racial and ethnic minorities. While the second federal trial resulted in the conviction of two of the four officers, our analyses revealed that the composition of the federal jury did not reflect a cross section of the community in a federal court jurisdiction of Los Angeles. In January 1990, in *Holland v. Illinois*, the Supreme Court reiterated the idea that no single jury need to be an accurate representation of the community. However, for a racially sensitive trial like the King beating case in Los Angeles, racially balanced juries could have provided much stronger legitimacy in representing collective community sentiments, especially in the eyes of racial and ethnic minorities.

The possible reforms and elimination of biases in the jury selection system include the following: (1) uses of multiple source lists (ROV, DMV, and other sources including property tax and social security lists) so that the compiled source list contributes to the enlarged jury pools available in the jurisdiction; (2) the change of venue to be granted to a new jurisdiction where the race and class makeup is similar to the original site; (3) securing abilities of prosecution and defense attorneys to directly question prospective jurors during voir dire;

(4) requiring mandated follow-ups of non-returned jury qualification questionnaires and jury summonses; and (5) increased payments to potential jurors. As our analysis pointed out, the use of ROV lists alone does not lead to a representative cross section of the community because voter lists automatically exclude large proportions of racial and ethnic minorities. Despite the obvious advantages of using multiple source lists, the majority of states, as well as virtually all federal courts, continue to use only the ROV list to identify potential jurors. The impact of narrowly defined source lists on minority representation is undoubtedly severe and the use of multiple source lists can improve judicial participation by members of racial and ethnic minorities.

Secondly, the change of venue plays an important role in deciding the trial site and the kind of jury pools available for the trial. We recommend that if the trial is to be granted, it should go to a new site where racial and social class compositions are similar to the original trial site. In California, since a single judge can determine the location of the new trial site, the judge should be required to consider extra-legal dimensions of the potential jury pool such as race and social class makeup of prospective jurors in the new jurisdiction.

Thirdly, since jury summonses and qualification questionnaires are generally sent by mail, it is important to require courts to follow up mailings to potential jurors to ensure their appearance for courtroom screening. For example, in Los Angeles, between 1983 and 1984, almost one million jury qualification questionnaires (963,836) were mailed to potential jurors. Approximately 44% (423,779) of them were not responded: 15% undeliverables (140,581) and 29% recalcitrants (283,198). While the follow-up of nonresponses is required by law, it has been virtually non-existent in almost all of state and federal courts (Fukurai et al., 1993, pp.119-122). Thus the follow-up of both undeliverables and recalcitrants becomes crucial in an attempt to obtain a cross sectional representation on jury trials.

Fourthly, Proposition 115 in 1990 eliminated the ability of prosecution and defense attorneys to directly question individual prospective jurors. Federal courts also rely on judge-conducted voir dire methods. While Proposition 115 supporters generally billed the measure as a way to speed up justice, recent research shows that the judge-directed voir dire methods cost as much as attorney-conducted voir dire and that judge-directed voir dire shows greater problems in impaneling "impartial" juries because judge-conducted voir dire is less successful in revealing jurors' potential biases (Johnson, 1990). Since the requirement of trials by impartial jurors is less likely to be met under the judge-conducted voir dire method, attorneys should be allowed to question individual prospective jurors in both state and federal courts.

Lastly, the prospect of getting five to ten dollars a day, less than half the minimum wage, is a disincentive to many potential jurors. Minorities and the urban poor are the least able to give up most of their income for a minimum of one or two weeks. Many of them consequently disregard their subpoenas or manufacture gimmicks to get excused. Thus the inadequate jury compensation contributes to class and race bias in the composition of jurors. There are two ways to cope with inadequate compensation problems. One way of compensating jurors is to make employers continue to pay regular salaries to their employees while serving on juries. In the past, attempts have been made to equalize the economic burden of jury duty by securing mandatory company compensations. For example, Hawaii, in 1966 and 1970, passed a statute requiring employers to continue an employee's salary during jury service. This law required every employer with more than 25 workers to continue the salary of any employee who served on a jury or participated on any public board. However, the law was later declared unconstitutional by the Hawaii Supreme Court as a violation of the equal protection clause and the taking clause of both the U.S. and the Hawaii Constitutions (*Hasegawa v. Maui Pineapple Co.*, 52 Haw. 327, 475 p.2d 679 1970). While it may not be unreasonable for large corporations who employ the bulk of Americans to subsidize jury functioning as a public service, this might be too big a burden for small businesses to afford. The statute also left out many potential jurors such as hourly-wage and daily-wage earners, the underemployed, and the unemployed. Prospective jurors whose livelihood depends on commissions were also inadequately compensated by mere salary-continuation plans.

Second, since payments to jurors represent a tiny fraction of the total expenses of the legal system, juror pay could be raised substantially. In 1992, although jury fees vary among counties, jurors were awarded $5 a day in most state and federal courts in California. Savings accrued from using modern techniques for making juror utilization more efficient and averting wasted hours spent sitting in the jury hall may be a important step to obtain the additional funds to pay for the increased wages for jurors. Adequate juror compensations will be an important incentive to the urban poor and contribute to greater jury participation by members of racial and ethnic minorities. After all, the judge and prosecutors are paid by the state because they are considered part of the system. Why not jurors?

After the 1967 summer "riots," the Kerner Commission Report (1968) had warned that the nation was moving toward two societies, one black, one white—separate and unequal—suggesting that the resourceful and imaginative use of available legal processes could contribute significantly to the alleviation of tensions—providing the black underclass a meaningful opportunity to influence events which affect them and their community. Yet, for the past thirty years, the step towards egalitarianism in the jury system and equal treatment by the law enforcement agency had not been carried out. Rather official violence and legal injustices have continued, with the 1992 acquittal of white police officers and the subsequent urban uprising in Los Angeles and many other urban cities, suggesting that no end is in sight. In order to establish the legitimacy of jury verdicts and win public confidence in police fairness, it is of great significance to eliminate biases in the jury selection process that contribute to the underrepresentation of minority jurors and to work for deep-seated reforms in law enforcement agencies like the LAPD.

Acknowledgment

This project was made possible by two Academic Senate intramural grants awarded to the first author. Appreciation is extended to Robert Thompson and John Brown Childs, Board of Studies in Sociology at the University of California, Santa Cruz for their continuing support and encouragement. For information, contact Hiroshi Fukurai at (408) 459-2555, FAX at (408) 459-3334, or e-mail at hiroshi@cats.ucsc.edu.

References

Abramson, Jill, McQueen, Michael, Kotlowitz, Alex, and Rigdon, Joan. 1992. "Ills of Urban America Return to the Spotlight in Politics and Offices." *Wall Street Journal*, May 1.

American Bar Association. 1983. *ABA Standards for Criminal Justice*. ABA: Standing Committee on Association Standards for Criminal Justice.

Butler, Edgar W. and Hiroshi Fukurai. 1992. "Computer-aided Evaluation of Racial Representation in Jury Selection," *Computers, Environment and Urban Systems*, 16(2): 131-155.

Butler, Edgar W., Hiroshi Fukurai, Jo-Ellen Huebner-Dimitrius, and Richard Krooth. 1994. *The Anatomy of the McMartin Trial*. New Brunswick, NJ: Rutgers University Press.

Cannon, Lou. 1992. "Policemen Win round in L.A. Beating Trial: Judge Excuses 10 Jurors Influenced by Tape." *Washington Post*, February 21.

Cannon, Lou. 1993. "L.A. Beating Trial Jury Chosen: Judge Refuses Defense Request to Bar Black Resident of Riot Area." *Washington Post*, February 23.

Contemporary Social Issues in Los Angeles: A Panel Discussion-Final Report. 1992. University of California, Santa Cruz, Social Science Division.

Cordell, LaDoris. 1992. "Rodney King Verdict Shakes A Judge Into

Questioning—In Horrified Disbelief—Her Faith In The System She's Part Of," *The Buffalo Soldier Newsmagazine* (East Bay Edition, Special to the Mercury News), May 10.

Crewdson, John. 1980. "10 Die in Miami Riot," *New York Times*, May 19.

Daniels, Lee A. 1992. "Some of the Jurors Speak, Giving Sharply Differing Views," *New York Times*, May 1.

Fukurai, Hiroshi and Edgar W. Butler. 1991. "Organization, Labor Force, and Jury Representation: Economic Excuses and Jury Participation," *Jurimetrics* 32:49–69.

Fukurai, Hiroshi and Edgar W. Butler. 1994a. "Sources of Racial Disenfranchisement in the Jury and Jury Selection System," *National Black Law Journal* in press.

Fukurai, Hiroshi and Edgar W. Butler. 1994b. "Black Jurors' Underrepresentation—Intentional or Institutional? Discriminatory Jury Selection Process, Gerrymandered Judicial Districts, and Racially Designated Verdicts," *Phylon*, in press.

Fukurai, Hiroshi, Edgar W. Butler, and Jo-Ellan Huebner Dimitrius. 1987. "Spatial and Racism Imbalances in Voter Registration and Jury Selection," *Sociology and Social Research*, 77: 33–38.

Fukurai, Hiroshi, Edgar W. Butler, and Richard Krooth. 1991a. "Cross-sectional Representation or Systematic Jury Representation? Simple Random and Cluster Sampling Strategies in Jury Selection," *Journal of Criminal Justice* 19: 31–48.

Fukurai, Hiroshi, Edgar W. Butler, and Richard Krooth. 1991b. "Where Did Black Jurors Go? A Theoretical Synthesis of Racial Disenfranchisement in the Jury System and Jury Selection," *Journal of Black Studies* 22(2): 196–215.

Fukurai, Hiroshi, Edgar W. Butler, and Richard Krooth. 1993. *Race and the Jury: Racial Disenfranchisement and the Search for Justice.* New York: Plenum Publishing.

Galloway, Laura A. and Ann Griffith. 1992. "Questionnaires reveal attitudes of King jury," *Los Angeles Times*, March 15.

Gross, Jane. 1992. "In Simi Valley, Defense Of a Shared Way of Life," *New York Times*, May 4.

Hans, Valerie and Niel Vidmar. 1986. *Judging the Jury*. New York: Plenum Press.

Johnson, Catherine M. 1990. *Felony Jury Selection: A Social Psychological Analysis.* Unpublished Dissertation. University of California, Santa Cruz.

Kairys, David. 1972. "Jury Selection: The Law, a Mathematical Method of Analysis, and a Case Study," *American Criminal Law Review*, 12: 771–806.

Kerner Commission. 1968. *Kerner Commission Report on Civil Disorders.* Washington. D.C.: U.S. Government Printing Office.

Kramer, Pamela. 1993. "King-case Juror Ill, But Trial Can Go On." *San Jose Mercury News*, April 15.

Levine, James. 1993. *Juries and Politics*. Pacific Grove, CA: Brooks/Cole Publishing Co.

Los Angeles Times. 1992a. "Understanding the Riots, Part 2: Images of Chaos." *Los Angeles Times*, May 12, Section T.

Los Angeles Times. 1992b. "Understanding the Riots, Part 4: Seeing Ourselves," May 14, Section T.

Margolick, David. 1992. "Switching Case to White Enclave May Have Decided Outcome," *New York Times*, May 1.

Mydans, Seth. 1992a. "Officers' Assault Trial Nears Opening,". *New York Times*, March 2.

Mydans, Seth. 1992b. "Los Angeles Policemen Acquitted in Taped Beating," *New York Times*, April 30.

Newsweek. 1992a. "The Siege of L.A.," May 11.

Newsweek. 1992b. "Crime: A Conspiracy of Silence," May 18.

Reinhold, Robert. 1992a. After Police-Beating Verdict, Another Trial for the Jurors. *New York Times*, May 9.

Reinhold, Robert. 1992b. "Acquittal of All 4 Officers Was Shock, Gates Says," *New York Times*, May 21.

Reinhold, Robert. 1992c. "Judge Sets Los Angeles for Retrial of Officer in Rodney King Beating," *New York Times*, May 23.

Report of the Independent Commission. 1991. The Independent Commission led by Warren Christopher, Los Angeles.

Smith, Danyel. 1992. "Justice for All: Searching in Vain After the Verdict," *Express*, East Bay, Vol 14, No. 30, May 8, 1, 14.

Smith, Leef. 1992. "Juror Selection Begins in Videotaped-beating Trial," *Washington Post*, February 6.

Stevens, Ann Sarah. 1992. "Deciding Moment of the Trial May Have Been Five Months Ago." *Wall Street Journal*, May 1.

Van Dyke, Jon. 1977. *Jury Selection Procedure.* Cambridge: Gallinger.

5

Public Opinion Before and After a Spring of Discontent[1]

Lawrence Bobo, Camille L. Zubrinsky,
James H. Johnson, Jr., and Melvin L. Oliver

Yet to do all of these things and spend the sums involved will all be for naught unless the conscience of the community, the white and the Negro community together, directs a new and, we believe, revolutionary attitude toward the problems of our city.

—The McCone Commission, 1965

This alternative will require a commitment to national action—compassionate, massive and sustained, backed by the resources of the most powerful and the richest nation on this earth. From every American it will require new attitudes, new understanding, and, above all, new will.

—The Kerner Commission, 1968

Can we all get along?

—Rodney King, 1992

The Los Angeles rebellion of 1992 differed from its predecessors of the 1960s and 1980s not merely in terms of the magnitude of the devastation and the level of the emergency response needed to quell the civil unrest, but in several other important respects (Johnson et al. 1992).[2]

First, the participants in the civil unrest represented a range of ethnic groups. For example, more Latinos were arrested and killed than were blacks.

Second, the violence had a much more systematic quality and was targeted at another ethnic minority: Korean entrepreneurs.

Third, events in Los Angeles ignited deep and powerful grievances across the nation. Many cities, some with quite small minority populations (e.g., Omaha and Minneapolis), experienced large scale protests and violence.

Fourth, the rebellion was conveyed to the rest of nation and the world with unparalleled speed and often in shockingly graphic detail. As a consequence of the highly sophisticated and dense media market in Los Angeles, and of the globalization of news events made possible by the Cable News Network (CNN), literally hundreds of millions of people could share the same events virtually as they unfolded on the streets of Los Angeles.

In part for these reasons, the beating of Mr. King, and the Simi Valley brutality verdict now stand as global symbols of the extent to which racial oppression is omnipresent in the U.S. For example, nearly four full months after the police brutality verdict and the rebellion a Pakistani woman who counsels victims of hate crimes in Great Britain was quoted as saying: "We all know about Rodney King and what happened in Los Angeles. But the problems are [in East London], they are everywhere, and the more we acknowledge that, the better for all of us" (Schmidt, 1992).

By any measure, the verdict and rebellion in L.A. were watershed events in the nation's experience, which are likely to leave a permanent imprint on the national consciousness and on how the rest of the world perceives the U.S. In this regard, world leaders were quick to comment on events in Los Angeles, some of them in quite strong terms. Some of the strongest criticism came from French President Francois Mitterand who said the riots were "above all a racial conflict and racial conflict is always wed to poor social programs. George Bush is a generous man, who embodies an extremely conservative political ideology, and American society is conservative and economically capitalist. Here are the results." Criticism of the Simi Valley police brutality verdict also came from a right-wing British paper which opined that "justice [has been] mocked by prejudice" (Los Angeles Times, 1992).

These dramatic events also raised fundamental questions about both the current and future state of race relations in Los Angeles, the nation's most diverse metropolis, and in the nation as a whole, which is rapidly becoming more ethnically heterogeneous. Few in-depth studies are available to answer these crucial questions. Most of the recent public opinion studies that sought to examine issues of interethnic relations were in the position of tapping individuals attitudes and beliefs strictly in the wake of the verdict and the subsequent rebellion. Thus most efforts to understand perceptions of how the criminal justice system treats minorities, basic racial attitudes and the like, are post-rebellion assessments based on quickly conducted media polls of limited scope.

The purpose of this chapter is to provide a crucial exception to the types of public opinion studies published in the aftermath of the Los Angeles civil unrest of 1992. UCLA's annual Los Angeles County Social Survey for 1992 had as its focus, prior to the civil unrest, the issue of "Ethnic Antagonism in Los Angeles".[3] The survey had been in the field for twelve weeks prior to the verdict and rebellion, and the interviewing continued for another twelve weeks after the civil unrest. As a result, we are able to paint a detailed portrait of the racial attitudes, beliefs and preferences of a random sample of Los Angeles County residents prior to the verdict/rebellion and of a random sample of residents immediately after the verdict/rebellion. In addition, shortly following the uprising we conducted a series of focus group discussions. These discussions were especially useful for understanding the unexpectedly high levels of Latino involvement in the uprising. With the survey and focus group data we can provide, in a way that no previous poll or social science survey has been able to do, answers to the following crucial research questions:

Did the most destructive civil unrest of this century harden ethnic antagonisms or open the door to mutual understanding?

Did the rebellion worsen stereotypes and prejudice, or did it break down the prevailing negative images and orientations?

Did the civil unrest greatly weaken, or did it fundamentally rekindle, a commitment to resolving the American Dilemma?

We know of only four other occasions where sample surveys provide close pre- and post- event measures of racial attitudes following dramatic social events. None of these previous instances combine the depth of topical coverage and large subsamples of several major ethnic groups characteristic of the 1992 LACSS. One such reading of opinion occurred at the time of President Eisenhower's decision to send troops into Little Rock, Arkansas in 1957 and another occurred at the time of the assassination of Dr. Martin Luther King, Jr. Both studies took place in Texas, included one or just a few racial attitude measures, and contained significant data on the attitudes of whites only (for a report on these data see Riley and Pettigrew, 1976). The third such reading also involved the assassination of Dr. Martin Luther King, Jr. and involved samples of black respondents in the Detroit area. In this case, the pre-event measurement included a small number of black respondents and only six questions (see Schuman and Hatchett, 1974). The fourth occasion involved the 1991 Los Angeles County Social Survey (formerly called the Southern California Social Survey) which conducted interviewing before and after the airing of the Rodney King Police Beating video (see Sidanius et al., 1991). The latter study, however, also contained few racial attitude measures and very limited data on the opinions of blacks, Asians, and Latinos. Hence, the 1992 LACSS data constitute a fortuitous but also genuinely historic assessment of public opinion on race and ethnic relations before and after a set of the most traumatic racial events in the nation's experience.

This chapter is divided into three sections. In the first section we provide more complete details on the scope, design, and content of the 1992 LACSS. The second section reviews the major findings of the research in several key topical domains. These domains include opinions on life in Los Angeles, fears and beliefs about crime, opinions on the nature of poverty and of black-white economic inequality, perceptions about the traits and abilities of different ethnic groups (i.e., stereotypes), and preferences for interethnic contact or separation. Our final section then reviews the main findings and identifies several major implications of the research.

The 1992 Los Angeles County Social Survey

Since 1986 the Survey Research Center at UCLA's Institute for Social Science Research (ISSR) has conducted an annual survey. From 1986 to 1991, the survey covered a three county area including Los Angeles, Ventura, and Orange counties and was thus labeled the Southern California Social Survey. Beginning in 1992 the area sampled was restricted to Los Angeles County and hence the project is now titled the Los Angeles County Social Survey. The 1992 LACSS was a countywide random digit dial telephone survey of adults living in households and was conducted by the Computer Assisted Telephone Interviewing unit of the Survey Research Center at ISSR. In addition to the general countywide sample, oversamples of telephone numbers in zip code areas of high black concentration (65% or more) and of high Asian concentration (30% or more) were used in order to efficiently generate larger numbers of black and Asian respondents. To fully capture the views and opinions of Los Angeles' very large Latino population, a Spanish language translation of the questionnaire was developed. Monolingual Spanish speakers and those preferring to conduct the interview in Spanish were interviewed in Spanish. A majority (56%) of the interviews with Latinos took place in Spanish. Overall, interviews averaged 38 minutes in length.[4]

The pre-verdict/rebellion interviewing took place from February 3, 1992 until April 29, 1992 at approximately 3:30 PM, yielding a total of 963 interviews. The Post- verdict/rebellion interviewing extended from that time until July 29, 1992, yielding a total of 906 interviews. Thus, 51.5% of the interviews were obtained prior to the verdict/rebellion and 48.5% in its aftermath.[5]

The core focus of the 1992 LACSS, as noted previously, was "Ethnic Antagonism in Los Angeles". In addition to measuring basic background and demographic characteristics of respondents (i.e., age, sex, race, ethnic ancestry, marital status, household composition, education, employment status, occupation, family income, religion, etc.), the study also measured a wide array of social attitudes, beliefs, and experiences. This chapter emphasizes results for topical areas including attitudes on: the death penalty, crime, social spending, confidence in institutions, beliefs about poverty and black-white economic inequality, life in LA, interethnic social distance, interethnic stereotypes, and the fairness of ethnic group experiences in America. We consider then whether the verdict/rebellion changed opinions about LA as a place to live, affected fear of crime and levels of punitiveness in response to crime, as well as how these dramatic events may have affected fundamental feelings of interethnic social distance, basic stereotypes, and how people think about the broader issues of poverty and black-white economic inequality.

Throughout the chapter we have two key interests. First, we wish to know whether the verdict/rebellion shifted opinions from what they were prior to these dramatic events. Second, we wish to know to what degree members of the major ethnic groups here in Los Angeles react differently in general, and with specific reference to whether the level of pre- events/post-events change is larger or smaller, or varies in direction, depending on ethnic background. In cases of no change in opinion, the figures will show results for the entire survey. In those instances of clear cut pre-events/post-events change, figures will be separated by pre- or post-conditions or report the post-events results only. We note a few cases where statistically reliable change occurred but where the direction of change was ambiguous thus leading us to rely on the overall (as opposed to pre versus post) figures.

Major Survey Findings

Life in Los Angeles

By and large feelings about life in Los Angeles were not affected by the events of spring 1992. Survey respondents were asked if, over the last five years, they felt that Los Angeles had "become a better place to live, a worse place to live, or stayed the same?" Overwhelming majorities, 70% or greater of each of the four major ethnic groups, felt that LA had become a "worse" place to live. There was no change in opinion among Asian, black or Hispanic respondents, but surprisingly, a small shift among whites toward saying that things had "stayed the same". In short, opinions on the general trend in the quality of life in LA were already so negative that there was little room for the verdict/rebellion to further shift opinion in a negative direction.

There has been widespread concern that the disturbance would worsen the economic fortunes for recession weary residents of Southern California. Our data, however, show no rise in economic uncertainty directly tied to the verdict/rebellion. For example, there was no change in level of concern that someone in the household might lose a job within the next six months. The lack of change was as true among blacks, Latinos, and Asians as it was among whites, even though the former more often live in neighborhoods that were affected by the disturbance. To be sure, there are important group differences in the level of worry about job loss. Hispanics were far more likely to express "a lot" of concern about someone in the household losing a job (41.8%) than were Asians (26.8%), blacks (19.9%), or whites (14.9%). This is not an unexpected finding given that Latinos are highly concentrated in low wage, service and craft specialty industry jobs in Koreatown and South Central Los Angeles, the region most adversely affect by the civil unrest. Further justification for the high level of concern over possible job loss in the Hispanic community is provided by data on the overall socioeconomic status of each group. A full 52% of Hispanic households in the survey reported family incomes below $20,000 annually. Given that Hispanic households tend to be larger as well this translates into a very low household per capita income figure (roughly $8,000), which is less than 50% that of white and Asian households in the survey and slightly higher than 50% that of black households.

As a second way of tapping economic insecurities the survey contained a question on whether it was a good or bad time to make large purchases of the type that require "downpayments and loans"? In the current recession it is no surprise that substantial fractions of all the major ethnic groups perceive it to be a "bad time" to make large purchases. In addition, there is no evidence of pre-events/post-events change in this perception.

The LACSS also tapped opinion about the performance of the local government in Los Angeles. In general, blacks expressed the least amount of confidence in the local government, followed by Hispanics and then whites, and lastly Asians who expressed slightly higher levels of confidence than did whites. Among Asians, blacks, and Latinos, there was no significant change in confidence in the local government in response to the verdict and disturbance. However, among whites, there was some shift toward more polarized views as the percentage expressing both "a lot of confidence " (+5.4%) and "not much confidence" (+5.3%) rose by about equal margins after the disturbance, leaving fewer people in the intermediate "some confidence" category (down from 56.5% to 45.7%).

When asked about the local police there was no significant change in opinion among Asians, Blacks, or Hispanics. There are, nonetheless, sharp group differences in opinion about the police. Fifty-six percent of blacks express "not much" confidence in the local police as compared to 31.1% of Hispanics, and 26.3% of Asians. Among whites, however, there is a significant decline in confidence in the local police following the disturbance. The percentage expressing not much confidence rose from 13% to 20.5%. Despite this decline, whites remained the least likely to give low confidence ratings to the police.

Crime and Punishment

Another common concern raised in the wake of the disturbance involves the level of fear of crime. All respondents were asked how likely it was that a member of their household would be a victim of a crime during the next 12 months. Among each group the level of fear of crime was relatively high. Surprisingly, there was no significant change among any of the ethnic groups. What movement there is appears, in fact, to be in the direction of slightly less fear of crime, particularly so among blacks. This slight trend may be a reaction to the declaration of a truce between the rival "Bloods" and "Crips" gangs who have been linked to much of the violent criminal activity in South Central Los Angeles.

Since personal fear of crime did not rise it is less surprising to discover that other indicators of concern with issues of crime and punishment also showed no change. When asked if we are generally spending "too much", "too little", or "about the right amount of money" on "halting the rising crime rate" our pre-events/post-events comparisons find no real movement. To be sure, large majorities of

Asians, Blacks, Hispanics, and Whites believe that "too little" is money is spend in this area. Yet this feeling did not increase in the wake of the disturbance.

There is also no indication that the disturbance led to greater feelings of punitiveness in response to crime among Los Angeles County residents. The LACSS included a question on support for the death penalty for persons convicted of murder. Pre-event responses to this question were not discernibly different from post-event responses among any of the major ethnic categories. Levels of support for the death penalty were highest among whites, followed closely by Asians, then Hispanics, and lastly blacks.

The Verdict and the Rebellion

Four questions were added to the survey immediately following the Simi Valley police brutality verdict and the eruption of violence in South Central Los Angeles.[6] We asked about opinions on the verdict acquitting the four LAPD officers who beat Mr. King, about the overall fairness of how the criminal justice system treats African Americans, about opinions on an amendment to the Los Angeles City Charter that would limit the police chief to two five year terms of office, and about whether the violence following the verdicts was mainly legitimate social protest or criminal behavior.

Consistent with the results of other local and national polls, the LACSS data show (Table 5.1) that substantial majorities of all the major ethnic groups disagreed with the jury's verdict in the police brutality trial (see Mathews, et al. 1992; Church, 1992; Elis, 1992; Lacayo, 1992; Kramer, 1992). But even here, there are large group differences. Fully 96% of blacks disagreed with the verdict as compared to roughly three-quarters of Asian and Latino respondents and just under two-thirds of white respondents. Indeed, one in five whites expressed agreement with the verdict. Although the absolute level of agreement with the verdict is low even among whites, it is important to note that the level of agreement with the verdict among whites is ten times the level found among blacks and approximately twice that found among Latinos and Asians.

Solid majorities of all groups expressed support for an amendment to the city charter to limit the Los Angeles Chief of Police to two five year terms. Blacks were the most likely to favor such a change (78.9%), followed closely by Asians (76.1%), who were followed, in turn by whites (70.9%), and then Hispanics (62.6%). These patterns are largely the same when attention is restricted to data for the four week period from May 2, 1992, when the questions were introduced, to

TABLE 5.1   Post Verdict/Rebellion Opinions on Criminal Justice System Issues

Now I have some questions to ask you about the Rodney King case. First, how did you feel about the jury verdict acquitting the four police officers accused of beating Rodney King? Do you personally strongly agree, agree, neither agree nor disagree, disagree or strongly disagree with the jury verdict?

Response	Asians	Blacks	Hispanics	Whites
Strongly agree	2.5	.5	1.0	4.0
Agree	10.6	1.4	9.4	17.25
Neither agree nor disagree	11.1	1.8	10.7	13.4
Disagree	36.4	20.6	45.8	32.8
Strongly disagree	39.4	75.7	33.1	32.3
N	(198)	(437)	(478)	(372)

How about the statement that blacks usually don't get fair treatment in the courts and criminal justice system? Do you strongly agree, agree, neither agree nor disagree, disagree or strongly disagree with that statement?

Response	Asians	Blacks	Hispanics	Whites
Strongly agree	8.4	44.2	7.9	9.2
Agree	36.6	35.5	37.1	30.3
Neither agree nor disagree	17.8	6.1	17.6	13.2
Disagree	31.7	11.1	32.8	36.5
Strongly disagree	5.5	3.1	4.5	10.8
N	(202)	(425)	(466)	(370)

Some people say these disturbances are mainly a protest by Blacks against unfair conditions. Others say they are mainly a way of engaging in looting and street crime. Which of these statements seems more correct to you? (IF VOLUNTEERED, 50/50 mixture).

Response	Asians	Blacks	Hispanics	Whites
Mainly protest	42.9	67.5	38.7	37.4
Half and half protest and looting	6.6	9.7	9.4	6.9
Looting and street crime	50.5	22.8	51.9	55.8
N	(196)	(412)	(470)	(364)

Source: Based upon 1992 LACSS.

June 2, 1992, when Los Angeles voters actually voted to pass Charter Amendment F to implement several of the Christopher Commission recommendations, including term limitations for the police chief. It is interesting to note that even a majority of self-identified political conservatives supported this change in the city charter.

Although most people disagreed with the jury verdict and were supportive of reforming the LAPD, there is less evidence of broad majority consensus and large group differences in opinion when respondents were asked if blacks usually do not receive "fair treatment in the courts and criminal justice system". Eighty percent of black respondents agreed that blacks usually do not receive fair treatment. This contrasts sharply with the 45% of Asian and Latino respondents who adopted this view, and with the 39% of white respondents who agreed that the criminal justice system usually treats blacks unfairly.

Views of the civil unrest also produced large differences between blacks and other groups. When asked whether the disturbance was "mainly a protest by blacks against unfair conditions" or "mainly a way of engaging in looting and street crime", only 22.8% of blacks gave the latter response with over two-thirds of blacks interpreting the disturbance as a protest against unfair conditions. In contrast, slightly more than half of whites, Asians, and Hispanics defined the disturbance as no more than looting and street crime. Only small fractions of any of the groups were inclined to volunteer that the disturbance involved an equal mix of social protest and criminal behavior.

The verdict in the police brutality trial was clearly seen as unjust and most residents of Los Angeles County saw a clear need to reform the LAPD as recommended by the Christopher Commission. However, on all of these questions there are important group differences, with a particularly sharp contrast emerging between the views of blacks and those of whites. On the whole, blacks appear to be strongly inclined to see the verdict as part of an on-going and systematic pattern of injustice that blacks face when dealing with the criminal justice system. Whites, and to a considerable degree Asians and Hispanics, see the verdict as wrong but also exceptional. One product of these widely different assumptions is widely diverging interpretations of the civil unrest that followed on the heels of the verdict. These patterns point to fundamental problems once again brought to the surface by these events, an issue to which we return in the conclusions to this report.

Poverty and Racial Inequality

Many commentators have suggested that one potential positive outcome of the civil unrest would be new ways of thinking about and renewed commitment to addressing problems of poverty and racial inequality. Unfortunately, the LACSS data provide no indication that such new thinking is taking place. All LACSS respondents were asked to agree or disagree with each of four different statements about "why there are poor people" in America? Two of these reasons explain poverty in terms of larger social barriers to opportunity such as the "failure of society to provide good schools" or a "failure of industry to provide enough jobs". Alternatively, two of these reasons explain poverty in terms of the shortcomings and weaknesses of individuals such as "loose morals and drunkenness" and "lack of effort by the poor themselves". Pre-/post-event comparisons reveal no significant change among Asians, blacks, Hispanics, or whites. Most people see poverty as involving both an element of societal blame and individual blame. Within this general pattern, however, it is clear that blacks are the most likely to believe that general societal barriers to opportunity are causes of poverty and are among the least likely to accept individual blame explanations.

Given the absence of change in basic assumptions about the underlying causes of poverty it is not surprising that support for social spending on the poor did not change in the wake of the disturbance. When asked whether "too much", "too little" or "about the right amount of money" was being spend on programs for the poor a solid majority of each group felt that "too little" was spent. Nonetheless, this initially favorable posture toward social spending on the poor was totally unaffected by the events of this spring. Again, we should note that blacks stand out in their support for greater spending on the poor, with Hispanics closely behind.

The 1992 LACSS also included a set of questions concerned with possible explanations for the large gaps in socioeconomic status between blacks and whites. Two of these reasons point to barriers encountered by blacks such as "discrimination" and lack of educational opportunity. Two of these reasons point to potential shortcomings of blacks such as "less in born ability" or a lack of effort and motivation. With one noteworthy exception (discussed below), the results suggest no change in how residents of Los Angeles county think about black-white inequality as a result of the verdict and civil unrest. Blacks more so than any of the other groups see racial discrimination as a cause of black-white economic inequality. Still, a majority of all groups agree that discrimination is one cause of black-white socioeconomic inequality. Blacks are the least likely to accept an explanation that emphasizes blacks' levels of motivation and effort. Hispanics and Asians, large fractions of whom are immigrants to the U.S., are the most likely to accept effort and motivation on the part of blacks as a cause of black-white economic inequality. In general, people resist explaining black-white inequality in terms of lower ability levels among blacks, though greater than 1 in 5 Asians did so.

The one clear sign of change following the verdict and the disturbance occurred among blacks. There was a significant rise in the percentage of blacks who felt that racial discrimination was a causal factor in black-white economic inequality. The proportion agreeing that discrimination was a reason for black-white inequality rose from an already high 75.2% to 83.6%. This confirms many of the speculations commentators made following the Simi Valley police brutality verdict that blacks would grow more pessimistic about the treatment they could expect from white dominated social institutions (Bobo, 1992).

Ethnic Group Alienation and Equity in America

One of the central concerns of the 1992 LACSS was to determine how the different ethnic groups in Los Angeles felt about the general social and economic opportunities available to them in the U.S.[7] To assess these views the survey included the following questions:

> Now I will read several statements. Please tell me whether you strongly agree, agree, neither agree nor disagree, disagree, or strongly disagree with the following statements.
>
> American society owes people of my ethnic group a better chance in life than we currently have.
>
> American society has provided people of my ethnic groups a fair opportunity to get ahead in life.
>
> I am grateful for all the special opportunities people of my ethnic group have found in America.
>
> American society just hasn't dealt fairly with people from my background.

The responses show no pre-verdict/rebellion to post-verdict/rebellion change among whites and Latinos. In sharp contrast, however, the responses of African-Americans show substantially more feelings of having been treated unfairly and deeper alienation across all four statements after the verdict and the rebellion (Table 5.2). The single largest change took place in response to the first statement concerning whether American society owed members of one's own ethnic group a better chance in life. Whereas 54.7% of blacks agreed with this statement prior to the verdict and disturbance, fully 75.4% agreed with it following these dramatic events. The proportion of blacks who disagreed with the statement that "American society has provided people of my ethnic with a fair opportunity" rose from 49.4% to 63.4%; the proportion who disagreed with the statement "I am grateful for all the special opportunities people of my ethnic group have found in America" increased from 24.1% to 32.5%; and the proportion who

TABLE 5.2 Ethnic Alienation Questions

American society owes people of my ethnic group a better chance in life than we currently have?

Response	Asians			Blacks			Hispanics			Whites		
	Pre	Post	Total	Pre	Post	Total	Pre	Post	Total	Pre	Post	Total
Agree	36.9	44.0	42.2	54.7	75.4	64.8	49.5	64.1	64.2	17.3	14.8	16.5
N	(73)	(209)	(282)	(243)	(228)	(471)	(224)	(245)	(469)	(409)	(209)	(618)

American society has provided people of my ethnic group a fair opportunity to get ahead in life?

Response	Asians			Blacks			Hispanics			Whites		
	Pre	Post	Total	Pre	Post	Total	Pre	Post	Total	Pre	Post	Total
Agree	65.7	66.2	66.1	42.9	27.1	35.4	68.6	62.1	131.9	84.4	83.8	84.2
N	(73)	(210)	(283)	(249)	(232)	(481)	(226)	(248)	(474)	(411)	(210)	(621)

I am grateful for all the special opportunities people of my ethnic group have found in America?

Response	Asians			Blacks			Hispanics			Whites		
	Pre	Post	Total	Pre	Post	Total	Pre	Post	Total	Pre	Post	Total
Agree	74.3	77.5	76.7	62.9	55.0	59.0	82.7	80.8	81.7	76.0	77.8	76.6
N	(70)	(209)	(279)	(245)	(231)	(476)	(225)	(250)	(475)	(405)	(207)	(612)

American society just hasn't dealt fairly with people from my background?

Response	Asians			Blacks			Hispanics			Whites		
	Pre	Post	Total	Pre	Post	Total	Pre	Post	Total	Pre	Post	Total
Agree	36.7	35.3	35.6	63.6	75.8	69.4	41.2	44.5	43.1	11.8	14.6	12.8
N	(71)	(207)	(278)	(245)	(227)	(472)	(221)	(246)	(475)	(467)	(211)	(617)

agreed with the claim that "American society just hasn't dealt fairly with people from my background" rose from 63.6% to 75.8%.

The absolute levels of ethnic alienation among blacks are very high, especially in the Los Angeles context. At the time of the survey, Tom Bradley was in his nineteenth year as Mayor of Los Angeles and a black man, Willie Williams, had been designated as the new police chief. To be sure, the specific ethnic alienation questions pose a national, as opposed to a local, frame of reference. It is nonetheless striking that in an area with a high level of black political empowerment locally that we find such high fractions of the black population expressing feelings of unfair treatment. Such patterns speak to the severe limitations of local black political empowerment when situated in a larger social context of racial inequality and ongoing discrimination (see Bobo and Gilliam, 1990, especially pp. 387-89).

This strong and uniform rise in black alienation from American social institutions is the single clearest and most consistent change observed for any of the items we have examined. Careful inspection of responses shows that this rising discontent occurred among black men and women, as well as across educational and income levels. With respect to the effects of income level, however, there is an unexpected twist. We combined responses to the four questions and generated a simple average score for all black respondents. Analysis of this "Ethnic Alienation from American Society" measure showed, critically, that the rise in discontent was strongest among black households whose incomes were $50,000 or higher. Mean alienation scores rose after the verdict/rebellion for all black income groups, but the increase was greatest among blacks in the highest income category. The magnitude of the change among the high income category is very nearly a full standard deviation unit increase.

Asians were the only other group to undergo significant movement in level of ethnic alienation. The change was not consistent across all of the items, however. As was true among blacks, Asians tended to become more pessimistic. The question asking whether one's ethnic group had had a "fair opportunity to get ahead in life" produced the clearest change. Following the verdict and rebellion the percentage of Asians who disagreed with this statement rose from 8.2% to 20.0%. The overall percentage of Asians who agreed with statement, "I am grateful for all the special opportunities people of my ethnic group have found in America", did not change much as one compares the pre-verdict/rebellion response (74.3%) to the post-verdict/rebellion response (77.5%). However, the percentage who "strongly agreed" with the statement was cut in half, falling from 25.7% (pre-verdict/rebellion) to 12.4% (post-verdict/rebellion).

Dimensions of Prejudice I: Stereotyping

Stereotyping is regarded as one of the fundamental elements of racial/ethnic prejudice (Allport, 1954; Pettigrew, 1982). The 1992 LACSS included a number of questions designed to tap group images, which parallel items included in a recent major national survey (Bobo and Kluegel 1993; Davis and Smith, 1990; Smith, 1991), and other statewide surveys (Bobo et al. 1992). Respondents were asked to rank on seven point scales members of their own ethnic group and the members of each of the other major ethnic categories. The end points of the scales were defined in terms of three key pairs of traits: intelligent to unintelligent, prefer to live off of welfare to prefer to be self-supporting, and hard to get along with to easy to get along with. This measure allows us to assess whether members of any given group (e.g., whites) rate members of other groups (e.g., blacks, Asians, or Hispanics) more positively (e.g., less likely to prefer living off of welfare), the same, or more negatively (e.g., more likely to prefer living off of welfare) than members of their own group. For example, fully 61.2% of whites rated blacks as more likely to prefer living off of welfare relative to whites, 35.5% rated the two groups as equally likely to prefer living off of welfare, and 3.3% felt that whites were more likely to prefer living off of welfare than blacks. Whites hold similarly negative stereotypes of Hispanics: 59.3% said that Hispanics were more likely to prefer living off of welfare than to be self-supporting. Whites' perceptions of Asians' preferences for welfare (only 21%) is considerably lower indicating a much more favorable image overall. Los Angeles County residents are, nonetheless, more racially tolerant in their views than the nation as a whole. These figures are more liberal or tolerant than those for whites' views of blacks and Hispanics as measured in the 1990 General Social Survey (Bobo and Kluegel, 1991).

In general, we found almost no evidence of change in racial stereotyping in Los Angeles among any of the groups following the verdict and the rebellion. The only sign of change occurred among Asians who, to a degree, became more hostile toward blacks. Asians were more likely to perceive blacks as having lower intelligence and less likely to perceive blacks as easy to get along with. Specifically, the percentage of Asians who rated blacks as more intelligent was 11.3% prior to the verdict/rebellion but fell to just 2.9% after the verdict/rebellion and the percentage rating blacks as lower in intelligence increased from 59.2% to 64.9%. Whereas 20.8% rated blacks as more likely to be easy to get along with prior to the verdict/rebellion this figure was cut roughly in half after the rebellion, falling to 9.5%.

It is important to note that negative stereotyping is fairly common, especially with regard to perceptions of blacks and Hispanics. To show this pattern we have averaged the proportion of respondents (e.g., blacks, Asians, and Hispanics) who rated members of each other group (e.g., whites) negatively on each trait dimension to produce an indicator of the average level of negative perception that each group faces from the other three groups combined. The results are telling.

Blacks (especially) and Hispanics face the highest degrees of negative stereotyping. On the average 45.1% of non-blacks in Los Angeles County rated blacks as lower in intelligence; fully 63.4% rated blacks as more likely to prefer living off of welfare, and 48.5% rated blacks more likely to be hard to get along with. On average among non-Hispanics, 44.6% rated Hispanics as less intelligent, 52.2% rated them as more likely to prefer living off of welfare, and 34.5% rated them than as more likely to be hard to get along with. Thus, for blacks and Hispanics, anywhere from a third to two-thirds of those individuals from non-black or non-Hispanic background, respectively, are likely to believe them inferior in intelligence, in determination to remain off the public dole, and in ease of common social interaction.

Such broadly shared negative perceptions do not hold where whites or Asians are at issue. The percentage rating whites negatively never exceeds 25% and is considerably lower for two of the traits (intelligence and welfare dependency). The only trait where an appreciable fraction (45.5%) of members of non-Asian groups rate Asians negatively is in terms of being hard to get along with.

The overall average level of group stereotyping masks, however, some important group variations. For example, a higher fraction of Asians than Hispanics or whites hold negative views of blacks with regard to intelligence and desire to live off of welfare. In the post-verdict/rebellion data, as noted previously, 64.9% of Asians rated blacks as less intelligent. These patterns may shed considerable light on the level of tension and conflict found between blacks and some segments of the Asian-American community. In addition, Hispanics were the most likely to rate blacks unfavorably in terms of being difficult to get along with.

Dimensions of Prejudice II: Social Distance

One reason scholars place significant emphasis on stereotyping is that such group specific beliefs and behavioral expectations should influence behavior toward them. To the extent members of a group are perceived negatively then it follows that others are likely to avoid social contact with them, especially if the contact might be of a prolonged and intimate nature. The 1992 LACSS contained two sets of questions on social distance feelings of this kind. Respondents from each ethnic group were asked separate questions on, first, whether they would favor or oppose living in neighborhood where half of their neighbors would, one group at a time, be members of each of the other groups. These questions are a relatively demanding test of openness to residential integration since they ask about substantially mixed settings (Farley et al. 1978; Schuman and Bobo, 1988). A second set of questions asked respondents whether they would favor or oppose an interracial marriage that involved a "close relative or family member".

The one clearly positive change in all of the items we have examined involves the level of openness among whites to residentially integrated settings. As contrasted to pre-verdict/rebellion figures (Table 5.3), whites expressed significantly greater openness to substantial integration with regard to blacks (+13%), Hispanics (+18), and Asians (+18%). The consistency of these data strongly suggest that many whites concluded that the high levels of residential segregation in Los Angeles, colloquially referred to as a distinction between city and suburb, were an important factor in the verdict in the police brutality trial outcome and the explosion of anger and resentment that followed it. One indication that this shift in openness to residential integration is not merely liberal lip service is that there is less movement on the issue of racial intermarriage. Among whites there was an increase in the percentage expressing openness to intermarriage with Hispanics (+9.3%), but no movement with respect to blacks or Asians. If people had merely been trying to sound more liberal then we would have found equally positive and consistent trends on the intermarriage questions as well. We do not, presumably because some barriers, especially at the level of intimacy involved here, are more deeply felt than others.

TABLE 5.3 Whites Favoring Social Contact

	Whites		
	Pre	*Post*	*Total*
Neighborhood that is half:			
Asian	22.0	40.1	28.2
Black	15.3	28.4	19.7
Hispanic	20.9	39.1	27.1
Family member intermarriage to:			
Asian	27.0	34.3	29.6
Black	23.5	28.0	25.0
Hispanic	30.8	40.1	33.9

Source: Based upon 1992 LACSS.

We found no evidence of significant change in social distance feelings among blacks, or among Asians. In general, the most common response to the social distance questions was neither one of clearly favor or clearly oppose contact, but rather the intermediate response of "neither favor nor oppose". Among Hispanics, however, there was a drop in openness to intermarriage with Asians as one compares the pre-verdict/rebellion results (40.6%) to the post-verdict/rebellion results (34.5%).

All the same, a clear set of patterns emerged with respect to social distance (Table 5.4). As with the stereotyping questions, we averaged the level of opposition to contact with any given group (e.g., blacks) across the responses of each of the other groups (e.g., Asians, Hispanics, whites). The results are telling. For both residential contact and for intermarriage the level of hostility to contact with blacks exceeds that found for all other groups. Strikingly, Asians express the highest level of opposition to residential contact with blacks.

Dimensions of Prejudice III:
The Hidden Conflict Between Asians and Latinos

Another part of the story that has yet to be told concerns what we call the Hidden Conflict: the growing tensions between Koreans and Latinos. Indeed, this tension probably helps account for the level of violence directed at Korean merchants and businesses.

As part of a larger research project at UCLA we scheduled a set of focus group discussions with blacks, whites, Latinos, and Asians on the subject of intergroup relations and residential segregation. We signed a contract for the groups two weeks prior to the verdict and the rebellion and scheduled the first round of groups for the second week in May. Overall, we sought to have gender balanced groups between 21 and 50

TABLE 5.4   Group Opposition to Social Contact

	Asians	Blacks	Hispanics	Whites
Neighborhood that is half:				
Asian	—	19.2	20..6	17.7
Black	46.2	—	32.8	30.8
Hispanic	24.9	21.4	—	20.7
White	6.1	8.3	8.6	—
Family member intermarriage to:				
Asian	—	14.8	20.4	25.8
Black	31.8	—	25.5	32.8
Hispanic	20.3	11.9	—	21.2
White	13.8	9.9	8.9	—

Source: Based upon 1992 LACSS.

years of age with a minimum annual household income of $15,000; and included participants residing in the Los Angeles area for at least a few years. Two of the four Latino groups were conducted in Spanish, and the Asian groups were conducted in Mandarin Chinese (2) and Korean (2). Groups ranged in size from 9 to 12 participants and lasted approximately two hours. Groups were ethnically homogeneous including the discussion moderator (for a complete description, see Bobo et al. 1994).

The results of our discussions with Latinos suggested that they harbored the same grievances against Korean merchants and business owners as did blacks. The discussions yielded examples of Latino-Korean conflict in patron/client relationships, the case most frequently publicized in the black-Korean conflict. However, Latinos also reported problems in employer/employee contexts, in co-worker relations, and in neighborhood settings with Koreans.

For example, when discussing shopping in Korean-owned stores, one of the Latino focus group participants complained:

> I live in Koreatown. And I know that that's where more damage was done than other places. Everywhere, but mostly there. And since [the Koreans] saw it was a lot of Latin people they're going to be discriminating more, even more.... We see the Korean people when we go to shop. They look at you. But maybe if the same race as theirs goes in they even bow for them. They think that we're going to steal from them. They see very much how one is dressed and they don't give us the same service they give to their own people.

While one person made these remarks, the others in the focus groups nodded in agreement. No one dissented or attempted to qualify her remarks, and there was general consensus on this point of Korean shopkeeper discrimination.

There are sometimes extremely tense relations between Korean employers and the Latino community. Many Korean businessmen prefer to hire Latinos because they are a readily exploitable labor pool. At least, this was the sentiment expressed in our focus group discussion with a group of Koreans. They made the following remarks:

> "It is not uncommon for Koreans to hire Mexicans because they will work for less."

> "Indeed, some Koreans felt that the preference for cheap Latino labor was so strong that it resulted in discrimination against fellow Koreans:"

> "Sometimes Koreans will not hire Koreans because they know they can

save money by using Mexican or Latino labor. Those people will work for less."

"Looking at it from a Korean owner's perspective, why pay more for labor than you have to, even if it means not hiring Koreans."

To put this more fully in context, we should note that our focus groups also discussed what people regarded as good or ideal jobs. The Korean group, even compared to the Chinese group—which was composed of an equal number of recent immigrants to the U.S.—showed a striking narrowness of focus on economic success. When asked what makes a job a good job, the following comments were made in the Korean focus group:

"Money is the first consideration. Money says it all in the U.S."

"I came to the United States to make money."

"Any job that offers good pay is a good job."

"It is not so much how good the job is, but what you get paid."

"The important thing on any job is the money."

Indeed, the discussion of ideal job characteristics would have stopped here in the Korean group. After prodding from the group moderator, a number of other qualities (e.g., benefits, relations with supervisors and co-workers) were ultimately mentioned. This apparent singularity of purpose helps account for some of the behavior of the Korean merchants and business owners. However, viewed from the Latino perspective, their employer/employee relations with Koreans are seen as exploitative. Two examples. One person explained that she had not personally been discriminated against by Koreans, however:

I met a girl. We used to go to the same school and she told me that she worked for Koreans and that she wanted to learn English because she wanted to overcome the handicap because it was the worst thing to do to work for a Korean. Because they called [them] with [derogatory] names. They made them work very hard and threatened them with firing if they don't do it fast. So you see, it's racist.

Another told the following story:

My son works in a factory in Koreatown. And he fell and he didn't say anything because of the need that we have right now. And the Chinese man . . . Korean . . . Chineseman bought a machine so that he could lay off three people. And he laid them off. And another person came and said, "don't be stupid. This was an accident and why you kept your mouth shut? You still have time to sue them." Who has brought them [the Koreans] up, helped them up? It's been us.

There were also signs of Latino-Korean conflict when they met one another as co-residents of the same neighborhoods. As one Latino explained:

When I moved into that area there were only [white] Americans and three Latino families. The [white] Americans started to sell and the Koreans started moving in and it changed a lot. . . . It changed in that with the neighbors we used to communicate with them, and you cannot communicate with the Koreans. Even a property where it is a house, they build a building and when there's a vacancy they don't put "apartment for rent." Not in English or in Spanish, but they put it in their own language. One knows that it's for rent, but they don't offer it for rent to anybody else.

For their part, sentiments expressed in the Korean groups suggested that they held very negative images of Latinos. For example, the following comments were made:

"Hispanics drink too much and play loud music. That disturbs the neighborhood."

"From past experience it is a common rule that if Black or Latino populations in a neighborhood increase, values in the neighborhood will eventually decrease."

Negative imagery of Latinos was even more pervasive in the focus groups we conducted with Chinese. For example:

"Mexicans tend to be noisy."

"Latinos are dirty and messy. They don't take care of where they live."

"Lower class Latinos and illegals are forced to live in terrible conditions. Unfortunately, it is a way of life for them and they know little else."

"It may be a terrible thing to say, but being dirty and messy seems to be a national characteristic."

This level of conflict and tension among Latinos and Asians, receives very little media attention. These focus group results go a long way toward helping to make sense of the very high level of Latino involvement in the violence directed at Korean businesses. We suspect that the Latino-Korean conflict remains hidden for several reasons. First, many of those Latinos who work for Koreans or live in neighborhoods where Koreans own the local stores are non-citizens or do not speak English, or both. Second, they are likely to be extremely poor, living under extremely strapped conditions. That was communicated directly in a comment summarized earlier where a woman's son continued working under abusive conditions, even though injured, because the family desperately needed the income he brought home. Third, relative to the black community, the Latino community doesn't have the same level of political networks and culture of protest politics to draw attention to their grievances (though this is changing, and rapidly so). But, these tense relations between Latinos and segments of the Asian community warrant close attention in the future.

Conclusions

It seems that the more things change the more they stay the same. Many commentators have referred to the police brutality verdict and rebellion as a strong "wake-up call". The implication of this metaphor is that the emotional, symbolic, and material toll of these events was sufficiently powerful to compel the nation to think and act differently; that they signaled a time to act with renewed resolve in addressing problems of urban poverty, racism, and bias in the criminal justice system. Sadly, our data provide no substantial indication that this "wake up call" has been heard.

This conclusion rests on three major patterns. First, we found no shift in public thinking about either the nature of poverty or the causes of black-white economic inequality. How people understand the sources of these problems is a powerful determinant of their willingness to support active efforts to ameliorate these conditions (Apostle et al. 1983; Bobo and Kluegel, 1993; Kluegel and Smith, 1986; Kluegel, 1990). If a change in public thinking about the nature of poverty and racial inequality are needed to create and sustain the political pressure necessary to truly solve the difficult problems and tensions revealed by the police brutality verdict and the events in South Central Los Angeles, then these data provide little encouragement that the needed "new thinking" has occurred.

Second, there is what might be termed a clear "rank order of discrimination" in Los Angeles (Table 5.5), as there appears to be in the nation as a whole (Myrdal, 1944). Considering just the responses to the stereotyping and social distance questions, the distinctive level of hostility that confronts African-Americans cannot be ignored. What is most important in the data are not the absolute percentages, but the clarity of who occupies the top and the bottom of the ethnic hierarchy. It should be borne in mind that very little, if any, of these patterns can be explained by individual concern over average differences in socioeconomic status between blacks and each of the other groups. Perceptions of differences in socioeconomic status do relatively little to explain social distances feelings. In addition, although our data show that blacks in Los Angeles are, on average, considerably more affluent and highly educated than Hispanics, they are subject to more negative stereotyping and much higher walls of social distance. The crucial point is that stereotypes are not simply a reflection of the socioeconomic characteristic of groups. We should also note that if the comparison is restricted to native born blacks and Latinos then the gaps narrow considerably. The household income figures then slightly (but nonsignificantly) favor Latinos, whereas the per capita household income figures favor blacks (marginal significance). In addition, even among the native born, our data indicate that blacks are significantly more likely to have completed college or hold a more advanced degree than Latinos and are significantly more likely to work in professional or technical occupations. If one wishes to understand the anger and frustration in black Los Angeles, we suggest that much of it is tied to the likely behavior and experiences that flow from the overall American "rank order of discrimination".

To be sure, there is one bit of evidence that points in the direction of positive change. White residents of Los Angeles County are much more willing to contemplate living in substantially integrated communities, including largely black or largely Latino neighborhoods. To the extent that hostility to residential integration and the actual patterns of separation that it helps to produce are part of the web of problems

TABLE 5.5 The Rank Order of Discrimination

Target Group	Average Percentage Who: Object to Residential Integration	Average Percentage Who: Object to Racial Intermarriage
Whites	7.7%	10.9%
Asians	19.2%	20.3%
Hispanics	22.2%	17.8%
Blacks	36.6%	30.0%

Source: Based upon 1992 LACSS.

that contributed to the verdict and the explosion of anger that followed it, then these are surely positive developments. What is now required is genuine initiative to break down the very high levels of residential segregation in the county, especially the tremendous isolation of blacks and whites from one another. Even this positive result, however, is immediately tempered by the lack of change on openness to interracial marriages. Some forms of interethnic social distance appear to be adamantine.

In addition, some potentially negative effects of this spring's dramatic events did not happen. Residents of Los Angeles County did not become more pessimistic than they already were about the quality of life in LA, they did not become more anxious about their own jobs, or the broader economy. With the exception of a decline among whites in confidence in the police—presumably attributable to the initially slow response to the rebellion and the horrifying Reginald Denny beating video—confidence in local government and the police did not further deteriorate. Perhaps most strikingly, given some of the political rhetoric immediately following the rebellion, there was no sign of an increase in fear of crime; no increase in support for spending to fight crime; and no increase in punitiveness as gauged by levels of support for the death penalty.

The other evidence of change, however, generally runs in a negative direction. Two findings standout in this regard. First, there has been a shift among Asians toward more negative stereotypic images of blacks. Second, and far and away the clearest and perhaps most important long-term consequence of the verdict/rebellion, African-Americans in Los Angeles county have become substantially more pessimistic about the problem of discrimination and whether, in a fundamental sense, they will ever be treated fairly in the United States of America (Prager, 1987). Of considerable note, it was the most economically successful blacks who were most likely to undergo this conversion to greater racial pessimism and alienation following the verdict and rebellion.

There is a broad consensus among social scientists that African-Americans and also Latinos continue to face substantial discrimination in many domains of life, ranging from the labor and housing markets, to educational institutions, to everyday "public spaces" (Jaynes and Williams, 1989; Turner, Fix, and Struyk, 1991). Yet, scholars have only recently begun to carefully examine the problem of discrimination as experienced by middle class blacks (Cose, 1994; Feagin, 1991). Our own data strongly confirm that middle class blacks continue to feel the burdens of discrimination. But further, these results suggest that the Rodney King beating, the Simi Valley verdict, and subsequent responses to the rebellion have left the vast majority of affluent blacks more certain than before that much of the American public, meaning a large fraction of white America, is not yet prepared to admit them fully to the broader social and civic community. As Andrew Hacker put it in his recent provocative book *Two Nations: Black and White, Separate, Hostile, Unequal*:

> Black Americans are Americans, yet they still subsist as aliens in the only land they know. Other groups may remain outside the mainstream—some religious sects, for example—but they do so voluntarily. In contrast, blacks must endure a segregation that is far from freely chosen. So America may be seen as two separate nations (Hacker, 1991:3).

The gulf between these "nations" has apparently grown wider. Where blacks and whites differed considerably prior to the discontents of this Spring, in believing that discrimination was a cause of black- white economic inequality, the gap between the two grew larger still after the rebellion. Blacks grew more likely to see racial discrimination as a problem and there was no movement among whites (or other groups for that matter). These pattern thus constitute our third major reason for concluding that the "wake up call" has not been heard.

Not only has the wake-up call gone unanswered, but some of the other lessons of the LA uprising do not appear to have fully sunken into public consciousness. In particular, we have in mind the growing evidence of tension and conflict between Latinos and segments of the Asian American community. Our focus group discussion results suggest that many of the same grievances voiced by the African American community in regard to Korean American businesses exist in the Latino community. Other research, based on sample survey data, has shown that blacks and Latinos express equal levels of feelings of group competition and threat from Asians (Bobo and Hutchings 1994). This sort of multiethnic polarization, especially among minority communities deserves more serious attention from scholars and policy makers than it has received to date.

To be sure, many studies suggest that the U.S. has seen important improvements in racial attitudes (Schuman, Steeh, and Bobo, 1988). History, nonetheless, appears to repeat itself. In 1965, as the embers from the Watts rebellion still smoldered, the McCone Commission called for a new and indeed, "revolutionary attitude toward the problems of our city". A similar clarion call for new attitudes was issued by the Kerner Commission in 1968 in the wake of major racial disorders in Newark, Cleveland, Detroit and a score of other cities. Just a few months ago a pained nation watched as police brutality victim Rodney King posed the achingly simple question: "can we all get along?"

Our own data may help explain why these problems arise again and again, and are never resolved. Events such as the LA rebellion of 1992 tend to be viewed as acute crises requiring immediate attention to the symptoms, such as violent disaffection, that are the razor's edge of the turmoil. Despite the commission reports and careful analyses produced after each round of major social rebellions, the underlying problems of negative attitudes and indifference, residential segregation and isolation of different groups, unfavorable labor market conditions and government policies that allow certain communities to fall ever farther behind, go on largely as before. One of the differences for the "fire this time" is that we have a careful record of how attitudes changed—and often failed to change. If we are to avoid "the fire next time", then this information must be added to our understanding of the range of issues that now require urgent, steadfast, and dedicated attention.

Three specific types of policy directions need to be pursued. First, political leadership at all levels of government must handle situations of racial/ethnic polarization and conflict with greater astuteness than occurred in Los Angeles both before and after the spring 1992 civil disorder. It is, of course, Pollyanna to expect that all public officials, especially those who must ultimately compete for votes, will eschew divisive rhetoric and actions when engaging in such tactics might increase one's electoral prospects. Absent some greater consensus among political leadership on the legitimate bounds of political discourse, however, it is easy for a few sharply polarizing voices to worsen strained intergroup relations. Unfortunately, the sort of language, symbols and talk that reassure one segment of the population, such as describing the uprisings as "riots", the work of "thugs", and as "wanton criminality" are likely to insult and further enrage other segments who might prefer to hear terms such as "rebellion", "militants", "payback", and "justice". When world views are so sharply divided over race/ethnic relations issues it is critical that leadership lean heavily in the direction of forging consensus and healing, not merely solidifying a particular constituency. If the later strategy prevails, however, then elemental problems of miscommunication, distrust, and tension are likely to continue.

Second, it is important that formal mechanisms of dialogue and more civil dispute be strengthened. Most major urban areas now have Human Relations Committees or councils. These groups are frequently poorly staffed, underbudgeted, and rarely consulted when consequential policy and spending decisions are made. Yet, such committees typically have rich ties to ethnically diverse communities and institutions and are well schooled in the diplomacy of modern urban interethnic relations. It is essential that such expertise, resource networks, and experiences play a more substantial role in local government decision making and in the managing of responses to crisis situations as the ethnic diversity of our urban centers increases. Some have even proposed that "human relations impact reports" become a regular part of any major resource expenditure by local government (Bobo 1992), in a way parallel to what current environmental impact reports now demand. Such evaluations would entail an explicit charge to assess how major policy decisions affected various ethnic communities and their interests. Increasing the influence of Human Relations Commissions, by charging them with this type of task would surely help reduce the chances that the needs of minority communities would be persistently overlooked or neglected.

Third, as any number of analysts of urban America have noted, a core issue in many cities is the problem of joblessness and low-wage work. Perhaps the single greatest need is for stable sources of employment that pay above poverty level wages (Jencks 1992). There is an urgent need for a national jobs policy that focuses on revitalizing our major urban centers. Otherwise, communities that bear the simultaneous burdens of ethnic minority status and economic marginality will remain powder kegs, awaiting the next spark to set them aflame.

Notes

1. The 1992 Los Angeles County Social Survey was supported by the College of Letters and Science at UCLA, by a grant from the Andrew Mellon Foundation-Yale University Project on "Blacks, Immigration and Race Relations," by the Center for the Study of Urban Poverty through its Ford Foundation Research and Training Grant, and by a grant from the Psychology department at Stanford University. Correspondence concerning this chapter should be directed to Lawrence Bobo, Department of Sociology, University of California, 405 Hilgard Avenue, Los Angeles, California, 90024-1551.

2. Johnson, et. al., recommend that the events in South Central and other parts of Los Angeles following the police brutality verdict be understood as a "rebellion", "uprising", or as "civil unrest" rather than as a riot. The nature of the precipitating event, the longstanding grievances and problems that provided the seeds of the rebellion, and the systematic nature of much of the violence provide the bases for this choice of terms. In addition, we use the terms Latino and Hispanic, as well as black and African-American, interchangeably throughout this report.

3. The first author of this report was the principal investigator for the 1992

LACSS. For an analysis of the demographic, political, and attitudinal roots of ethnic conflict in Los Angeles see Oliver and Johnson 1984 and Johnson and Oliver, 1989.

4. Interviews were conducted by trained student interviewers taking part in a survey research methods course (30%) and by the regular interviewing staff of SRC (70%). Student interviewers received 12 hours of training. The LACSS employs a twelve call back procedure, systematically varying the day of the week and time of day, before dropping any numbers from the sample. The study had an overall cooperation rate of 55% and an estimated response rate of 45%. Although far from ideal these figures are considered excellent for the Los Angeles County area, widely recognized as one of, if not the, most difficult area in the U.S. for conducting surveys, and exceed by a wide margin those accomplished in most media polls. It should be borne in mind, that not all households have telephones in them and telephone coverage varies by race/ethnicity, with whites more often living in telephone households than do blacks or Latinos (Thornberry and Massey, 1988). Telephone survey respondents are typically younger and somewhat better educated than respondents captured in face-to-face interview surveys (Groves and Kahn, 1976). Comparisons to 1990 Census data suggest that the LACSS data are well representative of the population of Los Angeles County.

5. We compared the pre-verdict/rebellion sample composition to the post-verdict/rebellion among each ethnic group in order to determine if any important changes had occurred. Within each group, the pre-events and post-events sample make-up is reassuringly similar. Out of 40 pre/post tests for change in sample composition involving 10 variables (nativity, sex, age, marital status, education, employment status, occupation, family income, party identification, political ideology) and the four major ethnic groups, we found only three noteworthy changes. One occurred among black respondents, where the post-verdict/rebellion sample had slightly higher incomes than the pre-verdict/rebellion sample. Two occurred among whites, where the post-verdict/rebellion sample was older and more often in the retired category than the pre-verdict/rebellion sample. This resulted from a cap, driven by cost considerations, imposed on the number of post-verdict/rebellion interviews with white respondents. Otherwise, we found no differences in composition among Asians and Hispanics nor among blacks and whites on any of the other measures including nativity, sex, education, occupation, marital status, party identification or political ideology.

6. The start date for the new items was May 2, 1992. These items were not only asked of all respondents given the full household interview, but anyone contacted as part of the screening effort was also asked these items. Thus the data reported in Table 1 include both data from respondents selected for the main household survey and those who were merely asked the screening questions.

7. Though they differ in exact content, these questions bear a strong conceptual resemblance to the "racial alienation" items examined by Schuman and Hatchett in their research on Detroit blacks (Schuman and Hatchett, 1974).

References

Allport, Gordon W. 1954. *The Nature of Prejudice*. Reading, MA: Addison-Wesley.

Apostle, Richard A. et al. 1983. *The Anatomy of Racial Attitudes*. Berkeley: University of California Press.

Bobo, Lawrence. 1992. "Jury's Verdict in King Beating Trial Sends Piercing Blow to Race Relations." *The Daily News*, Sunday, May 10, 1992, p. 1 (Viewpoint section).

Bobo, Lawrence. 1992. "Two Crucial Local Commissions That Receive Virtually No Money." *The Los Angeles Times*, Sunday, September 13, 1992, p. M6.

Bobo, Lawrence and Franklin D. Gilliam, Jr. 1990. "Race, Sociopolitical Participation, and Black Empowerment." *American Political Science Review*, 84: 344-393.

Bobo, Lawrence and Vincent L. Hutchings. 1994. "Black and Latino Conflict With Asians: Extending the Theory of Group Position." Paper presented at the 1994 Annual Meetings of the Western Political Science Association, Doubletree Hotel, Albuquerque, New Mexico, March 10-12, 1994.

Bobo, Lawrence, James H. Johnson, Jr., and Melvin L. Oliver. 1992. *Stereotyping and the Multicity Survey: Notes on Measurement, Determinants, and Effects*. Occasional Working Paper Series, Vol. 2, No. 8, Center for the Study of Urban Poverty, University of California, Los Angeles.

Bobo, Lawrence and James R. Kluegel. 1991. "Modern American Prejudice: Stereotypes, Social Distance and Perceptions of Discrimination Toward Blacks, Hispanics, and Asians." Paper presented at the Annual Meetings of the American Sociological Association, Cincinnati, Ohio, August, 1991.

Bobo, Lawrence and James R. Kluegel. 1993. "Opposition to Race-Targeting: Self-Interest, Stratification Ideology, or Racial Attitudes?" *American Sociological Review*, 58 (August): 443-464.

Bobo, Lawrence, Camille L. Zubrinsky, James H. Johnson, Jr. and Melvin L. Oliver. 1994. "Work Orientation, Job Discrimination, and Ethnicity: A Focus Group Perspective." Forthcoming in Research in the Sociology of Work, vol. 5, edited by Richard L. Simpson and Ida Harper Simpson. Greenwich, CT: JAI Press.

Cose, Ellis. 1994. *The Rage of a Privileged Class*. New York: HarperCollins.

Church, George J. 1992. "The Fire This Time." *Time*, May 11, 1992, 139(19): 20-25.

Davis, James A. and Tom W. Smith. 1990. *General Social Surveys, 1972:1990: Cumulative Codebook*. Chicago: National Opinion Research Center and University of Chicago.

Elis, David. 1992. "L.A. Lawlessness." *Time*, May 11, 1992, 139(19): 26-29.

Farley, Reynolds, Howard Schuman, Suzanne Bianchi, Diane Colasanto, and Shirley Hatchett. 1978. "Chocolate City, Vanilla Suburbs': Will the Trend Toward Racially Separate Communities Continue?" *Social Science Research* 7:319-344.

Feagin, Joe E. 1991. "The Continuing Significance of Race: Antiblack Discrimination in Public Places." *American Sociological Review* 56:101-116.

Groves, Robert M. and Robert L. Kahn. 1976. *Surveys by Telephone: A National Comparison with Personal Interviews*. New York: Academic Press.

Hacker, Andrew. 1992. *Two Nations: Black and White, Separate, Hostile, Unequal*. New York: Scribners.

Jaynes, Gerald D. and Robin M. Williams, Jr. (eds). 1989. *A Common Destiny: Blacks and American Society*. Washington, D.C.: National Academy Press.

Jencks, Christopher. 1992. *Rethinking Social Policy*. Cambridge: Harvard University Press.

Johnson, Jr., James H. and Melvin L. Oliver. 1989. "Interethnic Minority Conflict in Urban America: The Effects of Economic and Social Dislocations." *Urban Geography*, 10: 449-463.

Johnson, Jr., James H., Cloyzelle K. Jones, Walter C. Farrell, Jr., and Melvin L. Oliver. 1992. *The Los Angeles Rebellion, 1992: A Preliminary Assessment from Ground Zero*. Occasional Working Paper Series, Vol. 2, No. 7, Center for the Study of Urban Poverty, University of California, Los Angeles.

Kluegel, James R. 1990. "Trends in Whites' Explanation of the Gap in Black-White Socioeconomic Status." *American Sociological Review* 55:512-525.

Kluegel, James R. and Eliot R. Smith. 1986. *Beliefs About Inequality*. New York: Aldine dy Gruyter.

Kramer, Michael. 1992. "What Can Be Done?" *Time*, May 11, 1992, 139(19): 41.

Lacayo, Richard. 1992. "Anatomy of an Acquittal." *Time*, May 11, 1992, 139(19): 30-32.

Los Angeles Times. 1992. "World Reacts with Shock and Criticism to Los Angeles Riots." May 10, 1992, p. Bx)

Mathews, Tom et al. 1992. "The Siege of L.A." *Newsweek*, May 11, 1992, 119(19): 30-38.

Myrdal, Gunnar. 1944. *An American Dilemma: The Negro Problem and American Democracy*. New York: Harper.

Oliver, Melvin L. and James H. Johnson, Jr. 1984. "Inter-ethnic Conflict in an Urban Ghetto: The Case of Blacks and Latinos in Los Angeles." *Research in Social Movements, Conflict and Change*, 6:57-94

The Polling Report. 1992. "The King Verdict." 8(9): 1, 7-8.

Pettigrew, Thomas F. 1982. "Prejudice." Pp. 1-29 in *Dimensions of Ethnicity: Prejudice*, edited by S. Thernstrom, A. Orlov, and O. Handlin. Cambridge: Belknap.

Prager, Jeffrey. 1987. "American Political Culture and the Shifting Meaning of Race." *Ethnic and Racial Studies* 10:62-81.

Riley, Robert T. and Thomas F. Pettigrew. 1976. "Dramatic Events and Attitude Change." *Journal of Personality and Social Psychology*, 34: 1004-1015.

Schmidt, William E. 1992. "British Racial Attacks Grow, Alarming Minorities." *The New York Times*, August 20, 1992, p. A3.

Schuman, Howard and Lawrence Bobo. 1988. "Survey-based Experiments on White Racial Attitudes Toward Residential Integration." *American Journal of Sociology* 94:273-299.

Schuman, Howard and Shirley Hatchett. 1974. *Black Racial Attitudes: Trends and Complexities*. Ann Arbor, MI: Institute for Social Research, University of Michigan.

Schuman, Howard, Charlotte G. Steeh, and Lawrence Bobo. 1988. *Racial Attitudes in America: Trends and Interpretations*. Cambridge: Harvard University Press.

Sidanius, Jim, Lawrence Bobo, Felicia Pratto, and Michael Mitchell. 1991. "The Death Penalty, Confidence in the Police and the Beating of Rodney King: Some Implications of Social Dominance Theory." Department of Psychology and Institute for Social Science Research, University of California, Los Angeles.

Smith, Tom W. 1991. *Ethnic Images*. General Social Survey Topical Report 19. Chicago: National Opinion Research Center, University of Chicago.

Thornberry, Owen T. and James T. Massey. 1988. "Trends in United States Telephone Coverage Across Time and Subgroups." Pp. 25-49 in *Telephone Survey Methodology*, edited by R.M. Groves et al. New York: Wiley.

Turner, Margery Austin, Michael Fix, and Raymond J. Struyk. 1991. *Opportunities Denied, Opportunities Diminished: Racial Discrimination in Hiring*. Washington, D.C.: The Urban Institute Press.

6

A Profile of Those Arrested

Joan Petersilia and Allan Abrahamse

The riot[1] that took place in Los Angeles between Wednesday, April 29, 1992 and Monday, May 5, 1992 was sparked by the acquittal by an all-white jury of four white police officers charged with the 1991 beating of black motorist Rodney King. Other recent events in Los Angeles add to the impression that the riot was an instance of racial conflict—for example, a Korean grocer had recently shot and killed a black teenager but was given a probationary sentence instead of a prison term by a white judge. And in an eerie and perverse parallel, the televised images of the Rodney King beating were reflected in the televised images of a white truck driver, Reginald Denny, being beaten almost to death by blacks in the early hours of the riot. Moreover, memories of the "Watts Riots" of 1965 remain fresh in the minds of many, and in 1965 the area known as Watts was mostly black and the images that survive involve black rioters battling white policeman. All these facts contribute to an initial impression that the 1992 Los Angeles riot was a race riot—a conflict between races.

But while there can be little doubt that the anger felt by black people concerning the Rodney King verdict provided the spark that started the riot, there is considerable evidence that by the next day, April 30, the riot had spread well beyond the bounds of race. Plainly, it was not the case that only black people were rioting; television coverage of looting plainly showed non-black persons engaged in looting. Many of these non-black persons appeared to be Latinos. But, of course, television images provide only anecdotal evidence, at best.

Another critical theme raised early, and still a subject of vigorous investigation and debate, was the alleged lack of police response in the early stages of the riot. This allegation is supported, though hardly proved, by the searing television image mentioned above of the beating of the white truck driver: not a single policeman is in sight. Other images confirm the impression that citizens felt compelled to take security into their own hands, for example, the pictures of Korean businessmen defending their establishment with automatic weapons. But by the time the riot fully ended about six days later, many thousands had been arrested, so setting aside what might or might not have happened in the early hours of the riot, a massive police presence was eventually felt, although exactly when (and where) this presence was felt is somewhat difficult to know.

Understanding the dynamics of who was arrested, for what and where, and when the police became involved has become a significant challenge since many normal police recording practices were suspended during the emergency, and the justice records that were kept were more cryptic than usual. The riot-arrest reports often consisted of only a few sentences and did not specify what the individual did or give details about the person (e.g., home address). The absence of such information limits more detailed analysis of the arrestee characteristics. Nevertheless, given the importance of this event from a historical standpoint, preserving and reporting what descriptive information does exist seems quite worthwhile.

The article analyzes data on 7,056 adults arrested and held for arraignment on felony or misdemeanor charges between April 30, 1992, and May 9, 1992, within the Los Angeles Judicial District, the court serving the area in which the majority of the riot-related events occurred. Riot-related activities were essentially over by May 5, so a subset of the file—those 5,633 arrested between April 30 and May 5—is used for the analysis of riot-arrestee characteristics. However, the longer time period is used to examine police arrest patterns. The file describes the offender's age, race/ethnicity, gender, crime type, and date and location of arrest. The data are analyzed to answer the following questions:

- When did the police make most of the arrests?
- What was the impact of the emergency curfew put into effect during the riots?
- What were the demographic characteristics of those adults arrested?
- What crimes were arrestees charged with?
- How do the characteristics of the L.A.-riot arrestees compare with:
  - the 1990 South Central Los Angeles resident population;
  - adults arrested in the Los Angeles-Watts riots of 1965?

The results show that by far, the largest single group of arrestees were Latino men from 18 to 24 years old, accounting for 30 percent of all arrests during the riot period. Moreover, contrary to popular impression, the Los Angeles Police Department (LAPD) did not lie low for long: police made 1,417 arrests April 30, the first full day of rioting. In other words, whatever happened on the evening of April 29 when the Rodney King verdict was announced, whoever the rioters were and whatever the police response (or lack of it) was on that night, by the next day the rioters included persons throughout the affected communities, not just black persons, and law enforcement agencies were working vigorously to suppress the unlawful behavior of these persons.

The results raise interesting questions. For example, is the overrepresentation of Latinos in the arrest population due to higher riot-participation rates or bias exhibited by law enforcement? And why the lower arrest rate for black males, but not black females? Those questions, and others raised by this analysis, will likely be debated for years to come as the nation examines various aspects of the worst civil unrest in the United States in this century (51 dead, more than $1 billion in damages).

Description of the Los Angeles Riot-Arrestee Database

In late May, 1992, a machine-readable data file maintained by the Los Angeles County Municipal Court was obtained and analyzed by the authors. The database contains the records of all 7,056 adults arrested and held for arraignment on felony or misdemeanor charges within the Los Angeles Judicial District between April 30, 1992, and May 9, 1992 (inclusive).[2] For each individual arrested, the file contained the following information about the arrest:[3]

- date of arrest
- arrestee's birth year
- arrestee's race or ethnicity
- arrestee's sex
- arrest charge
- arresting agency.

The file is not a complete record of all persons arrested during the riots: it excludes juvenile arrestees (those younger than 18 years of age), and adult defendants whose cases were processed outside the Los Angeles (L.A.) Judicial District. The L.A. Judicial District is the largest in L.A. County, and the court of jurisdiction for the geographical area where most of the riot-related activities (and arrests) took place. However, it does not include courthouses in Compton, Long Beach, or

Inglewood, which also processed some (although not many) riot-related cases.

The data also do not include persons who were arrested on the evening of April 29. The first riot-related disturbances began around 6:00 p.m. on the 29th, so that including the full day April 29 cases would be misleading. The court database also does not include people who posted bail at police lockups or county jail facilities before they were arraigned. However, it had been reported that strict procedures regarding bail and own recognizance releases adopted during the emergency resulted in few releases of this type.[4] We also have no way of knowing for certain whether all of the arrests included in the database resulted directly from the riots, and certainly some of them did not. However, since the curfew was in effect throughout the city for most of the time period covered by the analysis, keeping most citizens in their homes and most commercial establishments closed, most arrests between April 30 and May 5 are presumed to be riot-related.

Although not a complete record of all persons charged during this period, the data appear to provide the most comprehensive single source currently available on persons arrested in conjunction with the riots.

Findings

Police Arrest Patterns

The Los Angeles Police Department (LAPD) has been much criticized for its lack of early presence in South-Central L.A., the geographic center of the riots. Some have argued that early police presence might have diffused the situation and stopped citizens from becoming victims. Clearly the police did not anticipate the quick and violent course the uprising would take. When the King verdicts were announced late in the afternoon of April 29, most of the LAPD's 1,000 detectives had gone home. L.A. Police Chief Daryl Gates himself was attending a police fund-raiser. On his way to the evening event, Gates stopped to comment to the local media that his officers were handling the situation "calmly, maturely, professionally." It appeared that the police had adopted a hands-off policy for the evening (Webster Commission, 1992).

Once the sun set, looting and burning began in earnest. The first fire call came in at 7:45 p.m., as rioters began torching buildings in South Los Angeles. By 9 p.m., normal life throughout Los Angeles had been derailed. By midnight it was clear that the violence and destruction had escalated and that police presence was desperately needed. At an early-morning news conference, Chief Gates admitted that the Police Department had been "simply overwhelmed" (Coffey, 1992).

Early Thursday morning, the LAPD dispatched all of its 8,000 officers, with orders to arrest rioters "for the most serious crime evident" (Coffey, 1992). Special law enforcement teams were dispatched to book suspects in the field, taking their mug shots and fingerprints before shipping them by busload to the L.A. County Jail. In some areas, suspects were being taken into custody a dozen or more at a time. At the height of the disorder, the police attempted to round up as many looters as possible. Often as many as 50 or 60 people were arrested at one time—the police literally placing barriers around a commercial area and rounding up everyone there. Many cases had 10, 20, and sometimes 40 or 50 people charged on one criminal complaint for looting offenses.

The Municipal Court data show that on Thursday, April 30, 1,417 arrests were made—a volume that the Court reports was unprecedented. Arrests for property crimes (burglary, receiving stolen property, theft, auto theft, forgery and looting) made up almost 70% of these arrests, followed by arrests for civil disturbance (curfew, disorderly conduct, false alarm, vandalism, trespassing, disturbing the peace, arson) which made up 16% of these arrests.

It is interesting to note the impact of the curfew imposed by Mayor Tom Bradley on April 30. At 12:15 a.m. on April 30, Mayor Bradley declared a dusk-to-dawn curfew in Los Angeles County in an attempt to limit the extent and geographical spread of the violence. The curfew declared public places off-limits, prohibited ammunition sales, and banned gasoline sales except for normal filling up. The curfews were portrayed as a way to clear the streets for fire and other emergency vehicles and as a tool to help police restore order in riot areas.

The Municipal Court data reflect the impact of this curfew. The total number of arrests on May 1 fell to 1,167, and property arrests made up only about 43% of the total, while the number of arrests for civil disturbance nearly doubled, accounting for about 39% of the total. On May 2, two days after the curfew had been imposed, property crime arrests made up only 11% of the total of 1,180 arrests, while arrests for civil disturbance soared to over 800, and comprised about 74% of the total (with few exceptions, arrests for civil disturbance were all curfew violations). The Court saw about a 20% drop in arrests on May 3, a 50% drop on May 4, and by May 9th, the last day for which we have data, only 265 arrests were made, probably near or even below the daily average (in 1991, the LAPD alone made about 470 arrests per day).

As these data suggest, it looks as though in the three days from April 30 through May 2 a sort of "substitution" occurred: arrests for property crimes fell while arrests for civil disturbance crimes rose. It is impossible to tell if this represents a change in behavior on the part of the rioters or on the part of law enforcement agencies.

Furthermore, setting aside the issue of whether law enforcement agencies were slow to react in the initial stages of the riot, at least by April 30 they were fully engaged, and they made probably at least three times the number arrests they normally make on an average April day.

Such large numbers of arrests quickly overwhelmed the already crowded Los Angeles criminal justice system. About 600 convicted felons in the county jail system awaiting transport to state prison were hustled off early to make room for new arrestees. The Los Angeles Municipal Court stayed open over the weekend to handle the arraignment rush.

The Demographic Characteristics of Persons Arrested

As noted above, state and local officials—including Mayor Bradley and Governor Pete Wilson—declared the riot over on May 4. Hence, the remainder of our analysis focuses on the subset of 5,633 who were arrested and held for arraignment between April 30 and May 5. Table 6.1 describes those arrested during this time period by gender, race/ethnicity, age, and crime type.[5] Males comprised 88 percent of those arrested, women, 12 percent. Fifty-one percent of those arrested were Latino; 36 percent, black; and 11 percent, Anglo. The arrestees were also quite young, 44 percent being between the ages of 18-24. Most crimes—42 percent—were for civil disturbance crimes, primarily curfew violations.

Almost 90% of those arrested from April 30 through May 5 were males, and most of them were young: about 45% were under 25 years of age. Most males were charged with civil disturbance and property crimes, as were females.

About 53% of the arrested males were Latino; contrary to this pattern, slightly more black women were arrested than Latino women (about 43% vs. 35%). One explanation for the racial disparity among males, discussed more fully below, is that the black male looked like a very volatile population and police stayed away from them.

Contrary to the pattern observed with males, slightly more black women were arrested than Latino women (281 black females vs. 233 Latino females). It was only in the arrests of men that the racial/ethnic disparity emerged: with far more Latinos than blacks taken into custody (2,619 Latino men vs. 1,756 black men). One explanation, discussed more fully below, is that the black male looked like a very volatile population and police stayed away from them.

TABLE 6.1   Characteristics of Los Angeles Riot Arrestees

	Number	*Percent*
Sex		
Male	4976	88
Female	657	12
Total	5633	
Race		
Black	2037	36
Latino	2852	51
Anglo	601	11
Other	143	3
Age		
18-24	2464	44
25-34	2046	36
35-44	869	15
Over 44	254	5
Crime Type		
Drug possession/sale	244	4
Other/misc	68	1
Property	1964	35
Curfew/civil disturbance	2361	42
Traffic	426	8
Violent	570	10

Source: Based upon Los Angeles County Municipal Court data file.

More noteworthy than their race/ethnic breakdown is the crime type distribution for females. A higher percentage of women were arrested for property related crimes: 27 percent vs. 23 percent for men. Men were more likely to be arrested for civil disorder: 33 percent vs. 20 percent for women. Latino women were more than twice as likely to be arrested for property offenses (mostly looting) as for civil disturbance violations. Charges against black women were distributed about evenly between property and civil disturbance crimes.

Arrests of Latino males exceeded that of black males throughout the 6 days from April 30 through May 5. Arrests of Latino and black females were practically tied during the first three days of the riot, but May 3rd saw a surge in arrests for black females while arrests for Latino women continued to drop. We have no explanation for this phenomenon.

Earlier results showed that overall, the age distribution of persons arrested during the L.A. riots is similar to general arrest patterns: younger people are arrested more, and the rate falls off sharply for populations over 35 years of age. But Latino arrestees in the L.A. riots constitute a younger group than blacks: they were about four years younger on average (Latinos, 26 years old; blacks, 30 years old), and the median age was about 6 years younger (Latinos, 23 years old; blacks, 29 years old). In fact, 30 percent of all those arrested during the six-day riot period were Latinos, between the ages of 18-24 (comparable figure for blacks is 10 percent; for whites, 2 percent).

Comparing L.A.-Riot Arrestees to Other Relevant Populations

Arrestees Compared to South Central L.A. Resident Population. The data show higher arrest rates for Latinos than blacks, and interpretations of what this means are many. Do the high Latino arrests reflect the group's higher participation in the riot, a general failure or reluctance of Latinos to flee or resist arrest, a concentration of police arrest efforts on Latino rather than black men, or some other possible cause?

Some have attributed the high Latino arrest totals to simple demographics—Latinos are the largest group in Los Angeles, according to the 1990 U.S. Census figures, making up 39 percent of the city's population and narrowly outnumbering blacks in South Los Angeles, where most of the riot took place. And regardless of their representation in overall county statistics, young Latinos are normally arrested at high rates—so the riot-arrest patterns may not be all that different from what occurs normally.[6]

Several Latino organizations complained early on that there was discrimination in law enforcement during the riots, and that the police concentrated on Latinos specifically, using the riots as an opportunity to arrest and identify illegal immigrants. Another possible explanation for the relatively low level of black arrests may be that police deliberately "under-arrested" blacks, possibly as a tactic to avoid inflaming a bad situation further, or possibly because the black neighborhoods were perceived as being too dangerous to enter.

Existing information cannot resolve these interpretations, particularly those alleging discriminatory practices. This database tells us who was arrested, and as is true with all arrest statistics, such data are only proxies for criminal behavior, and are not the same as measuring the criminal behavior directly (as would be possible with offender self-reports, for example).

It is possible, however, to compare the demographic characteristics of the arrest population with the characteristics of persons living in South Central Los Angeles. Data for the residential population were obtained from the U.S. Census of Population for 1990 (U.S. Bureau of the Census, 1992). The data reveal that the black population in South Central Los Angeles is somewhat older than the Latino population: for example, over 40 percent of the black population, but less than 20 percent of the Latino population, is aged 45 or over. But for both blacks and Latinos, few such persons were arrested: in both groups the arrestees were drawn heavily from the younger age groups.

Table 6.2 points out another difference between the black and Latino population. The "relative incidence" displayed there is the ratio of arrestees to population, each measured as a percentage of the relevant total. For example, black males aged 18-24 represent 15.9 percent of the residential population, and 30.0 percent of the arrestees, so the relative incidence for this group is 30.0/15.9, or 1.8. Table 2 shows that for both blacks and Latinos, and for both males and females, young people are heavily overrepresented among arrestees, with a relative incidence close to 2.0 for all groups. For the middle age groups (age 25-34 and 35-44), the picture for blacks is different from that of Latinos. Here, arrested blacks are somewhat overrepresented, but Latinos are somewhat underrepresented. Finally, older persons are hardly arrested at all compared to their distribution in the population. Thus, the table gives the impression that among Latinos, the youngest were more heavily engaged in the riot than older members, while among blacks, participation was somewhat more widespread. Unfortunately, as noted earlier, these comparisons must be regarded tentatively. The database did not include the exact location of the arrests, or the arrestees' address, so it is impossible to know whether the residents lived in the riot area or drove into the area once the riot began.

Arrestees Compared to 1965 Watts Riot Arrestees. To residents of Los Angeles, the massive destruction and loss of life that began on April 29, 1992, must have seemed unparalleled, but sadly, such an uprising had occurred in much the same way and location just over 25 years ago. An excerpt from the final report of the Governor's Commission on the Los Angeles-Watts Riots of 1965 reveals strikingly similar parallels.

TABLE 6.2   Residents and Arrestees, Relative Incidence by Age, Gender and Age/Ethnicity

Age	Gender	Blacks	Latinos
18-24	Male	1.82	1.93
	Female	2.34	1.99
25-34	Male	1.76	0.84
	Female	1.81	0.83
35-44	Male	1.31	0.50
	Female	1.30	0.64
Over 44	Male	0.14	0.18
	Female	0.18	0.29

Source: Based upon Los Angeles County Municipal Court data file.

The rioting in Los Angeles in the late summer of 1965 took six days to run its full grievous course. In hindsight, the tinder-igniting incident is seen to have been the arrest of a drunken Black youth.

. . . the crisis began near the district known as Watts, at seven o'clock on the evening of 11 August, a Wednesday. The crisis ended in the afternoon of 17 August. In the ugliest interval, perhaps 10,000 Negroes took to the streets in marauding bands. They looted stores, set fires, beat up white passersby whom they hauled from stopped cars, many of which were turned upside down and burned, exchanging shots with law enforcement officers, and stoned and shot at fireman.

. . . had to be controlled with the aid of military. . . . When it was all over, 34 persons were dead . . . 3,952 persons were arrested, including 500 persons under the age of 18 . . . one of the causes seemed to be a resentment, even hatred, of the police, as the symbol of authority." (McCone report, summary, 1965)

A summary description of the 3,438 adults arrested during the 1965 Watts was prepared by the California Department of Justice for the McCone Commission (California Bureau of Criminal Statistics, 1965). Unfortunately the raw data no longer exist for the 1965 riots, so we had to rely on published tables, and the crime categories reported in 1965 are not as detailed as in 1992. Nonetheless, it is informative to compare the two arrest populations, and interesting differences quickly emerge.

The main difference we observe between the two riot arrest populations is the different race/ethnic mix. A far higher fraction of those arrested in the 1992 riots were Latino than in the 1965 Watts riots. In 1965 blacks comprised nearly 94% of the arrested population; Latinos only 2%. As we have seen, in 1992 blacks made up a little over a third, while Latinos more than half, of the arrested population. Other demographic characteristics, however, were quite similar. In 1965 about 37% of the arrested population were aged 18-24, while in 1992 this fraction rose barely to 39%. In both riots, females made up just 13% of the arrestees.

It should come as no surprise that the residential population of South Central Los Angeles has seen dramatic demographic changes since 1965. In 1965, according to the U.S. Census, blacks made up over 80% of the population, while Latinos made up only about 10%; in 1990 the black

TABLE 6.3   Relative Incidence of Arrestees by Race/Ethnicity in 1965 Watts Riot and 1992 Riot

Race/ethnicity	1965	1992
Black	1.15	0.70
Latino	0.20	1.12

Source: Based upon Los Angeles County Municipal Court data file for 1992 figures; California Bureau of Criminal Statistics, 1965.

population had fallen to just over half the total, while the Latino population had risen to about 45%. Table 6.3 compares the relative incidence of arrests in the two riots, by race/ethnicity. As it shows, it appears that in each riot, the predominant racial/ethnic group was "over arrested". The rise in the Latino population *plus* an increase in Latino participation serve jointly to explain the increase in Latino arrests seen in 1992.

Conclusions

The causes and consequences of the 1992 Los Angeles riots will be studied for years to come. The role of the criminal justice system—as provoking, controlling, and escalating the disorder—will undoubtedly figure prominently into the research—as it has in all other civil disorders.[7] This analysis has documented police arrest trends and the characteristics of persons arrested. Given the importance of the event, much more analysis should be done. For example, it would be useful to compare the criminal histories of riot-arrestees with those normally arrested in these areas. Were rioters essentially opportunistic offenders or were they essentially protesters? Court disposition information would also illuminate how various types of crimes and offenders were dealt with at sentencing. And, self-report studies of rioters might illuminate whether Latinos were overrepresented in arrests, or simply participated at higher rates.

Regardless of such analysis, it is clear that the conditions that spawned the riots remain, and that there are continuing deep frustrations about the problems of class and racial division, poverty, and police abuse in Los Angeles. It is also clear that the riot was much more than a protest by blacks against an injustice to a fellow black. Such an interpretation would vastly oversimplify and misrepresent the unrest. The heavy involvement of Latinos suggested that they too used this opportunity to vent their frustrations. Testimony reported by the Webster Commission showed that both Latinos and blacks in Los Angeles feel powerless to change their position and have lost faith in the leaders and institutions of the community (Webster Commission, 1992). While they hope the violence will not return, they also recognize for those without means and political power, violence is a means of communicating with such leaders and the larger community. For those who participated in the 1992 Los Angeles riots, anger was expressed and control exerted—if only for a brief six-day period.

Notes

1. According to Spilerman (1970), for inclusion as a "riot," a disorder has to have the following characteristics: (1) involve a racial or ethnic minority, or minorities and the police, as opposed to interethnic fighting, (2) incur some detectable level of property destruction or interpersonal violence, (3) involve at least 30 riot participants, and 4) occur outside a school setting (many of the school riots involve interracial and interethnic fighting). According to this definition, the Los Angeles disturbance qualifies as a riot.

2. The arraignment is the first time that a person is given notice of the actual charges filed, and bail is set. In normal circumstances, a person arrested and placed in custody must be arraigned within two court days. The volume of arrests, particularly at the beginning of the Los Angeles riots, quickly swamped the arraignment system and the two-day time-limit was extended to 96 hours.

3. The file also contained a bond dollar amount, but this data element was deemed too unreliable to be used. The arrestee's age at time of arrest was estimated (although since only the year of birth was known, that age may be off by one year); the race variable was collapsed into four categories (white, black, Latino, other); the over-250 arrest charges were reduced into eight different categories; and the many (over 100) arrest agency codes were collapsed into eight categories. Missing values (e.g., three persons were coded as sex="X") were assigned to the largest non-missing category (e.g., the sex="X" codes were assigned to "Male", which already made up about 88 percent of the file).

4. The American Civil Liberties Union reported (ACLU, 1992:29) that during the emergency, both the City Attorney and District Attorney disregarded their usual policies regarding bail and own-recognizance (O.R.) release and demanded high bail on all cases. Although the established bail schedule that applied to Municipal and Superior Courts recommends $250 for non-violent misdemeanors—including curfew violation, petty theft and misdemeanor burglary—the City Attorney demanded $15,000 and up on disorder-related misdemeanors for all offenders, regardless of criminal record, ties to the community, etc. Thus, release on O.R. or bail was practically non-existent for both misdemeanor and felony cases regardless of verified information, and very few people were able to gain release from custody pending trial.

5. Race and ethnic classifications were recorded by the arresting officer.

6. It would have been interesting to learn how the characteristics of the LA-riot arrestees compare with those normally arrested in the same geographical area. Unfortunately, that question can't be answered solidly because the LAPD does not release arrestee characteristics (race, age) by neighborhood. The LAPD was only able to provide information on the total sample of persons arrested in Los Angeles in 1990. In 1990, 33 percent of all persons arrested by the LAPD were Latino (as compared with 51 percent of the riot arrestees), and 33 percent were aged 18-24 (as compared with 44 percent of the riot arrestees)(LAPD, 1991).

7. The Kerner Commission (1968) found that the typical incident sparking a black riot during the 1960s was an interaction between a black person and the police (e.g., a car-stopping or an arrest), and the perception on the part of blacks

witnessing the interaction that the police were abusing the suspect or acting unjustly. Analysis of Hispanic riots also has shown that 42 percent of Hispanic riots between 1967-1971 were in reaction to perceived police brutality and abuses, the most common type of riot-precipitating incident (Carter, 1992).

References

American Civil Liberties Union Foundation of Southern California,1992. *Civil Liberties in Crisis: Los Angeles during the Emergency*, Los Angeles, CA.

Carter, Gregg Lee, 1992. "Hispanic Rioting During the Civil Rights Era," *Sociological Forum*, Vol. 7, No. 2, pp. 301-322.

California Bureau of Criminal Statistics, 1965. "Summary of a Preliminary Report of Persons Arrested in the Los Angeles Riots," *Governor's Commission on the Los Angeles Riots*, Vol. 2., Washington, DC: Library of Congress.

Coffey, Shelby, III (ed.), 1992. *Understanding the Riots*, Los Angeles, CA: Los Angeles Times.

Kerner Committee, 1968. *Report of The National Advisory Commission on Civil Disorders*, Summary, March 1, Washington, DC.

Lieberman, Paul, 1992. "51% of Riot Arrests Were Latino, Study Says," *Los Angeles Times*, June 18, p. B3.

Los Angeles Police Department, 1991. *Statistical Digest, 1990*, Los Angeles, CA.

McCone Commission, 1965. *Violence in the City—An End or a Beginning*, A Report by the Governor's Commission on the Los Angeles Riots, Los Angeles, CA: Governor's Commission on the Los Angeles Riots.

Oberschall, Anthony, 1968. "The Los Angeles Riot," *Social Problems*, Vol. 15, pp. 322-341.

Spilerman, Seymour, 1970. "The Costs of Racial Disturbances: A Comparison of Alternative Explanations," *American Sociological Review*, Vol. 35, pp. 627-649.

U.S. Bureau of the Census, 1967. "Special Census Survey of the South and East Los Angeles Areas: November 1965," *Current Population Report*, Technical Studies, Series P-23, 17, March 23.

_____, 1992. *Selected Population and Housing Characteristics for South Central Los Angeles, 1990*, Washington, DC.

Webster Commission, (October) 1992. *The City in Crisis*, Los Angeles, CA.

7

Property Damage and Violence: A Collective Behavior Analysis

Kathleen J. Tierney

The Los Angeles unrest is widely considered to be the most serious episode of race-related crowd violence in the U. S. in this century. In the aftermath of the disturbance, the city continues to face major challenges related to community recovery and reconciliation.

In many respects, the unrest was almost a textbook case, the prototypical big-city riot, resembling episodes of collective violence that occurred in Washington, D. C., Detroit, Newark, and scores of other U. S. cities during the 1960s. Like many of these earlier racial disturbances, including the 1965 Watts riot, the 1992 unrest was triggered by an event that highlighted conflicts between a minority community and the law enforcement/justice system (see National Advisory Committee on Civil Disorders 1968 for a discussion of common features of these earlier riots). The unrest also closely resembles the 1980 Miami riot, which followed the acquittal of police officers in the killing of Arthur McDuffie, a black man. That case also involved a change of venue—to Tampa. The jury, which was all white and all male, discounted the testimony of eyewitnesses, including police officers, who testified that McDuffie had been beaten to death by police following a high-speed chase. (For accounts of the origins and dynamics of this collective violence episode, see Ladner et al. 1981 and Porter and Dunn, 1984.)

As was the case with the riots of the 1960s, including Watts, and like Miami in 1980, the 1992 Los Angeles unrest was initiated within the minority community by local residents, and the looting and burning of business establishments were the major forms of property crime. And like these earlier episodes, most of the people killed in the unrest were black.

These similarities notwithstanding, it is the premise of this chapter that in other important respects the Los Angeles episode constituted a new form of race-related collective violence. Just as significant shifts occurred earlier in this century between the race riots that broke out around the time of the First World War, those of the Second World War, and those of the 1960s, the U. S. may well be in the midst of a transition to a more complex form of unrest, of which the 1992 riot is a precursor. The origins and dynamics of this new form of unrest derive from large-scale changes that have occurred in the U. S. since the 1960s: major demographic shifts, increased immigration, increased population diversity, and the declining investment in the cities.

These ideas will be expanded on in the sections that follow. I will first discuss the distinctive features of the Los Angeles unrest, and then outline factors at the societal and community levels that influenced the dynamics of the unrest. The chapter will close with a discussion of the implications of this case for collective behavior research and for the future of Los Angeles and other urban centers.

Distinctive Features of the 1992 Disturbance

Following the release of the verdict in the police brutality trial in mid-afternoon on April 29 (a Wednesday), crowd actions began taking place almost immediately. The unrest started in the relatively stable, comparatively well-off Hyde Park neighborhood. The area around the intersection of Florence and Normandie, which became notorious for the Reginald Denny beating, was a similar neighborhood (*Los Angeles Times* July 5, 1992). Among the first acts of the rebellion were attacks on persons—mainly white and Hispanic motorists who were perceived as outsiders from the perspective of the African-American community. Looting began by about 6:00 pm., and the burning of buildings started less than two hours later. Outside the South Central area, police headquarters at Parker Center in downtown Los Angeles was another focal point for crowd activity (mainly peaceful protests) on the night following the verdict.

Caught by surprise and unable to muster a sufficient number of officers to the initial flashpoints, the police were not successful in bringing the first crowds that formed under control. Police officers sent to South Central fell back to a field command post to reorganize, but found that they lacked the communications equipment and other resources necessary to manage all the incidents that by then were occurring. This inability to act decisively in the early hours was a factor in the growth of the disturbance, which by the second day

(Thursday) covered a larger geographic area. The situation was exacerbated by continuous media coverage that focused on areas where looting and other crowd actions were taking place and conveyed the impression that law enforcement agencies were not actively present in the riot area.

The unrest was most intense on Wednesday night and Thursday, April 29 and 30. It was during this period that most of the deaths and injuries occurred and most of the fires were set. Activity tapered off on Friday and over the weekend (May 1-3), and the community gradually began returning to normal during the next week. State and local officials declared the unrest over on May 4.

Two features are important to note in considering both the dynamics and the conditions underlying the Los Angeles unrest: the selective damage done to Korean-owned businesses; and the widespread participation in the riot by non-black minority group members.

Targeting of Korean Businesses

Previous studies indicate that in civil disturbances property crimes such as the looting and burning of buildings are selective rather than random, reflecting emergent norms that define particular types of property as deserving of community retaliation or expropriation. The properties most often attacked are typically businesses, as opposed to schools, churches, other community institutions, and homes. The businesses that are most often targeted are those that are operated by persons the community considers outsiders (Dynes and Quarantelli 1968; Quarantelli and Dynes 1970). In the urban riots of the 1960s, the victimized businesses tended to be owned by whites; in the Watts riot, for example, Jewish store owners were singled out. However, the norms that develop during a situation of unrest can define a range of groups as deserving of attack. For example, Porter and Dunn (1984: 144) noting that a number of black businesses were among those looted by blacks in the 1980 Miami riot, explain this pattern by arguing that "[t]o the very degree that black merchants achieve commercial success . . . they are perceived as having become just as bad as the white merchants."

Following the unrest the Disaster Research Center obtained records from the Los Angeles Department of Building and Safety and the City Clerk's office that contain information on both buildings and building tenants that sustained damage in the unrest. The records indicate that, consistent with the patterns of property crime observed in earlier U. S. riots, businesses were overwhelmingly targeted in the 1992 unrest; an exceedingly small number of residential dwellings were damaged. In preliminary analyses, an effort was made to code the 1,530 business establishments included in the records according to business type (using SIC codes), owner ethnicity, and the extent of the damage to the business. From the records, it was possible to determine business type for 1,079 of the cases and to determine owner ethnicity for the majority of the businesses. Unfortunately, it was impossible to distinguish white and black owners, since an owner's race was not included the record, and owners' names don't provide a basis for differentiation. Businesses that were owned by corporations could also not be categorized according to owner ethnicity. Despite these limitations the data are still useful for suggesting patterns of riot victimization.

Tables 7.1 and 7.2 summarize damage patterns in the 1992 unrest. The data indicate that the Los Angeles disturbance was similar to other U. S. riots in terms of the types of businesses that were looted, burned, and otherwise damaged. Retail stores were most frequently attacked; clothing stores, eating and drinking establishments, markets, and discount stores were the most frequent retail targets. The service establishments that were damaged in the disturbance include personal service businesses (e.g., beauty salons, barber shops) and services grouped as "health, educational, and social," which mainly included medical offices of various types (see Table 7.1).

The data also suggest that, consistent with earlier patterns, businesses whose owners were easily identified as non-community residents were singled out for attack. In this case, it was Korean merchants who suffered disproportionately. As Table 1 indicates, approximately one-third of the businesses that had riot damage were Korean-owned, with apparel stores, markets, and eating and drinking establishments hardest-hit. Just under 9% of the damaged businesses had owners who were Chinese or members of other Asian nationalities. Some of these owners could have been mistakenly identified as Korean, or the attacks on these businesses could have reflected general anti-Asian sentiment.

Table 7.2 presents data on business type and owner ethnicity for establishments that were totally destroyed. Korean representation is even higher in this category, constituting 46% of the 403 businesses in the "100% loss" group; and again, a number of businesses owned by members other Asian groups were also destroyed. According to the 1990 Census, there are just over 73,000 Koreans in the city of Los Angeles, and Koreans constitute only two percent of the city's population of

TABLE 7.1 Businesses with Losses Related to the 1992 Unrest, by Business Type and Owner Ethnicity

Business Type	Korean	Other Asian	Hispanic	Other	Corp.	Unknown	Total
Retail:							
Apparel	107	8	9	17	24	1	166
Eating & Drinking	32	28	16	25	34	0	135
Market & Grocery	48	15	8	15	15	1	102
Discount & General Merchandise	23	6	3	15	23	1	71
Jewelry	8	4	10	28	3	0	53
Furnishing & Appliances	13	6	6	6	18	0	49
Automotive	12	3	0	14	19	0	48
Liquor	28	6	0	3	3	1	41
Other Retail	27	3	8	24	29	0	91
Services:							
Personal Services	26	15	16	25	7	0	89
Health, Education & Social Services	3	9	7	28	27	0	74
Entertainment & Lodging	21	5	4	2	14	1	47
Business Services & Accounting	7	1	6	8	7	1	30
Other Services	5	2	10	5	9	0	31
Finance, Insurance & Real Estate	4	0	2	17	20	0	43
Other Establishments	2	0	0	4	3	0	9
Sub-total	366	111	105	236	255	6	1079
Percent	33.9	10.3	9.7	21.9	23.6	.6	
Business Type not Ascertained	151	22	80	146	49	3	451
Total	517	133	185	382	304	9	1530
Percent of All Business	33.8	8.7	12.1	25.0	19.9	.6	100.1

Source: Based upon data from the Los Angeles Department of Building and Safety and the City Clerk's Office.

approximately 3,485,000. Relative to their numbers in the population, Korean losses far exceeded those of the city's other ethnic groups.

Part of the reason for these high losses is the fact that Koreans were more likely than whites or other non-black minority group members to be doing business in South Central and adjacent downtown areas. Ong and Hee suggest in a recent paper that as many as one-third of all Korean-owned stores in the city are located in South Central Los Angeles, noting that "Koreans are the latest immigrant group to operate in South Central, replacing the Jews who left in large numbers after the Watts Riots" (1992: 8). Using data from the California State

TABLE 7.2   Businesses with 100% Loss, by Business Type and Owner Ethnicity

	Owner Ethnicity						
Business Type	Korean	Other Asian	Hispanic	Other	Corp.	Unknown	Total
Retail:							
Market & Grocery	29	5	1	4	3	0	42
Apparel	26	3	2	0	6	0	37
Discount & General							
Merchandise	9	2	1	4	9	0	25
Eating & Drinking	7	6	2	4	4	0	23
Liquor	12	1	0	0	1	0	14
Automotive	5	0	0	1	6	0	12
Furnishing &							
Appliances	3	1	2	0	4	0	10
Jewelry	1	0	1	2	0	0	4
Other Retail	9	0	1	5	6	0	21
Services:							
Personal Services	6	4	3	6	0	0	19
Health, Education &							
Social Services	0	1	2	3	2	0	8
Entertainment &Lodging	3	1	0	0	2	0	6
Business Services &							
Accounting	1	0	1	1	2	0	5
Other Services	3	1	4	1	0	0	9
Finance, Insurance &							
Real Estate	1	0	1	2	6	0	10
Other Establishments	0	0	0	1	2	0	3
Sub-total	115	25	21	34	53	0	248
Percent	46.4	10.1	8.5	13.7	21.4	0	
Business Type not							
Ascertained	72	9	19	43	10	2	155
Total	187	34	40	77	63	2	403
Percent of All							
Businesses	46.4	8.4	9.9	19.1	15.6	.5	99.9

Source: Based upon data from the Los Angeles Department of Building and Safety and the City Clerk's Office.

Insurance Commissioner's office (which contains information only on businesses that had insurance), they also found Koreans to be highly overrepresented among victimized businesses, with Latino businesses the second-hardest-hit. Observing that "[t]he economic niche created by Koreans exposed them disproportionately to the violence" (1992: 10), they also argue that Koreans in South Central may have suffered such drastic losses in part because, unlike many Korean merchants in other parts of the city, they were forced to abandon their stores during the riots, since "most owners felt it was unsafe to stay and protect their property . . . [g]iven the anti-white and anti-Asian nature of the attacks on persons by the rioters" (1992: 10).

Attacks on Korean businesses (particularly liquor stores and convenience stores) began in South Central Los Angeles very soon after unrest broke out, most likely in the late afternoon on Wednesday. When crowd activity began to spread beyond the South Central area where the initial outbreaks occurred, one prominent pattern was movement northward along Vermont Avenue, in the direction of commercial centers in Koreatown, which is just north of the Santa Monica Freeway and west of the central business district.

Many of the businesses in that area are Korean-owned and cater to a Korean clientele; however, the residential population is predominantly Hispanic. The Pico-Union district adjacent to Koreatown is home to the largest community of Central American immigrants in the United States, and it was Pico-Union residents who became involved in looting in and near Koreatown on the second and third days of the unrest. It is likely that damage would have been even more widespread in Koreatown if armed groups composed primarily of Korean men had not formed to defend property in that area (for a detailed description of how this emergent group activity was organized, see Yu 1992).

At the present time, these data are merely suggestive. Without being able to classify all the business owners in the areas of the city that experienced collective violence (including those whose businesses were not damaged) in terms their of race and ethnicity, it is not possible to say how much more likely Koreans were to be attacked than were other business owners, and the underlying causes for the pattern of violence are still not entirely clear. Koreans may have suffered such heavy losses not only because of their ethnicity and their presence in and proximity to South Central Los Angeles, but also because they tended disproportionately to own the kinds of businesses that typically become targets in episodes of civil unrest: liquor stores, markets, and apparel stores. Members of the Korean community have also argued that when the unrest broke out, the City failed to move decisively to protect Korean merchants, sacrificing areas like Koreatown in order to protect the more affluent Anglo parts of the city. A number of lawsuits seeking damages from the City have been filed, mostly by Korean business owners (*Los Angeles Times* Oct. 27, 1992). An emergent group, the Korean-American Victims Association, is spearheading this effort. Despite gaps in the data, the riot damage data make a strong *prima facie* case for the selectivity hypothesis. Perhaps more importantly, community residents and leaders in both the African-American and the Korean communities acknowledged after the unrest that many of the attacks on businesses contained an element of hostility against Asians.

Non-Black Minority Participation

Most of the early violence in the 1992 rebellion was initiated by blacks in predominantly black neighborhoods. However, the unrest was by no means confined to predominantly black areas of the city or to African-American participants. Unlike the 1965 Watts riot, the 1992 unrest extended well beyond South Central Los Angeles, to areas north and west of that part of the city. With respect to participation in the unrest, media coverage clearly showed that those looting and protesting were a racially mixed group, and fourteen of the 51 persons killed in the unrest were Latinos—the second largest group of fatalities after blacks.

Arrest records are almost certain to be a biased indicator of who participated in the rebellion, but in the absence of survey data they may shed some light on the question of participation. In their analysis of data on approximately 5,600 adults arrested in the Los Angeles judicial district during the unrest (April 30 through May 5), Petersilia and Abrahamse (1993) found that in contrast with the Watts riot, in which the majority of arrestees were black, over half of those arrested in 1992 were Latinos. Young Latino males accounted for fully 30% of those arrested, and this group was overrepresented relative to their numbers in the general population. Their analysis also indicates that Latino arrests outnumbered African-American arrests throughout the duration of the riot, including April 30, the first full day.

Analyzing population composition and change over time and comparing arrest statistics between the Watts riot and the 1992 unrest, Petersilia and Abrahamse conclude that Latino participation was higher and black participation lower in 1992 than their numbers in the population would predict. Characterizing the unrest as a "minority riot," not a "black riot," these authors argue that "the riot was much more than a protest by blacks against an injustice to a fellow black. Such an interpretation would vastly oversimplify and misrepresent the unrest" (1993: 21).

Petersilia and Abrahamse suggest that the arrest statistics may reflect a tendency on the part of police to selectively arrest Hispanics, while avoiding confrontations with black lawbreakers during the disorders, but I know of no research that addresses this question. The arrest patterns could also reflect selective deployment of police resources, or law enforcement agencies may have used the unrest as an occasion for rounding up Latinos suspected of being in the country illegally. During the uprising, police turned over a number of undocumented arrestees to the Immigration and Naturalization Service, and nearly 500 persons, most of whom were from Mexico, were subsequently deported. But even if police were selective in rounding up Latinos, it is still clear that the participants in the unrest were a diverse group.

General Observations

These data suggest that the 1992 Los Angeles rebellion differed in important ways from earlier episodes of civil unrest in the U. S. Whereas in the past such outbreaks could be analyzed in terms of relations between members of the dominant white society and members of specific racial or ethnic minorities, the Los Angeles unrest involved clashes among a range of groups, including blacks and whites; blacks and Asians; Latinos and blacks; and Latinos and Asians. In a broader sense, the unrest constituted a collective attack by minority group members both on Anglos and on minority business proprietors. The section that follows attempts to put the Los Angeles disturbance into a broader historical context and to identify the sources of the patterns of collective violence that emerged.

Conditions Affecting the Unrest

The trial verdict was the precipitating factor for the outbreak of civil unrest, and the inability of the Police Department to respond adequately in the early hours had a major influence on its subsequent dynamics. However, many aspects of the disturbance can only be understood in the context of changes that Los Angeles has undergone in population composition and intergroup relations in recent years. These changes helped determine the direction the unrest would take once the triggering event occurred. Among the most important contributing conditions were demographic trends in inner-city Los Angeles, particularly those related to immigration; inter-ethnic hostility; and recent U. S. urban policy.

Demographic Trends and Immigration

As other chapters in this volume show, one of the main reasons why the participants in the 1992 unrest were not predominantly black is that South Central Los Angeles is no longer predominantly black and hasn't been for some time. As was the case with patterns of participation in earlier U. S. urban riots, African-American and Latino participants in the 1992 unrest reflected the demographic characteristics of the neighborhoods in which the unrest occurred, except that they were younger and predominantly male.

Media accounts tended to depict the unrest as an African-American uprising against the white justice system, or secondarily as a black-Korean clash. However, the disturbance was much more complex. Some journalistic analyses suggest that a significant number of black-Latino clashes also occurred during the 1992 unrest. For example, Miles (1992) argues that during the riot many blacks engaged in intentional hostile actions against Hispanics, especially recent immigrants. According to his analysis, these attacks occurred because blacks resent Latino immigrants who compete with and undercut them in the labor force and who are moving into their neighborhoods in increasing numbers. Latino participation in the rebellion is accounted for, according to Miles (1992: 59), by the fact that Latinos who originally came to the U. S. in the hope of taking part in the American dream never had a chance to do so and ended up looting when the opportunity presented itself, to "steal what they once thought they could earn."

In a 1984 article on South Central Los Angeles, Melvin Oliver and James Johnson pointed out that the Latino population of that area had been growing rapidly, while the black population was declining, resulting in heightened levels of inter-ethnic conflict. They hypothesized that "the influx of Spanish speaking households into south central Los Angeles has created the conditions ripe for considerable conflict between blacks and browns" (1984: 75). Their examination of survey data from the early 1980s revealed that Latinos held prejudiced attitudes towards blacks, and that blacks, although not expressing high levels of hostility generally, did resent Hispanics—many of whom were recent immigrants—for taking jobs away from them. Oliver and Johnson identified this situation as one that could develop into overt intergroup conflict, adding that (1984: 86)

> . . . researchers should be sensitive and concerned with the potential for social conflict that exists between the have-nots who are increasingly forced to live together in our nation's ghettos...The impact of the "new immigration" is that the new groups, for the most part, are ethnically and culturally different from the traditional inhabitants of these areas and therefore, each are perfect targets for the others displaced hostility.

In a parallel case, Ladner, et al., (1981) have argued that large-scale Cuban immigration formed part of the context for the 1980 Miami riots. The pre-riot pattern they describe is similar to what has occurred in Los Angeles: white flight from the city, combined with a large influx of refugees and other migrants that competed with blacks for increasingly scarce jobs and housing, resulting in intergroup hostility and conflict. The Cubans in Miami, like Asian immigrants in Los Angeles, were also perceived as having greater access to business and credit opportunities, placing black businesses at a competitive disadvantage (Porter and Dunn, 1984).

Sharply increased rates of Asian immigration combined with the tendency for Asians (particularly Koreans) to operate businesses in inner-city neighborhoods clearly affected the character of the 1992 Los Angeles unrest. Los Angeles has been the destination of choice for recent waves of Korean immigrants who have established themselves primarily as small-business owners (Light and Bonacich 1988). Koreans make up a thriving immigrant enclave that has invested heavily in the small retail business sector: liquor stores, grocery stores, gas stations, and similar enterprises (Portes and Manning 1986; Light and Bonacich 1988). And in Los Angeles, as in many other U. S. cities, the presence of large numbers of Korean entrepreneurs in inner-city neighborhoods has sparked African-American hostility. Cheng and Espiritu (1989), focusing specifically on the situation in Los Angeles, argue that while both Hispanics and blacks might have reason to resent the presence of Korean-owned businesses in their neighborhoods, black Los Angeles residents are more likely than Hispanics to do so. African-Americans see recent immigrant business owners (in this case, Koreans) as having an unfair advantage over them; in contrast, Latinos, who tend to be immigrants themselves, are more likely to view competition from other immigrants as fair.

Hostility between Korean merchants and black community residents constitutes an important element in the social context that shaped the 1992 uprising. Particularly significant was the case of Soon Ja Du, a 51-year old Korean liquor store owner in Los Angeles, who killed a black 15-year-old customer, Latasha Harlins, shooting her in the back of the head with a .38 caliber revolver following an argument in which Du accused the girl of attempting to shoplift. In November of 1991, Du was convicted of voluntary manslaughter and given probation by a Los Angeles judge—a verdict and sentence that enraged many members of the black community and heightened hostility against Koreans (Neuman 1992; Coleman 1993).

Since the unrest, it appears that, if anything, the antagonism between blacks and Koreans has deepened. Many Koreans not only consider themselves uniquely victimized by the unrest, but also strongly resent recovery-related policies that make it difficult for liquor stores in South Central to get back into business. The Community Coalition for Substance Abuse Prevention and Treatment, a social movement organization that had been active for a number of years before the unrest, is leading the effort to reduce the number of liquor stores in inner-city black neighborhoods. In the aftermath of the riots, Korean merchants have come to interpret this activity as directed specifically against them, and the community has banded together to fight the new regulations (see Yu 1992 and *New York Times* 1992 for more details on this controversy). The Black-Korean Coalition, set up to improve relations between the two groups, disbanded in December, 1992, partly as a result of these conflicts.

As Los Angeles has become increasingly diverse, with Anglos now in the numerical minority, the stage has been set for increased competition and conflict among ethnic groups occupying different niches in the local economy, housing market, and labor force. Often, as is the case with blacks and immigrant Latinos, these relationships involve competition for increasingly scarce resources such as jobs and housing. Or, as is the case with blacks and Korean merchants, hostility develops out of perceived relationships of exploitation. Deep cultural misunderstandings further complicate the relationships among these groups.

Blacks, Latinos, and Asians are currently among those suffering most as a result of large-scale changes in the U. S. economy and the broader capitalist world system. Yet they are forced to compete for jobs, housing, resources, and political power, and that competition engenders hostility. In Los Angeles in 1992, Korean business owners became a "middleman minority" (Bonacich 1973) in a very literal sense: perceived as outsiders and exploiters by African-American inner-city residents, they bore the brunt of attacks by African-Americans and Latinos when the violence erupted.

Urban Policy and the Riots

Like residents of other large cities in the U. S., Los Angeles residents experienced a worsening economic situation in the two decades leading up to the unrest. In South Central Los Angeles, which had never really recovered from the Watts riots, levels of poverty and joblessness were high. In the late 80s, per capita income in South Central was less than half that of Los Angeles county as a whole, and poverty and unemployment rates were more than double. More than one-fourth of the households in South Central were on public assistance, as compared with about 10% for the county as a whole. For those few who were fortunate enough to find work, the average hourly wage only amounted to 58% of the countywide wage (Ong 1992).

Throughout the 1980s, Los Angeles portrayed itself as the new financial and cultural capital of the Pacific Rim, and foreign capital poured into the city for costly development projects and high-profile real estate purchases in the downtown area (Davis 1992). City government aggressively pursued development downtown and in the predominantly Anglo westside, while just south of the booming downtown business district, South Central Los Angeles lost jobs and economic activity on a massive scale. By any standard, the area constitutes a pocket of underdevelopment. The economic policies of the Reagan-Bush era hastened the flight of jobs from many inner city areas, including Los Angeles; between 1982 and 1989, 131 plants were closed in Los Angeles, and 124,000 workers lost their jobs. These plant closings disproportionately affected African-American and Latino communities (Johnson, et al. 1992; Oliver, Johnson, and Farrell, 1993). By the end of the 80s, economic activity was depressed in the retail, manufacturing, and service sectors in South Central. The small number of manufacturing jobs that remained were in low-wage industries like garment manufacturing, and these jobs were more likely to be held by Latinos than by blacks. Oliver, Johnson, and Farrell (1993: 122) observe that "[w]hereas joblessness is the central problem for black males in South Central Los Angeles, concentration in low-paying, bad jobs in competitive sector industries is the main problem for the Latino residents of the area." Large retail stores and supermarket chains avoid South Central (Ong 1992)—which is one reason the opportunities were so good for Korean liquor and convenience stores owners.

Although touted on the grounds that it would provide more jobs, the development frenzy of the 1980s didn't deliver on that promise in Los Angeles and many other U. S. cities. Tax advantages accrued to developers, not cities or community residents, and whatever new revenues were generated were typically diverted to pay for services that the Federal government was no longer supporting. Moreover, new construction in cities like Los Angeles may actually have increased urban blight, as tenants in older buildings near the city core deserted them in favor of newer, more prestigious addresses (*Washington Post*, May 10, 1992).

At the same time the economic situation worsened, the ability of cities to provide public welfare and safety services to residents declined. Drugs, crime, gang violence and other social problems were rampant in South Central Los Angeles and other inner city areas, but Federal programs to address these problems had been systematically cut as a part of the strategy to dismantle the social programs of the 1960s (Johnson, et al. 1992). In the decade leading up to the riots, Urban Development Action Grants, revenue sharing, and assistance to local law enforcement agencies were either eliminated or severely cut.

Police departments in cities like Los Angeles also became increasingly estranged from the communities they were supposed to be protecting, and critical resources were weakened. For example, at the time of the unrest in 1992, the Los Angeles Police Department had a force of about 7,800 officers—down from 8,400 two years before (*Los Angeles Times*, Oct. 22, 1992). The ratio of police officers to residents was about 2 to 1,000. Los Angeles was capable of deploying only 15 officers per square mile, compared with 89 per square mile for New York (Miles 1992). Of a police force of nearly 8,000, in early 1992 the city reportedly had only about 300 officers on the street at any given time to respond to radio calls; by the fall of 1992, that number had dropped to 279 (*Los Angeles Times*, Oct. 22, 1992). A large proportion of the police force held desk jobs and non-patrol duties, many of which could have been handled by civilians.

The analysis conducted for the Webster report (Special Advisor to the Board of Police Commissioners 1992) following the unrest revealed a police department that was overinvested in elite units like the SWAT team and a gang-suppression unit called CRASH (Community Resources Against Street Hoodlums). These units became the main avenue for promotion in the force, to the detriment of ordinary patrol activities and other crime-fighting efforts. The Commission noted that setting up these highly specialized units took more and more officers out of daily contact with the community, and it recommended that officers from these units be redeployed into community patrol duties. This pattern of chronic understaffing in the face of escalating community problems, along with lack of training and deeply ingrained racist attitudes that high management tolerated, may explain why police officers in Los Angeles were notoriously quick to resort to excessive force with minority suspects (for discussions of cases of police brutality involving the Los Angeles Police and Sheriff's Departments, see Amnesty International 1992).

The situation in which the Los Angeles Police Department found itself at the time of the unrest was indeed ironic. LAPD officers were originally responsible for the beating that became the occasion for the unrest. The LAPD's use of excessive force and its callousness toward the minority community caused many community residents to sympathize with Rodney King, focused community attention on the trial, and fueled the rage against the verdict. The police department's relationship with the South Central community was evidently so poor it was unable to gauge the magnitude of the resentment and riot potential that existed. And when the unrest began to escalate, the LAPD was too short-handed and disorganized to contain it. One is reminded of Carter's (1988) discussion of the relationship between police force size and riot severity, which suggests the cities in which the most serious rioting occurs are those in which the police force is large enough to generate a significant number of hostile encounters with community residents, but not large enough to exert control when a collective violence episode begins to escalate. This was certainly the case in Los Angeles.

Discussion

Grievances and the Los Angeles Unrest

The 1992 disturbances could lead to renewed discussions among collective behavior scholars concerning the role of grievances and discontent in collective violence. Such questions have been thoroughly addressed in previous research, the general thrust of which has been to downplay the importance of shared attitudinal predispositions like deprivation and frustration and to emphasize instead differential motivation and differential participation in collective behavior episodes (see McPhail 1971; Gurney and Tierney 1982; Rule 1988). Action-in-common need not stem from common underlying sentiments or goals; nor are attitudes automatically expressed behaviorally. In Los Angeles, many of the people who rioted were upset and outraged about the verdict, but clearly so were many of the people who didn't. Not everyone who burned a building during the period of unrest did so to protest the verdict; for example, fire department investigations attributed some arson cases to opportunism—that is, property owners using the uprising as a cover to unload unprofitable pieces of real estate. Reasons for looting likely included not only anger over the verdict and resentment of Korean shopowners and business owners in general, but also the desire for consumer items, basic food and clothing needs, and fear that the supply of goods would run out or that stores wouldn't reopen.

The acts of physical violence that were committed during the unrest undoubtedly stemmed from complex motivational sources as well. For example, some accounts suggest that the Reginald Denny beating was attributable in part the manner in which the police who first responded at the intersection of Florence and Normandie treated local residents. In other words, it may have been both the King verdict and subsequent actions by the police that triggered crowd violence against Denny and others who were attacked at that location. Other acts of violence that were considered part of the riot may actually have been unrelated to it. For example, in one homicide attributed to the unrest, two people got into a fight in a grocery store, and one person strangled the other. A stabbing death that was included in the toll occurred in a community where no other violence had been reported, and no one actually saw the killing. Several of the deaths included in the overall toll were heart attacks in which pre-existing medical conditions were judged to have been exacerbated by the verdict and the unrest (see *Los Angeles Times*, May 6; Koehler, et al. 1993). Like all statistics, riot statistics are social constructions.

Not everyone who takes part in crowd violence or collective lawbreaking does so because of anger against injustice. In their study of prison riots, for example, Useem and Kimball (1991) find that while such riots originate in objective conditions like the abuse of inmates, and while grievances arising from these conditions do play a role in the genesis of riots, a great deal goes on in actual riot situations that is by no means grievance-related or protest-oriented. Inmates may use a riot as an opportunity to steal food and other goods, set fires, or exact vengeance against "snitches." Useem and Kimball argue that a prison riot can be political in origin but lack explicit political content; it may be a political event for some participants, but not for others. The same argument can be made about episodes of urban unrest like the 1992 uprising.

Unrest as Protest

It would thus be an oversimplification to argue that the riot was purely expression of pent-up African-American grievances; both the data and previous research argue against such a perspective. At the same time, there is no question that black outrage did play a major role the genesis of the unrest. That outrage was generated not only the Rodney King verdict, but perhaps more importantly by the history of negative experiences that so many South Central residents— especially black males—had with law enforcement officers. The frequency of hostile encounters between police officers and blacks doubtless led many residents to empathize with Rodney King and made the trial and the verdict especially salient to a broad segment of the African-American community. The beating of Rodney King and the acquittal of the police officers would not have had such a large impact had they not resonated with what many African Americans in Los Angeles already knew from their own life experiences about law enforcement and the justice system.

There is a body of collective behavior theory and research that characterizes crowd violence as a form of protest or collective retaliation against an unjust social order. Historical and comparative studies suggest that events like the Rodney King verdict, which underscore a dominant group's lack of fairness, can trigger spontaneous and violent responses by members of subordinate groups (Hobsbawm 1959; Rude 1964; Oberschall 1973; Tilly 1975; 1978; Piven and Cloward 1977). These short-lived disturbances, which may be intensely violent, are typically engaged in by relatively unorganized groups that have few alternative avenues for expressing discontent or pressing for change. As Piven and Cloward (1992: 311) argue, the riot is an enduring form of collective behavior that appears and reappears throughout history:

> . . . preindustrial food riots, grain seizures, land invasions, and machine smashing have rough parallels in the modern period with urban riots, mob looting, squatting, sit-downs, sit-ins, rent strikes, and industrial sabotage.
> . . . Even as changing modes of social organization bring into being new forms of protest, certain persisting features of social organization facilitate continuities in other protest forms.

Several analyses of the 1960s urban riots characterized those episodes primarily as a form of protest against racial inequality and injustice (Fogelson 1971; Feagin and Hahn 1973). To some degree, the 1992 unrest can be interpreted in that same light. Many Los Angeles residents have in fact made that interpretation: a survey conducted after the 1992 unrest, using a sample of Los Angeles County residents, asked (as had several earlier riot studies) whether respondents considered the riots mainly protest, mainly a chance for participants to loot and commit crimes, or both. Not unexpectedly, different ethnic groups interpreted the riots differently; 67% of black respondents considered the riots mainly protest, as compared with about 43% of the Asians, 39% of the Hispanics, and 37% of the Anglos (Bobo, et al., 1992).

The "Assembling Process" and the Riots

While the unrest cannot be understood without taking into account black outrage against police brutality and other forms of injustice, the unrest was a complex event whose dynamics were also influenced by other factors. Work by Clark McPhail and his collaborators provides a useful perspective for understanding the crowd actions that constituted the unrest (see McPhail 1971; 1991; McPhail and Miller 1973; McPhail and Wohlstein 1983). Like many collective behavior scholars, McPhail argues that it is incorrect to assume that organized actions like crowd violence and looting stem from common psychological predispositions like frustration, anger, or feelings of deprivation. Rather, he claims, riots, like other types of collective gatherings, take place when participants have received various kinds of "assembling instructions" that indicate a gathering is occurring or about to occur. Persons who consider the gathering relevant, are able to participate, and don't have competing obligations that would rule out participation are most likely to join these collective behavior episodes.

Participation in riots and other "nonperiodic assemblages" can also be explained by taking into account ecological factors such as the spatial distribution of ongoing patterns of behavior, typical daily routines, and the propensity for particular groups to gather at particular locations. In other words, to understand patterns of riot involvement, one must first understand social behavior under routine conditions. Crowds will have a tendency to form in locations where people typically gather. Individuals who spend a lot of time on street corners with friends will likely congregate on street corners during times of crisis. People who have a history of hostile encounters with police will be more interested than others in the results of a verdict like the one in the Rodney King case and more likely to consider gatherings related to such issues as relevant. Densely populated, bustling areas like the Pico-Union district, or intersections like the one at Florence and Normandie, will be more conducive to crowd formation than more sparsely populated, less trafficked areas, simply because any unusual action that is initiated in such settings is more likely to "draw a crowd."

Seen from this perspective, the extensive media coverage of the King beating itself and of the trial, combined with black residents' experiences with the LAPD over time, other cases of police brutality, and incidents like the Latasha Harlins shooting, produced a social climate in which large numbers of black Los Angeles residents were involved with the King case and interested in the verdict. On the day the unrest broke out, the assembling instructions that led to the formation on unruly crowds included the news of the verdict, news reports that clashes with police had occurred or that looting had begun at a particular location, and direct visual evidence of looting and other crowd activity. The verdict was announced at approximately 3:30 pm on a weekday, a time when many community residents were at work or on the streets, which made for rapid transmission of the news and also facilitated crowd formation. The message was reinforced by the constant media coverage of the crowd's actions that subsequently developed.

The timing and manner in which the verdict was released and the media coverage that followed created conditions that were ideal for the formation of crowds. The fact that the police were unable to respond rapidly enough to contain the crowds that initially formed contributed to the spread of the unrest in part because it lowered the costs of participating in crowd activities. These important points were recognized by city authorities, who following the second police brutality trial in 1993 first withheld the verdict, which came on a Friday afternoon, from the general public; then released it at approximately

7:00 am the next day; and made sure there was a visible law enforcement presence on the streets when the verdict was announced.

Intergroup Competition and the Unrest

The work of Susan Olzak provides another useful framework for understanding the structural sources of the 1992 unrest. Olzak's analyses point to the important role played by immigration and labor markets in the genesis of collective violence. She argues that violence increases in periods characterized by both high rates of immigration and declining economic conditions (Olzak 1983; 1986; 1987). Her work also suggests that the existence of ethnic enclaves like those established by Koreans in Los Angeles may be associated with higher levels of intergroup conflict (see Olzak 1986). However, Olzak's work to date, like other recent scholarship on riots (e.g., Carter, 1990; 1992) analyzes collective violence as a situation involving two groups—typically whites and some other minority group, usually blacks—that are in conflict with one another. The Los Angeles case involved multiple interracial and interethnic antagonisms that are not easily reducible to a single model. Conflicts between African-Americans and Latinos in South Central can be analyzed from a split labor market perspective (Bonacich 1972), for example, but this is not the case for conflicts existing between African-Americans and Anglos or African-Americans and Koreans.

Conclusions

The foregoing analysis suggests that the Los Angeles unrest was considerably more complex than earlier episodes of racially-motivated collective violence in the U. S., and that future episodes of unrest in urban communities may well follow this new pattern. Recognizing that the form collective violence takes varies over time, earlier writers made a distinction between the "communal" riots of the first half of the twentieth century and the "commodity" riots that came later (Janowitz 1969). The 1992 unrest constitutes a new type of collective violence, involving multiple groups (rather than only two) as well as elements of both communal and commodity forms. Given the increasingly diverse range of potentially solidaristic ethnic, enclave, and class groupings in our cities, the Los Angeles unrest may well be a precursor to future episodes of collective violence.

The Los Angeles unrest had its origins in the ongoing experiences, daily activities, and collective definitions of minority community residents. These experiences included not only hostile encounters with law enforcement agencies but also increasingly uneasy and competitive relations with members of other ethnic groups. And these daily contacts and interactions had their roots in turn in broad structural changes—immigration, the internationalization of major urban centers, the globalization of the economy, and deindustrialization—that differentially impacted the various ethnic groups in Los Angeles.

Los Angeles in the Wake of the Unrest

In the two years since the Los Angeles unrest, some hopeful changes have taken place, but the picture remains bleak. On the positive side, the police department has a new chief, Willie Williams, who wants to improve police-community relations by instituting community-based policing practices. The newly-elected mayor appears to have a much better working relationship with the new chief than his predecessor, Mayor Bradley, had with Chief Gates.

On the negative side, economic conditions, already poor for blacks and Latinos, have generally worsened, and the downturn has now affected the middle classes. The economic climate in Los Angeles is not one that is conducive to the kinds of recovery projects the community needs, and the Clinton Administration pays just as little attention to inner city problems as did its Republican predecessors. "Rebuild LA," a post-riot reconstruction effort that was based on the notion that recovery can be privatized, has brought few tangible results. The effort to rebuild ultimately mirrored the intergroup antagonisms that characterize Los Angeles politics generally, government support was virtually nonexistent, and business enterprises that were not inclined to locate in areas like South Central Los Angeles prior to the unrest were generally even less willing to do so afterwards.

In May of 1993, the *New York Times* reported the results of a study it had conducted, based in part on data from the city's Department of Building and Safety. At that time, fewer than half the riot-damaged properties had been repaired or rebuilt, and compared with other hard-hit areas of the city, recovery was progressing most slowly in South Central Los Angeles. Among the reasons cited for the slow pace of recovery were:

> lack of money, problems collecting insurance and getting loans, heavy winter rains, bureaucratic delays with permits, compliance with modern seismic and disability codes, opposition to liquor stores, a depressed local economy and, for many owners, sheer fear and weariness (*New York Times*, May 10: 1).

In January of 1994, the city confronted yet another crisis. The

Northridge earthquake caused widespread damage and disruption throughout the greater Los Angeles area and impacted neighborhoods, residents, and businesses that were still in the process of trying to recover from the riots. Besides creating additional financial burdens for a city that was already facing considerable economic difficulty, the earthquake may well exacerbate intergroup tensions. Within a few days of the earthquake, for example, complaints were raised that the needs of earthquake victims in South Central were being ignored, while the attention of the media and public officials was focused mainly on victims in the San Fernando Valley. Anti-immigrant interests moved swiftly to try to limit undocumented residents' access to certain disaster assistance programs. Controversies developed around the provision of HUD "Section 8" rent vouchers to disaster victims, since thousands of low-income families had already been on the long waiting list for subsidized housing prior to the earthquake. Post-earthquake recovery is likely to further erode what little interest there is in the needs of riot victims and black inner city residents, rechannel the energies of city officials, and place a further drain on public finances.

Implications for Other U. S. Cities

A short commentary that appeared in the *Los Angeles Times* a few days after the disturbances argued that what it termed the nation's first "multiethnic riots" ought to be seen in the context of large-scale economic and social changes in which labor and capital were internationalized (May 10, 1992: M4):

> It was the simultaneous arrival of new money and new people that created, in the enthusiasm of the late 1980s, the vision of Los Angeles as capital of the Pacific Rim. That vision, we are learning, has a dark side.

Over ten years ago, Ladner et al (1981) made a similar point about the Miami unrest of 1980, an event that parallels the Los Angeles disturbances in numerous ways—except that it was Cuban immigrants who were the main competitors against blacks in Miami, and Koreans were not present in that city in large numbers (for a detailed analysis of that episode of unrest, see Porter and Dunn 1984).

Anyone familiar with U. S. urban centers today knows that the background conditions that gave rise to the 1992 unrest are in no way unique to Los Angeles. The restructuring of the U. S. economy, the globalization of labor and capital, and the policies of the Reagan-Bush years have affected communities across the country. And although it is probably very near the end of the continuum in terms of racial and ethnic diversity, Los Angeles is not the only city with a multi-racial, multi-ethnic population. The patterns of civil unrest observed in Los Angeles are almost certain to be repeated elsewhere. U. S. cities are becoming increasingly diverse, and members of minority groups are beginning to outnumber members of the white "majority." Overall, the future does not look promising. As cities nationwide have become less white and less important politically, there has been a corresponding national decline in public investment—including the types of investment that prevent and contain collective violence (Blakeley and Ames 1992).

References

Amnesty International. 1992. *Torture, Ill-Treatment and Excessive Force by Police in Los Angeles, California.* London: Amnesty International.

Blakely, Edward J. and D. L. Ames. 1992. "Changing Places: American Planning Policy for the 1990s." *Journal of Urban Affairs* 14: 423–446.

Bobo, Lawrence D., James H. Johnson, Jr., Melvin L. Oliver, James Sidanius, and Camille Zubrinsky. 1992. "Public Opinion Before and After a Spring of Discontent: A Preliminary Report on the 1992 Los Angeles County Social Survey." Los Angeles: University of California, Los Angeles. Center for the Study of Urban Poverty. Occasional Working Paper Series, Vol. 3, No. 1.

Bonacich, Edna. 1972. "A Theory of Ethnic Antagonism: The Split Labor Market." *American Sociological Review* 37: 547–559.

Bonacich, Edna. 1973. "A Theory of Middleman Minorities." *American Sociological Review* 38: 583–594.

Carter, Gregg Lee. 1988. "Local Police Force Size and the Severity of the 1960s Black Rioting." *Journal of Conflict Resolution*, 31, 4: 601–614.

Carter, Gregg Lee. 1990. "Black Attitudes and the 1960s Black Riots: An Aggregate-Level Analysis of the Kerner Commission's '15 Cities' Data." *Sociological Quarterly* 31: 269–286.

Carter, Gregg Lee. 1992. "Hispanic Rioting During the Civil Rights Era." *Sociological Forum* 7: 301–322.

Cheng, Lucie and Yen Espiritu. 1989. "Korean Businesses in Black and Hispanic Neighborhoods: A Study of Intergroup Relations." *Sociological Perspectives*, 32, 4: 521–534.

Coleman, Wanda. 1993. "Remembering Latasha: Blacks, Immigrants and America." *The Nation*, Feb. 15: 187–191.

Davis, Mike. 1992. *City of Quartz: Excavating the Future in Los Angeles.* New York, Random House.

Dynes, Russell R. and E. L. Quarantelli. 1968. "What Looting in Civil Disturbances Really Means." *Trans-Action* (May): 9–14.

Feagin, Joseph R. and Harlan Hahn. 1973. *Ghetto Revolts: The Politics of Violence in American Cities.* New York: Macmillan.

Fogelson, Robert M. 1971. *Violence as Protest: A Study of Riots and Ghettos.* Garden City, NY: Anchor Books.

Gurney. Joan N. and Kathleen J. Tierney. 1982. "Relative Deprivation and Social Movements: A Critical Look at Twenty Years of Theory and Research." *Sociological Quarterly* 23: 33–47.

Hobsbawm, Eric J. 1959. *Primitive Rebels: Studies in Archaic Forms of Social Movement in the 19th and 20th Centuries.* New York: W. W. Norton.

Janowitz, Morris. 1969. "Social Control of Escalated Riots." Pp. 501–515 in Allen D. Grimshaw (Ed.) *Racial Violence in the United States.* Chicago: Aldine.

Johnson, James. H., Jr. Cloyzell K. Jones, Walter C. Farrell, and Melvin L. Oliver. 1992. "The Los Angeles Rebellion, 1992: A Preliminary Assessment from Ground Zero." Los Angeles: University of California, Los Angeles. Center for the Study of Urban Poverty. Occasional Working Paper Series, Vol 2, No. 7.

Koehler, Gus, Darlene Isbell, Calvin Freeman, Daniel Smiley, and Joseph E. Morales. 1993. *Medical Care for the Injured: The Emergency Medical Response to the April 1992 Los Angeles Civil Disturbance.* Draft report. Sacramento, CA: California Emergency Medical Services Authority.

Ladner, Robert A., Barry J. Schwartz, Sandra Roker, and Loretta S. Titterud. 1981. "The Miami Riots of 1980: Antecedent Conditions, Community Responses and Participant Characteristics." *Research in Social Movements, Conflict and Change* 4: 171–214.

Light, Ivan and Edna Bonacich. 1988. *Immigrant Entrepreneurs: Koreans in Los Angeles, 1965–1982.* Berkeley and Los Angeles: University of California Press.

Los Angeles Times. 1992. "Were All Deaths in Toll Really Riot-Related?" May 6: B1.

Los Angeles Times. 1992. "Globalization of Los Angeles: The First Multiethnic Riots." May 10: M4.

Los Angeles Times. 1992. "Unlikely Flash Point for Riots." July 5: A1.

Los Angeles Times. 1992. "Call for More Patrol Units Faces Hurdles." October 22: A1.

Los Angeles Times. 1992. "1,800 File Claims Against City Over Riot Injuries, Losses." October 27:B3.

McPhail, Clark. 1971. "Civil Disorder Participation: A Critical Examination of Recent Research." *American Sociological Review* 36: 1058–1073.

McPhail, Clark. 1991. *The Myth of the Madding Crowd.* New York: Walter de Gruyter.

McPhail, Clark and David Miller. 1973. "The Assembling Process: A Theoretical and Empirical Examination." *American Sociological Review* 38: 721–735.

McPhail, Clark and Ronald Wohlstein. 1983. "Individual and Collective Behavior within Gatherings, Demonstrations, and Riots." *Annual Review of Sociology* 9: 579–600.

Miles, Jack. 1992. "Blacks vs. Browns." *Atlantic Monthly* (Oct.): 41–68.

National Advisory Committee on Civil Disorders. 1968. Report. Washington, DC: U. S. Government Printing Office.

Neuman, Elena. 1992. "Stores of Rage." *Insight*, August 22.

New York Times. 1992. "Under Siege: Liquor's Inner City Pipeline." November 29: 3–1.

New York Times. 1993. "Rebuilding Lags in Los Angeles a Year After Riots." May 1: A1; A14.

Oberschall, Anthony. 1973. *Social Conflict and Social Movements.* Englewood Cliffs: Prentice-Hall.

Oliver, Melvin L. and James H. Johnson, Jr. 1984. "Interethnic Conflict in an Urban Ghetto: The Case of Blacks and Latinos in Los Angeles." *Research in Social Movements, Conflict and Change,* 6: 57–94.

Oliver, Melvin L., James H. Johnson, Jr., and Walter C. Farrell. 1993. "Anatomy of a Rebellion: A Political-Economic Analysis." Pp. 117–141 in Robert Gooding-Williams (Ed.) *Reading Rodney King: Reading Urban Uprising.* New York: Routledge.

Olzak, Susan. 1983. "Contemporary Ethnic Mobilization." *Annual Review of Sociology* 9: 355–374.

Olzak, Susan. 1986. "A Competition Model of Ethnic Collective Action in American Cities, 1877–1889." Pp. 17–46 in Susan Olzak and Joane Nagel (Eds.) *Competitive Ethnic Relations.* Orlando: Academic Press.

Olzak, Susan. 1987. "Causes of Ethnic Conflict and Protest in Urban America, 1877–1889." *Social Science Research* 16: 185–210.

Ong, Paul M., with Wendy Belcher and Ji-Young Lee. 1992. "The Economic Base of South Central Los Angeles." Unpublished draft report. Los Angeles: University of California, Los Angeles, Graduate School of Architecture and Urban Planning.

Ong, Paul and S. Hee. 1992. "The Los Angeles Riots/Rebellion and Korean Merchants: Analysis and Comments." Unpublished manuscript. Los Angeles: University of California, Los Angeles. Graduate School of Architecture and Urban Planning.

Petersilia, J. and Allan Abrahamse. 1993. "The Los Angeles Riot of Spring, 1992: A Profile of Those Arrested." Unpublished manuscript. Santa Monica, CA: The Rand Corporation.

Piven, Frances Fox and Richard . Cloward. 1977. *Poor People's Movements: Why They Succeed, How They Fail.* New York: Random House.

Piven, Frances Fox and Richard A. Cloward. 1992. "Normalizing Collective Protest." Pp. 301–325 in A. D. Morris and C. M. Mueller (Eds.) *Frontiers in Social Movement Theory.* New Haven: Yale University Press.

Porter, Bruce and Marvin Dunn. 1984. *The Miami Riot of 1980: Crossing the Bounds.* Lexington, MA: D. C. Heath and Company.

Portes, Alejandro and Robert D. Manning. 1986. "The Immigrant Enclave: Theory and Empirical Examples." Pp. 47–68 in S. Olzak, Susan and Joane Nagel (Eds.) 1986. *Competitive Ethnic Relations.* Orlando: Academic Press.

Quarantelli, E. L. and Russell R. Dynes. 1970. "Property Norms and Looting: Their Patterns in Community Crises." *Phylon* 31: 168–182.

Rule, James B. 1988. *Theories of Civil Violence.* Berkeley: University of California Press.

Special Advisor to the Board of Police Commissioners. 1992. *The City in Crisis:*

A Report by the Special Advisor to the Board of Police Commissioners on the Civil Disorders in Los Angeles. Los Angeles: SABPC.

Tilly, Charles. 1975. "Revolutions and Collective Violence." Pp. 483-555 in F. I. Greenstein and N. W. Polsby (Eds.) *Handbook of Political Science*, Vol. 3. Reading, MA: Addison-Wesley.

Tilly, Charles. 1978. *From Mobilization to Revolution*. Reading, MA: Addison-Wesley.

Useem, Bert and Peter Kimball. 1991. *States of Siege: U. S. Prison Riots 1971–1986*. New York: Oxford University Press.

Washington Post. 1992. "The Urban Boom: Who Benefits?" May 10: H1.

Yu, Eui-Young. 1992. "Community Based Disaster Management: The Case of Los Angeles Koreatown During the April 29 Riots." Paper presented at the Korean Studies Conference, North Park College, Chicago, October 16–17.

8

Black-Korean Conflict

Regina Freer

The startling video-taped shooting of a young African American woman by a Korean American grocer; the portrayal of contentious relations between an African American customer and a Korean American merchant in Spike Lee's "Do The Right Thing"; and the sight of Korean American merchants in predominantly African American neighborhoods desperately attempting to defend their stores with guns during the recent Los Angeles rebellion are all images which served to bring the long-standing conflict between the members of the African American and Korean American communities into the nation's consciousness. Such conflict is an unfortunate reality in this nation's cities. Urban residents who simultaneously cope with decreasing federal funds for cities and a nationwide economic downturn are also coping with the challenges engendered by increasing diversity and population growth. Cultural misunderstanding, coupled with the perception and reality of competition for scarce resources, unfortunately ensures that the path leading to conflict is the one most frequently travelled. As reflected in the aforementioned images, a recent example of such explosive conflict is the flaring of tensions between African American customers and Korean American merchants in Los Angeles before and during the recent rebellion. On the heels of the shootings of two African Americans by Korean American merchants, leaders in the black community organized boycotts of selected Korean American-owned stores. Tensions flared on all sides of the conflict; one such boycott lasted for more than 90 days, eventually shutting down the store. While this conflict can be and has been painted simply as an example of cultural misunderstanding, I believe that it is far more complex and multifaceted. While cultural insensitivity and ignorance do play a significant role in the conflict, it

175

is important to view this conflict in the context of the economic disparity and racism which stretch well beyond the interaction of these two groups alone.

I argue that this conflict has a fundamentally economic root cause and that it is merely the latest symptom of a much larger problem with a very long history. Competition for scarce resources is akin to metaphorical competition over a single slice of an entire pie. Too often the fight between two individuals, or in this case groups, over that single slice detracts from any efforts to enlarge the pie itself, or to question the distribution scheme in the first place. It seems that this metaphor is an appropriate one to describe the case of blacks and Koreans in Los Angeles. While these two groups are engaged in a struggle over the scarce resource of economic opportunity in the city, those responsible for slicing the pie remain outside of the conflict, as do others who may be receiving unduly large portions of the pie. This metaphor recognizes that governmental resources are limited, thus it appropriately transmits that cities are in fact operating under severe economic constraints. However, it also properly identifies the fact that there is some flexibility in how existing resources are allocated. Decisions are made on how the shrinking pie should be sliced. It is this process which I examine in this chapter.

While there is evidence of general disparity between the African American and Korean American communities, they are both constrained by a lack of economic opportunities. This constraint ensures that the economically depressed inner-city is the meeting-place for these two marginal groups. The language and cultural barriers facing newly arrived Korean immigrants keeps them from pursuing economic advancement through professional careers that many of them trained for in Korea. One outlet that has proved available for Korean immigrant professionals has been to invest in small businesses in economically depressed and blighted areas such as South Central Los Angeles. Unlike those in more affluent, predominantly white areas, these businesses require a relatively moderate capital investment and very minimal expertise to run. However, they are extremely labor intensive, thus making them an unattractive investment for many. Low inventory, poor selection, and high prices on the merchant's side, coupled with joblessness, and persistent poverty on the consumer side, make for a volatile situation. This is all exacerbated by cultural differences and misunderstanding. Yet, these two relatively resource-poor groups are being asked to develop the solution to the inevitable conflict, a problem which does not begin with them. They are attempting to solve a crisis that grew out of decisions made by others.

The central questions then become: *Why* are these two resource-poor groups alone expected to develop solutions to a conflict that did not begin with them? Who are these "others" who have predetermined the existence of conflict, and why aren't they the focus of these conflict resolution efforts?

Some hint of an answer to these questions unfolds in an examination of the actors involved in the mediation efforts undertaken in the Los Angeles case. A complex web of entangled alliances between the "leaders" of the African American and Korean American communities who participated in negotiations of a "settlement," the mayor and economic elites in the city suggests why the agenda of proposed resolutions to the conflict between the African American and Korean American communities has been so narrowly defined as to exclude any real challenge to existing economic power. Additionally, this analysis suggests why efforts toward mediating a settlement have focused solely on the two communities, in isolation of a larger set of economic actors. Finally, it is suggestive of how it was that, four months after the mediation efforts concluded, the city erupted in flames, with African Americans and Koreans again finding themselves engaged in explosive conflict.

Los Angeles is clearly not the only city that has experienced conflict between African Americans and Korean Americans. A highly publicized case that occurred in Brooklyn, New York in 1990 involving a dispute over an alleged assault by the owner of the Red Apple grocery store against a Haitian female customer exploded as black residents engaged in a boycott that lasted over a year (Kim, forthcoming). The fact that this case, the one in Los Angeles and those that occurred in Atlanta, Baltimore, Washington D.C. and Philadelphia all involved Korean American merchants and black customers speaks to the importance of the economic character of these conflicts (Kim, 1981). Additionally, African Americans and Korean Americans are not the only two communities of color to experience these tensions and conflicts. In Detroit, for example, a similar conflict erupted between black residents and Arab American merchants. Unfortunately, this is a story which readily travels to other urban areas in the country. The Los Angeles case is compelling, however, because of the city's position as a trendsetter for the rest of the nation. In terms of demographic change and increasing diversity, Los Angeles is already experiencing shifts that have been predicted for the nation as a whole. In many ways, exploring the Los Angeles case may lend insight into the future for cities across the country.

I view this chapter as being a first step in an attempt to understand the nature of intra-ethnic conflict in urban settings. Hopefully it will establish hypotheses and generalizations that can be tested in other contexts and other groups. The competition over a slice of pie demonstrated in this particular case is undoubtedly and unfortunately being played out in dozens of different settings.

Before addressing those questions most central to this chapter, it is necessary to establish a history of the parties involved as well as of the city of Los Angeles itself. After exploring the common and divergent histories of the black and Korean American communities, I will spend some time describing the governance of the city. This effort will focus primarily on the mayor of Los Angeles at the time of the explosion of conflict, Tom Bradley, detailing his rise to power and shedding light on the many constituencies he serves. Later, I will turn to a discussion of the role of the current mayor, Richard Riordan. I have chosen to focus on Bradley, as opposed to other government officials and institutions such as the city council because of the mayor's standing as the symbolic leader of the city as well as the considerable power he has over key appointments to city agencies. Most notably, the mayor has the power to appoint the seven board members of the Community Redevelopment Agency, an agency that wields considerable power over the allocation of resources in the city. Overall, I believe that the mayor and the choices he's made in terms of policy are representative and illustrative of the public sector's role in economic development in the city.

Having laid the groundwork in terms of context, I will then proceed to give some descriptive attention to recent incidents of conflict and mediation between African Americans and Korean Americans in the city. While most of this effort will be focused on the period prior to the recent rebellion, activities during and after the rebellion will also be highlighted. Throughout this section I will be drawing upon the histories of the two groups as well as the economic development strategy of the city and economic elites to help to answer the question which drives this research, namely; Why are the African American and Korean American communities being held solely responsible for developing solutions to a conflict that is as much between them and the lack of economic opportunity as it is between the two of them alone?

The Setting

Obviously there is an expansive history to draw from for both the African American and Korean American communities in this country and even in Los Angeles itself. However, in attempting to make sense of their conflicted relationship, the 1970's are perhaps best viewed as a watershed period for both groups. Massive economic re-structuring internationally, coupled with the aftermath of the civil rights movement, the rebellions of the late sixties, and the effect of the immigration reform of the late sixties, all combined to create a complex and often depressing environment for the interaction of the African American and Korean American communities.

Much scholarly discussion has focused on the relative lack of power of cities in determining their own fate in a global economy (Peterson 1981; Logan and Swanstrom, eds. 1990). Irrespective of these differing perceptions of the range of mobility and self determination for cities, what is indisputable is that cities have been affected by the increased mobility of capital in the post-industrial age (Soja 1987). Los Angeles, while unique in some ways in its reaction to this change in capital flow, is no different from other large urban economic centers in its need to respond. During the 1970's, an estimated 75,000 heavy manufacturing jobs were lost, as large industrial plants closed and moved to foreign countries. A number of smaller firms also caused job loss in the city, as they relocated to suburban outposts (Davis 1990; Johnson and Oliver 1989; Soja 1987). The segment of the labor market that was most affected by these closures and relocations was highly unionized and included a high proportion of workers of color (Soja 1987:182). Blacks in particular, who had depended on these relatively good-paying jobs, suffered greatly as the majority of the plant closures were concentrated in the low-income African American and Latino communities (Johnson and Oliver 1989). Cities all over the country were experiencing similar scenarios as major industries sought cheaper labor and higher profits in the suburbs and abroad (Bluestone and Harrison 1982 ; Wilson 1980).

The Korean American community was not only affected by this economic dislocation, in some ways the Korean American community in Los Angeles was in fact created by changes in international capital flows. Light and Bonacich sketch out the extensive history of Korean emigration from Korea and immigration to the U.S. Much of this history is tied directly to the role of both the U.S. government and U.S. based multinational corporations (Light and Bonacich 1988). South Korea was one of the foreign countries that received much of the industry dislocated from the U.S. Even prior to the Korean war, the U.S. government had established a presence in the country as a safeguard against communist expansion, but the corporations arrived later (Light and Bonacich 1988). The relatively low wages in South Korea made it an attractive site for U.S. investment. Corporations that located there helped to shift the economy toward a solid export base. The dislocation and demographic change brought about by the rapidly industrializing export-led economy is one of the major factors in the decision of many Korean Americans to emigrate. Rapid urban population growth, housing shortages, depressed wages, un- and underemployment in the professional fields, and decreasing educational opportunity resulted in the departure of those individuals who could afford to leave (Light and Bonacich 1988). Because of a long-standing relationship with the U.S. and exposure to U.S. culture as a result of military presence in Korea, the U.S. represented the choice destination for many emigrants (Chang 1990; Light and Bonacich 1988). Only Japan received more Korean immigrants than the United States between 1971 and 1977 (Light and Bonacich 1988). Coupled with a liberalized U.S. immigration policy toward Asians, economic change in Korea led to an increase in the Korean American population in the U.S. from 69,510 in 1970 to 354,529 in 1980. The trend of Korean immigration to the U.S. has continued to the present (Light and Bonacich 1988).

Upon arriving in the U.S., the mostly middle-class, college graduates who immigrate often find their professions closed to them. In some cases immigrants are not even allowed to take professional qualifying exams, in others the tests weight English proficiency significantly, thus placing immigrants at a disadvantage. Research has demonstrated that even Korean immigrant professionals who were educated in the U.S. suffer job discrimination (Light and Bonacich 1988). On top of these factors, the tenuousness of immigrant status also serves to constrain opportunity for some Korean immigrants. The threat of deportation and the relative inaccessibility of federal aid weakens the position of new immigrants and serves to constrain their behavior and their choices. Without the ability to use their educational capital, many immigrants are forced to rely upon other resources to survive. It is this reality which puts them in direct contact with the African American community in Los Angeles; a community facing desperate economic conditions.

The flight of capital from South Central Los Angeles has not been confined to large industry. Smaller retail businesses have left as well. Gains from the civil rights movement made it possible for some black residents to open businesses elsewhere and to enter corporate America for the first time. As many African Americans who owned businesses took advantage of this opportunity, white businesses were leaving the area as well. The Watts rebellion of 1965 precipitated this exodus. As an editorial in the Los Angeles Times (29, November 1991, p.B4) noted, " One of the bad long-term consequences of the urban uprisings of the 1960's was that major retailers began to write off central cities, judging them too risky—too much crime, too many high insurance bills."

The Watts rebellion is an important event in another sense

considered in the context of the current conflict between blacks and Korean Americans. A comparison between the 1965 uprising and that of April 1992 is compelling. White-owned businesses in Watts were targeted for destruction by participants in the rebellion. As the Kerner Commission investigating the Watts rebellion indicates, resentment over absentee ownership of a large number of firms in the black community provided fuel for the rebellion (Dominguez 1976). The same frustration is echoed in complaints from black residents about Korean merchants who do business in South Central Los Angeles, but live elsewhere and give little back to the community. This illustrates that conflicts similar to the black-Korean American one have a precedence. For comparative purposes, it will be well worth watching to see if Korean American merchants leave South Central Los Angeles in the same numbers as Jewish merchants did after the Watts rebellion. Already there are indications that Korean American merchants are looking to relocate to areas such as Orange County (Needham 1992).

Considering the deteriorating economic state of the South Central Los Angeles area brought on by the dislocation of industry, the area represented a largely abandoned market. Compounding the flight of industrial employment, the 1970s also saw skyrocketing housing prices, further limiting the opportunities for black residents to leave South Central Los Angeles (Johnson and Oliver 1989). Spatial isolation for the poor black community in South Central , the tragic result of these two economic factors, was further compounded by the exodus of smaller black and white businesses alike.

The ultimate result of this economic dislocation was a relative vacuum of private investment in the South Central community. This provided an ironic opportunity for the first- generation Korean immigrant population. Having been shut out of other labor market sectors, self-employment represented one of the only opportunities remaining for Korean immigrants to advance economically. Their ability to rely on resources other than their professional training allowed them to step in and fill the void of private investment in South Central Los Angeles. One of the most important resources immigrants from Korea rely upon are the monetary assets they bring from Korea. According to Ivan Light, more than half of Korean immigrant entrepreneurs arrive with assets ranging from $60,000. to $250,000 (Treadwell 1991). In addition to arriving with capital or borrowing it from family, friends or other formal lending institutions, immigrants are also able to tap into collective community resources. Rotating credit associations, or "Kye" have a strong tradition in the Korean American community and they are often used to finance small businesses (Chang 1990). Shared business information accessed through church and alumni groups also represents a form of collective resource available to Korean immigrants. Finally, the ability and willingness to rely upon unpaid family labor also represents an available resource for potential Korean immigrant entrepreneur. Employing family members decreases overhead costs and increases the number of hours which can be worked (Light and Bonacich 1988). All of these resources combine to put Korean immigrants in a position to afford to open businesses. It is important to note, however, that while these resources represent an opportunity for the Korean immigrants, they are usually only sufficient to open businesses in economically depressed communities abandoned by other investors. The resources available to most Korean immigrants are not sufficient to open businesses in predominantly white areas, where the initial capital investment is often prohibitive. Additionally, these resources are not sufficient for overcoming the discriminatory barriers faced by Korean immigrants in other sectors of the labor market. These resources do, however, represent a key distinction between the African American and Korean American communities in terms of opportunity. In many ways this difference is an important one in determining and defining "otherness" for the two communities. The apparent economic success of the Korean community distances them from the economically-pressed residents of the South Central Los Angeles area. Of course the economic disparity between these two groups is not a sufficient explanatory variable in the determination of "'otherness." If it were, it would be difficult to explain why African American businesses were able to rely upon signs proclaiming black ownership in order to escape destruction in the recent rebellion. Cultural and racial differences also play a significant role in the creation of "other." This "otherness", is a critical variable in explaining just how it is that two relatively, but not identically, resource-poor groups can come to view their differences as being more important than their similarities.

While the business opportunities present in South Central Los Angeles may not represent the optimal opportunity for Korean immigrants, they are still well beyond the reach of most of South Central Los Angeles' black residents. Considering that more than one in every three South Central Los Angeles residents lives below the annual-income poverty threshold (Curran 1988), that the median income in South Central Los Angeles is $20,820 (Silverstein and Brooks 1991), and that unemployment among black youth in Los Angeles county was 45 percent through the late 1980's (Davis 1990), Korean immigrants are in a far better position for upward mobility than are the majority of South Central Los Angeles residents. According to a sample survey conducted by Eui-Young Yu, the median household income for Korean

Americans is $41,730 (Kim 1990). Additionally, the capital accumulated by many Korean immigrants also distinguishes them from the majority of even middle-class African Americans whose wealth (as opposed to income) accumulation pales in comparison (Oliver and Shapiro 1989). This disparity carries over into comparisons of business owners from different racial backgrounds as well. According to a study published in The Review of Black Political Economy, all else being equal, black business owners face greater discrimination in their efforts to obtain bank loans than do whites, Latinos, and Asians (Ando 1988). Such disparity helps to explain the relative scarcity of African American-owned businesses in areas like South Central Los Angeles.

As a result of taking advantage of this entrepreneurial opportunity, Korean American small businesses have flourished. Korean-owned liquor stores, grocery marts, clothing shops, gas stations, auto-repair shops, real estate agencies, etc. reportedly comprise almost 50% of small businesses in South Central Los Angeles .[1] As Korean American merchants often represent the only signs of economic investment in South Central Los Angeles, they find themselves in what Edna Bonacich terms a "middleman minority" position (Bonacich 1973; Light and Bonacich 1988). They are simultaneously exploiting and exploited participants in the economy of impoverished areas like South Central Los Angeles. For large corporations and franchises, the Korean American entrepreneur represents an opportunity to penetrate a largely neglected market without having to absorb the costs of hourly wages, benefits, or overhead costs associated with high insurance premiums (Light and Bonacich 1988). The store owners bear these costs by working extremely long hours and employing non-wage family members. Thus, the Korean American merchants represent a form of indirect cheap labor for larger corporations. In this sense they are exploited. They are in a position to exploit because of the high prices, low inventory, poor selection and absence of competition endemic to small businesses in poor communities. According to a Los Angeles Times study, there was one store for every 415 residents in South Central Los Angeles, compared to one store for every 203 residents countywide (Silverstein and Brooks 1991). Of particular concern to many residents in South Central Los Angeles is the fact that so many of these stores are or were liquor stores. This sentiment is reflected in recent attempts by South Central residents to limit the rebuilding of liquor stores destroyed in the rebellion (Krikorian 1993). The absence of choice for residents' shopping needs is a source of great frustration. In occupying this paradoxical position, Korean American merchants bear the brunt of black hostility and frustration rooted in their lack of economic opportunity.

To add fuel to this fire, African Americans and Asian American immigrant groups are often stereotypically compared by the media and society at-large. While African Americans are portrayed as being lazy, undeservedly poor, and inclined towards criminality, Asian Americans, particularly immigrants, are portrayed as being a "model minority." As Ron Takaki (1993, p. 417) explains, adherents of the "model minority" thesis proclaim, "Look at the Asian American! They did it by pulling themselves up by their bootstraps." He goes on to observe that, "For blacks shut out of the labor market, the Asian American model provides the standards of acceptable behavior; blacks should not depend on welfare or Affirmative Action." The juxtapositioning of these two groups without regard to their respective histories, reinforces what Michael Omi and Howard Winant (1986) refer to as the "ethnicity paradigm." Rooted in sociological theory, this paradigm suggests that all minority groups in this country should melt into American society, much like European immigrants have. Grounded in the values of the Protestant work ethic and self sufficiency, this paradigm sets the standard for appropriate assimilation, or the "model." If groups are perceived as having achieved some degree of success in climbing the economic ladder without undue assistance, they are considered "model minorities"; if the perception is that they have not, they are considered deviant. This paradigm is inadequate and dangerous because it ignores the role of race as distinct from the concept of ethnicity in the history of this country, and it normalizes the white ethnic experience. The significance of slavery, colonization, racially-based exclusion and near-extirpation are ignored in this melding of race and ethnicity (Omi and Winant 1986). Racial categories have, to a large extent, shaped and limited the life chances of racial minority groups, thus distinguishing them from European immigrants. This paradigm has received a great deal of attention lately, as neo-conservatives such as Thomas Sowell (1980) and Nathan Glazer (1983) praise its usefulness in analyzing conditions for African Americans. This is an uncritical adoption of a flawed and inappropriate paradigm. Aside from its failure to account for the role of race and racism, it is also inadequate in its failure to account for the economic history of various minority groups as well. As indicated above, the economic security of Korean immigrants is very different from that of African Americans in South Central Los Angeles. Additionally, the lumping of all Asians and comparing them to all African Americans ignores different intra-group historical social and economic experiences. The insistence on making such unfair comparisons places yet another strain on relations between African Americans and Korean Americans, as both are exposed to these confining stereotypes. For blacks in particular, the comparison to a "model minority" feeds animosity towards Korean Americans.

In sum, the set of cultural and economic conditions that prevail in South Central Los Angeles serve to pit African American residents against Korean American merchants. Because they so often represent the only economic activity in the black community, and are thus held up as examples of success by larger society, Korean merchants come to represent the economic exploitation felt by South Central Los Angeles residents. While the flight of capital strained relations between blacks and Korean Americans, Los Angeles' city government did little to change this situation.

The 1970's represent a watershed period for exploring city involvement in the economy of South Central Los Angeles. Tom Bradley, an African American city councilperson and ex-police officer, was elected mayor of Los Angeles in 1973. At just the time when economic power seemed to be decreasing as industry left the largely black community, black political power seemed to be on the rise with the election of one of the first black mayors in the country. This is not an uncommon phenomenon as blacks became mayors in a number of large industrialized cities with shrinking tax bases (Keller 1978). What does distinguish the Los Angeles case is the support the first black mayor received from white voters. Tom Bradley's election has been widely attributed to his success in mobilizing a coalition of liberal white voters from the Westside of Los Angeles and black voters from South Central (Davis 1990; Payne and Ratzan 1986; Sonenshein 1990). Major community organizers supported Bradley's candidacy because of his active support for federal anti-poverty and community development funds during his ten-year tenure as a councilperson (Curran 1989). These same community organizers quickly became disillusioned with Bradley's performance as mayor, however. Many point to the mayor's disbanding of the city's Community Development Advisory Committee as an indication that those who helped elect him were not necessarily going to be included in policy-making decisions once he took office (Curran 1989). This particular committee was poised at the time of Bradley's election to help the city launch a large-scale re-development strategy targeting many of the blighted areas of the city, including South Central Los Angeles. Clarence Stone's (1989) conception of a "governing coalition" which forms around city officials once they are elected offers insight into the apparent change in Bradley's allegiances. As Stone (1989, p. 5) defines it, the coalition, an informal arrangement, represents ". . . a core group—typically a body of insiders—who come together repeatedly in making important decisions." For the case of Atlanta, the governing coalition represents an informal, yet stable, policy advisory group comprised of economic elites, members of the black middle class and city officials, most notably the mayor. A similar coalition exists around Bradley in Los Angeles. Just as the Community Development Advisory Committee was disbanded, the mayor began courting the city's business community. In particular, the Committee of 25, a steering committee of some of downtown's biggest corporate heads, became an important advisory group for the mayor (Davis 1990). This committee expanded to include some Westside developers and eventually became the economic elite component of the city's governing coalition. As powerful members of this coalition, the economic elite proposed a downtown development strategy. Instead of adopting the re-development strategy put forth by the Community Development Advisory Committee, the mayor adopted this downtown development strategy aimed at revitalizing the central city by providing commercial space and major developments such as the Wells Fargo Headquarters building, Crocker Center, and the Los Angeles Bonaventure hotel (Payne and Ratzan 1986).

In Atlanta, like Los Angeles, neighborhood and community groups had one vision of development aimed at meeting resident's needs, while economic elites had another vision aimed at securing maximum private profit. The informal alliance between the mayor and business elite in both Los Angeles and Atlanta formed governing coalitions able to make and carry out governing decisions regarding economic development. These coalitions did not expand to include neighborhood and community groups. As Stone (1989, p. 135) describes in the case of Atlanta, "Andrew Young's mayoralty quickly demonstrated that the neighborhood movement was outside the governing coalition . . . it no longer played a major part in forging the city's policy effort. Instead . . . neighborhood groups found themselves reacting to, not formulating, policy initiatives." This is a strikingly similar scenario to the one played out in Los Angeles. In both cases, black mayors found the resources of the economic elite more compelling than those of the community activists. In so doing, they bought into the notion that a corporate-led development model was the only way to assure economic growth, irrespective of the possible ramifications of ignoring social welfare needs in the process. Again in both cases, the respective mayors were able to secure reciprocal benefits from the economic elite for members of the black middle class in the form of contracts and contacts. The poor, however, did not benefit from the governing coalition's negotiations, as they were not participants.

In justifying this decision, Bradley has argued that because the causes of poverty and community reclamation are national and regional, their eradication is not the charge of the city (Curran 1989). While it is true that fiscal constraints imposed by a shifting global economy and decreasing federal funds, especially under Reagan, have limited the ability of cities to respond to poverty and economic decline in inner cities, cities are not helpless in the face of these problems. The decision to focus on downtown development aimed at pleasing the cities' business community involved the expenditure of city resources in the form of incentives, such as publicly financed infrastructure and transportation construction. These are city funds which were not available for direction at the problems of the inner city. Claims made by the City's Redevelopment Agency (CRA) (a board entirely appointed by Mayor Bradley) that this downtown development strategy meets the section of its mandate calling for the creation of new employment opportunities, are dubious at best. Despite its reliance on this development strategy to reach its own job-creation goals, the CRA has no accurate mechanism to access its efforts. In fact, A current CRA manager, formerly in charge of the central business district project, ". . . confessed in an interview that the agency has no idea how many jobs for women or minorities have been created, or what has been their per capita cost in public subsidies." (Davis 1990). Thus, any claim that such a strategy does in fact benefit residents of areas most in need of economic opportunity is specious. Such failure to provide data essential to assessment of city benefits gained from public-private partnerships follows a pattern typical in cities that have adopted a corporate-led development strategy. Such cities seem to give minimal consideration to whether or not the city's most needy residents benefit from the subsidization of corporate development. In some cases, cities fail to even articulate performance criteria for companies benefitting from city subsidization.[2] In accepting the argument that the economic elite's demands must be met in order to maintain economic viability in the city, the mayor has prioritized development in areas other than South Central Los Angeles, most notably downtown and the predominantly white Westside of the city. This strategy changed very little during Bradley's tenure, as shown by his continued support for downtown development. In recent years, the governing coalition has expanded to include foreign business elites, including a large number of business elites from the Pacific Rim countries. These new coalition partners also advocate city subsidization for downtown economic ventures (Davis 1990). With the strong support of Bradley, these foreign investors have moved the city's economic development toward a Pacific Rim strategy of increased Asian investment in the downtown area. In a related development, Bradley found himself under investigation for ethics violations, including illegal deposits of city funds in the Far East National Bank, which is owned by a major downtown developer (Davis 1990).

The mayor's prioritization of other areas of the city at the expense of South Central Los Angeles appear to be mirrored in city agencies other than the CRA as well. Those agencies which do provide services aimed at alleviating poverty and economic disparity, also prioritize other parts of the city over South Central Los Angeles. Again we see the importance of how the pie of economic opportunity is sliced and divided. According to the city's own figures, in 1989 South Central ranked last among six city regions in per-person-in-poverty and per-family-in-poverty human services funds distributed by the city. Additionally, job-training funds are also disproportionately awarded to areas of the city with less poverty than South Central. This is particularly startling considering that 37 percent of the city's families-in-poverty were concentrated in South Central Los Angeles in 1989 (Curran 1989) Even as South Central residents are neglected from an economic development standpoint, so too are they neglected in terms of social programs. Thus, city government becomes an important partner in the blight of South Central Los Angeles and a key participant in the dividing of the economic pie as well. The few small businesses which do remain in South Central, most notably the Korean American merchants, come to represent both the exploitation and the neglect of the area's residents. In this sense they bear a burden which could be shared by numerous other parties, including the city's economic elites and local government officials.

The Conflict

On March 16, 1991 in South Central Los Angeles, a Korean American merchant, Soon Ja Do shot and killed a thirteen year-old African American girl, Latasha Harlins, in a dispute over a container of orange juice. As media attention focused on this case, it came to symbolize the long-standing animosity between black patrons and Korean merchants. Coming at a time when the racial climate in the city was already charged by the videotaped beating by four white police officers of Rodney King, a black motorist, the African American community viewed this shooting as the last straw in the context of a history of abuse of the black community.[3] Sporadic boycotts of Korean American merchants by members of the black community ensued as leaders sought to focus the anger of the black community on what they viewed as a general lack of respect for black customers by Korean American merchants (Katz and Chavez 1991). The boycott efforts galvanized in

June of 1991 around a single Korean American-owned store, when another shooting of a black customer by a Korean American merchant occurred. Police investigators concluded that Lee Arthur Mitchell's death in John's Liquor Store was justifiable homicide. This conclusion was unsatisfactory for leaders in the black community, namely Danny Bakewell and Rev. Edgar Boyd, who pointed to what they believed was a history of mistreatment of black customers by the owner of John's Liquor Store.

The Brotherhood Crusade, an African American charity organization, under the leadership of chairperson Danny Bakewell, joined with Rev. Boyd, of Bethel African Methodist Episcopal church, to coordinate the boycott effort. (see note 3) Bakewell and the Brotherhood Crusade were active in organizing efforts around the Latasha Harlins case, so they were poised to assume leadership of the boycott efforts with Rev. Boyd. Together they formed the African American Honor Committee, the official organization behind the boycott. Rev. Boyd, whose church is directly across the street from the store, had a long-standing conflict with the store's owner because the owner sold liquor on Sundays, an act the Reverend found offensive to his congregation.(see note 3) Additionally, Rev. Boyd and members of his congregation were disturbed by merchandise sold in the store, ranging from pornographic materials to paraphernalia associated with (see note 3) drug-use. In addition to expressing outrage over the killing itself, organizers including Bakewell and Boyd viewed the boycott of John's Liquor Store as an opportunity to send a message to all merchants doing business in the black community, and particularly Korean American merchants, that the black residents of South Central Los Angeles would not tolerate "disrespectful" absentee shopkeepers who give little back to the community. "We are not against Koreans as such. We are against Koreans, and anybody else doing business who are disrespectful to black people . . ." (Boyarsky 1991). The animosity directed at Korean American merchants was not solely confined to the boycott effort. On a number of occasions, firebombs were thrown at Korean American-owned stores (Rutten 1991). This, of course, foreshadows the firebombings of Korean American-owned stores that occurred during the insurrection almost a year later.

As the boycott took hold and virtually eliminated the store's business, members of the Korean community, including the owner, expressed outrage and contempt for the boycott's organizers. As Tae Sam Park, the store's owner, explained in a Los Angeles Times interview (2, July 1991, p.A1), "The fact is we didn't do anything wrong, and we worked hard to get this far. If we walk away from this, they'll find reasons to pick on more Korean markets. It won't end with us." Many Korean Americans also expressed frustration over the lack of attention given to past killings of Korean American merchants (see note 1). There was a great deal of resentment on the Korean American side of the conflict rooted in their belief that they were being wrongly scape-goated, blamed and silenced by the boycott efforts (Bong and Oh 1991). The sentiment that the Korean American community was silenced by the boycott carried over into their response to the rebellion, as many Korean Americans pointed to the need for their voices to be heard as victims of the destruction. Many leaders in the Korean American community pointed to the need for a political awakening of their community, in order to ensure that they received the attention they deserved in the relief effort and beyond (Lee 1992).

The language and description used by those involved directly in the conflict indicate that both African Americans and Korean Americans were sensitive to the role played by economic disparity in the tensions between the two groups. As Annie Cho, former-Executive director of the Korean American Grocers Association (KAGRO), a non-profit membership organization established to serve the interests of Korean American grocery and liquor business owners, describes, ". . . the economy has been very bad, people are loosing jobs, there's a threat of welfare cuts, people are worried about being evicted because they can't pay their rent, so people are very edgy and their tolerance level has become very low. This simply boiled over last year (see note 1)." Ralph Sutton, public relations director for the Brotherhood Crusade, expressed similar sentiment in that the source of the conflict was a combination of things including, ". . . the volatility of the inner-city and the economy, the unemployment rate and the fact that industry has left (see note 3)." But there was a heavy emphasis on the role of cultural differences and misunderstanding in the tensions. Echoing the concerns about "disrespectful" merchants, individuals on both sides of the conflict pointed to ignorance of "American customs" on the part of first generation Korean Americans as being a crucial piece of the conflict puzzle. Again quoting Cho, "Newly arriving immigrants need to be educated about American customs . . . something as trivial as looking a person in the eye. In Korea to look someone in the eye you are accusing them of something. So to be polite you don't do that. They are trying to be polite in their own way, but in this country that is not what American culture dictates." (see note 1).

Sutton also believed that cultural differences were a main source of the conflict between African Americans and Korean Americans. "Cultural differences and intolerance are a problem. Not from the third generation . . . but from the new arrivals who are still steeped in Korean culture . . ." (see note 3). More strident language was used, however, by other African Americans involved in the boycotts themselves, in describing their assessment of what the problem was. As reported in the Los Angeles Times (2, July 1991, p.A1) a sign held by one protester at John's Liquor Store declared, "GET OUT OF OUR COMMUNITY!" A rap song by L.A. based rapper Ice Cube (1991), "Black-Korea", which became popular in the wake of the publicity around the Harlins killing echoes this sentiment. The lyrics in this rap encapsulate a number of the issues that members of the black community point to when expressing their resentment toward Korean American merchants. Frustration over lack of choices in where to shop; outrage at the criminalization and stereotyping of members of the black community; demands for respectful treatment; and resentment over the perceived encroachment of Korean Americans into the black community, are all given voice by Ice Cube in this rap. The xenophobia apparent in the lyrics also gives voice to sentiment that exists in the black community. This is an explicit example of how racist and xenophobic messages and images from mainstream media and culture are utilized by people of color. In the quest to achieve recognition as full citizens themselves, African Americans have often historically viewed the distinction between themselves and foreigners as an important signifier of citizenship, loyalty, and American-ness.

The use of xenophobic language by the black community in the context of the black-Korean conflict seems to express the frustration of many African Americans that they are denied access to the American dream, while newly arrived immigrants seem to not only access the dream easily, but do so at the expense of the black community. People of Color's adoption and reformulation of images and messages from dominant society is an important phenomenon to consider in terms of the perpetuation of the "model minority" myth, as well. While the myth is a frustrating reminder that American society blames African Americans for their plight, it is none the less used by the black community as a motivational tool. Calls for the black community to "Be more like Jews and Asians" in their efforts to get ahead echo or appropriate the model minority message. This is an ironic denial of the very different historical experiences and present-day circumstances of the African American and Korean American communities in this country. Korean immigrants are also subjected to racist messages which they also appropriate. According to Edward Chang (1990, p.167), ". . . many Korean immigrants are exposed to American values and culture and thus may come [to the U.S.] with negative images of blacks. They have learned and accepted the stereotypes of blacks as criminals, welfare recipients, drug addicts, and/or lazy through American movies, T.V. shows, and American

Forces Korea Network (AFKN) programs." Thus, even as they struggle with racism themselves, Korean immigrants participate in the process of constructing racist ideology and racial identities. This appropriation has been pointed to as the source of many of the merchants' suspicious attitudes toward all black customers (Ice Cube 1991). As the appropriation process feeds cultural misunderstanding, distrust and resentment between the two groups, it simply adds to the challenge they are already facing in confronting racial and cultural barriers in the larger society. Again, the "otherness" of each group is reinforced by this appropriation process.

The emphasis on the need for respect from Korean American merchants reflects the underlying frustration in the black community over lack of opportunity in almost every aspect of their lives. In fact, the Brotherhood Crusade characterized its boycott efforts as being part of an overall "disrespectful merchant strategy (see note 3)." A community that was more economically secure would not be as affected by the apparent disrespect of the Korean merchants. For one thing, they could take their business elsewhere. Poor residents of South Central however, have no such option. Because of the general economic abandonment of the inner city, Korean American merchants represent one of the only tangible perpetrators, aside from the police, of the disrespect they feel in their everyday lives.

The cyclical distrust that appropriation of racist images breeds between the two groups serves to narrow the scope of their conflict. Again the characterization of 'otherness' becomes important. The conflict itself hinges on this characterization. In reacting and responding solely to each other, members of the two communities are identified as the source of the problem between them. This is the metaphorical fight over the slice of pie. Other actors, namely economic elites and city officials, are thus relieved of responsibility for the role they played in the evolution of the conflict. Thus the bakers of the pie are ignored. They are similarly absolved of any responsibility for bringing resources to the settlement table. This course of events is unfortunately the one that transpired in the mediation effort and settlement agreement reached by the negotiating parties representing the black and Korean American communities.

The Settlement

After sustaining the boycott for 90 days, as promised, Bakewell and Boyd agreed to sit down at the table to negotiate a settlement to bring about the end of the boycott. The major players involved in negotiation efforts were representatives of the Brotherhood Crusade, most notably

Danny Bakewell, representatives of the Korean American Grocers Association (KAGRO), most notably President David Kim, and representatives from the mayor's office, including Deputy Mayor Mark Fabiani and Gary Boze, special assistant to the deputy mayor. According to Boze, the mayor's office played a purely facilitative role in the negotiations.[4] Thus, the respective leaders of the African American and Korean American communities were the focus of expectations for a settlement. While to some degree this was necessary to bring about an end to the boycott itself, it also meant that city officials were not viewed as participants in any way in the conflict. In fact, participants from Brotherhood Crusade and KAGRO said that the solution to the conflict had to come from the two communities alone. As Annie Cho of KAGRO noted, "What can the mayor do over problems that the actual customers and businessmen were having? They had to work it out themselves. These problems must be addressed and solved by people that are involved."(see note 1).

While there was agreement between Sutton and Cho on the fact that the mayor had to become involved formally in the mediation process, they did not conceptualize Bradley's involvement beyond the role of facilitator. Sutton expressed a view similar to Cho's above, namely that the problem ultimately began and ended with blacks and Korean Americans alone. (see note 3).

The immunity from responsibility given to the mayor and other city officials explains to some degree the absence of city resources in the settlement that was eventually reached. The drafting of the 10-point "KAGRO Statement of Good Business Practice Principles" was one portion of the settlement. This document highlighted a variety of merchant vows ranging from a pledge to increase use of English whenever possible, to a pledge to train staff to resolve disputes peacefully . According to Boze, there was also an agreement to end the "selective buying campaign" against John's Liquor Store, a thirty-day opportunity for black investors to purchase the store, a suspension of the liquor license for the store so that liquor could no longer be sold there, and the establishment of a Dispute Resolution Process to prevent future "selective buying campaigns (see note 4)." A jobs program was also launched as an effort to ". . . embark on a new era of mutual cooperation regarding economic goals and interethnic relations." (Press Release, Mayor's Office November 14, 1991) This plan called for Korean American merchants to provide 100 jobs for South Central Los Angeles residents. It called upon the Urban League and other black organizations to identify potential employees.

While these principles and the larger settlement agreement

certainly address concerns expressed by members of the African American community ranging from joblessness to disrespectful merchants, they do not in any fundamental way address economic issues raised earlier in the chapter. Of course this failure became painfully evident in the wake of the rebellion. The 100 jobs program hints at the economic challenges that fuel black dissatisfaction with Korean American merchants, but it is merely a token gesture considering the number of unemployed residents in South Central Los Angeles. And in its total reliance on Korean merchants to provide the jobs, it ignores the relatively resource-poor position of the majority of Korean American merchants. In effect, it is an admission or acceptance of the distortion that Korean merchants are to blame for joblessness in South Central Los Angeles.

The mayor and other city officials were thus not held accountable for their role in failing to give priority to development in South Central Los Angeles. Those economic elites who advocated a downtown development strategy were not held accountable for their role in steering funds away from South Central. Those corporations and firms that chose to relocate to the suburbs or abroad in search of cheap labor were not being held accountable either. The only avenue of accountability left open for consideration was the one that travelled between the African American customers and the Korean merchants. Thus, the settlement reached focused solely on the behavior and resources of these two groups.

In highlighting the narrowness of the proposed solutions to the conflict, it is also important to consider who was doing the negotiating. Bakewell, although staunchly against accepting government assistance for the Brother Crusade, has life-blood ties to corporate sponsorship, and has relied upon access to public officials, particularly the mayor, to support not only the Brotherhood Crusade, but himself as well (Stolberg and Clifford 1991). Considering his own partnership in a major downtown development, his past presidency of a downtown municipal securities firm, and his close ties to Mayor Bradley, it is doubtful that he would challenge the city's prioritization of a downtown development strategy (Stolberg and Clifford 1991). In fact his promotion of a self-help philosophy, "We must not expect others to do for us that which we can and should do for ourselves!" (Bakewell 1991) fits well within the ethnicity paradigm and the model minority myth discussed above. There is an implicit acceptance in this message of the argument that the black community is responsible for its plight and thus must solve it alone. Bakewell's own vision for self-help economic development is crystallized in his establishment of the Mom and Pop Economic Development

Corporation. The objective of this venture is to assist African Americans in opening small businesses in South Central Los Angeles. According to Ralph Sutton, Bakewell views this as the path to economic empowerment for the black community (see note 3). Considering the simultaneously exploited and exploitative position Korean American merchants are in, and considering that the proliferation of these stores to date has left the economic condition of South Central Los Angeles virtually unchanged, it seems unlikely that this strategy will lead to the empowerment Bakewell envisions. A few store-owners may benefit, but it is doubtful that the larger black community will. Corporations, on the other hand, stand to benefit from this strategy in three ways. First, as in the case of Korean American merchants, they will obtain a form of indirect cheap labor through the Mom and Pop ventures. Secondly, they will receive positive publicity for donating to the Mom and Pop effort via the Brotherhood Crusade. The list of corporations who currently support the Brotherhood Crusade includes; The Adolph Coors Company, ARCO Foundation, Northrop Corporation, Lockeed Corporation, Coca Cola Bottling Company, Sony Pictures Entertainment, and many more. (Brotherhood Crusade 1991). Finally, corporations will benefit as they are relieved of pressure to make a substantial capital investment in the blighted South Central area. Instead of creating large-scale gainful employment, the corporations can support the community by simply donating a token amount to a charitable organization.

Similar to Bakewell's presence, the participation of KAGRO president David Kim in the bargaining efforts also foreshadows a narrow set of solutions to the conflict. Like the Brotherhood Crusade, KAGRO also relies on corporate sponsorship to some degree (KAGRO 1992). Recognizing that the liquor companies and other corporations and distributors who contribute to KAGRO-sponsored activities and events benefit greatly from the presence of cheap Korean American immigrant labor in the black community, it is doubtful that Kim would suggest they shoulder any of the blame for the conflict. This would be comparable to biting the hand that feeds him.

Finally, the mayor's office is wedded to its downtown development strategy as well as to the contention that the systemic problems of poverty and lack of economic development are well beyond the control or policy reach of city government. Thus, participants from the mayor's office are content to be facilitators and managers for conflicts such as these. In doing so, they also avoid criticism for not doing anything about the conflict.

After the Rebellion

Despite the dramatic wake-up call given by the 1992 Los Angeles Rebellion, sadly, little has changed in South Central Los Angeles to alter the roots of racial conflict. The city's official, high-profile response to the rebellion was the mayor's formation of the Rebuild LA committee (later shortened to RLA) headed by Peter Ueberroth. Officially, this organization was charged with providing the leadership for redeveloping and rebuilding Los Angeles, focusing on urban economic ills (Estrada and Sensiper 1993). Considering the importance of economic roots in the African American-Korean American conflict, RLA's apparent focus on economic development in neglected areas seems right on target. However, an examination of the organization's conception, mission, membership, and method illustrates how its status quo approach has yielded little in the way of meaningful change.

Bradley's appointment of Ueberroth foreshadowed the problems which eventually beset RLA. Appointed on the basis of his success in organizing the 1984 Olympics in Los Angeles. Ueberroth, a white resident of Orange County, Calif., was greeted with skepticism from residents of the inner-city who doubted his ability to adequately resolve the crises exposed by the uprising (Peterson 1992). In answer to these criticisms about unrepresentative leadership in RLA, Asians, blacks and Latinos were brought on board as co-chairs with Ueberroth and as staff members (Kim 1992; Weinstein 1992b; Estrada and Sensiper 1993). Ueberroth eventually resigned from his post, citing controversy surrounding him as being part of the reason for stepping down (Rivera and Murphy 1993). Additions to the board of directors for RLA also became a racially charged political struggle, with various groups fighting for adequate representation (Weinstein 1992a). Ironically, these struggles were fought for representation in a less-than-successful effort.

Ueberroth's business background was also indicative of the corporate-led character RLA assumed as corporate interests were heavily represented in board appointments (Weinstein 1992a). This dominance is reflected in the efforts undertaken by the organization as well. Instead of exploring options for developing a comprehensive plan for improving the economic climate in areas like South Central Los Angeles, RLA turned its attention to helping damaged businesses re-build and to luring corporate donations to the inner city. While RLA leadership touts its success at bringing economic development to the inner city, its record is questionable at best. A Los Angeles Times investigation revealed that many of the corporations RLA claimed to have secured $500 million in investments from actually had no plans to invest in the inner city (Rivera and Murphy 1993). And, what money has been secured from corporations is largely in the form of donations, not investment in job-creating enterprises (Labor/Community Strategy Center 1993). Thus, again the corporations responsible for deserting the inner city have been able to remain unscathed by contributing charitable donations instead of development and jobs. The point is not that corporate gifts are not needed and appreciated, but instead, that such gifts offer little hope of translating into lasting economic change. Additionally, such gifts in no way compensate for the devastation of corporate abandonment. They are, however, excellent public relations gestures and an income tax write-off.

The direction of RLA perhaps could have been predicted by examining the list of those participating in the organization as staff and as board members. In addition to corporate representatives, it is worth noting that the committee includes many of the same players as were involved in the aforementioned mediation efforts in the African American-Korean American conflict. Both Danny Bakewell of the Brotherhood Crusade and Annie Cho of the Korean Grocers Association are involved in the RLA effort (Kim 1992; Weinstein 1992). But the story of RLA is as much in who is not participating as it is in who is participating in the effort. There is virtually no representation in the formal structure of RLA of grassroots organizations or community activists who had been working in areas like South Central Los Angeles prior to the rebellion. Apparently such individuals did not have skills, resources, or experience that was considered valuable for the RLA mission.

On the whole, RLA represents the loss of a significant opportunity to alter the economic context that underlies the black-Korean conflict. Instead of seizing the opportunity to bring together government and private corporate resources with community activists experienced in economic development and interracial relations, RLA has largely maintained the status quo approach to economic development in the inner city, relying on economic elite to do whatever they deem appropriate and adequate. Bradley's reliance on RLA, a private entity, to offer leadership in rebuilding was an abdication of city responsibility to address the problems of the areas affected by the rebellion. This abdication is unfortunately reminiscent of the city's hands-off approach to mediation of the African American-Korean American conflict. Again, the status-quo seems to have prevailed.

The election of Richard Riordan to succeed Tom Bradley as mayor of Los Angeles also represents a perpetuation of the status quo. Despite his campaign image as a political outsider, a brief examination of

Riordan's history reveals that he is an experienced insider, and most notable here, a player in the downtown development strategy pursued under Bradley.

Prior to his election as mayor in 1993, Riordan, an attorney and venture capitalist, made over $2 million as a consultant on various land issues for the city and county of Los Angeles (Curran 1993). Additionally, after making a $300,000. interest-free loan to Tom Bradley's failed 1982 gubernatorial campaign, Riordan was appointed by the mayor to a number of city commissions, including the Recreation and Parks commission, where his duties included working on development of an important historical section of downtown Los Angeles (Curran 1993). Of additional note, Riordan was also appointed to the board of RLA (Weinstein 1992). All of these activities, ranging from working for the city and performing public service to financing political campaigns, establish Riordan's familiarity with Los Angeles politics. Of particular significance to the African American-Korean American conflict, however, are Riordan's own business ventures in downtown Los Angeles. In the early 1980's Riordan was involved in what proved to be highly profitable speculation on several parcels of property downtown. As explained in a LA Weekly article:

> Riordan bought his second of four parcels on the downtown block on March 18, 1981. Just eight days later, the city's Community Redevelopment Agency informed owners of the targeted properties that it was considering purchasing their lots for its "South Park" residential complex. The following year, Riordan sold his properties to the CRA for a $3.5 million profit (Curran 1993).

Thus, Riordan benefitted directly from the downtown development strategy that utilized CRA resources which could have been directed at revitalizing areas like South Central Los Angeles.

Looking at Riordan's mayoral record thus far does not offer much hope that he will be turning his attention to the needs of South Central residents. In his appointments to city commissions, Riordan has half as many appointees from the Central, South Central and Southwest areas of the city as Bradley did (Connell 1993). This reveals that residents of South Central are also losing some of the little influence they had on city policy-making under the Bradley administration.

All in all, the relationship between the economic and political elite in Los Angeles has not been significantly altered in the wake of the rebellion. Perhaps the most significant change has been the replacement of Bradley with Riordan in the governing coalition. If Riordan's personal history and record to date as mayor are any indication, it is doubtful that much will change in how economic development decisions are made in the city of Los Angeles. This unfortunate likelihood does not bode well for the eradication of interracial conflict in the economically devastated inner city.

Conclusions

An examination of the actors and environment involved in the conflict between African Americans and Korean Americans in Los Angeles reveals the economic roots of their tense relationship. Were it not for their respective economic vulnerabilities, it is possible that the cultural misunderstanding between them could be replaced by a respectful alliance. However, as long as this misunderstanding is fed by their own insecure economic positions in society, it is doubtful that cultural sensitivity will improve their relationship much. The fact remains that those who have the most to offer in the way of real economic opportunity, namely the economic and political elite, are not throwing their weight and resources into the solution of the conflict, nor have they been proactive in preventing the economic conditions which undergird this conflict. In fact, because they are so tied to those negotiating the resolution, economic elites in particular needn't even be present at the negotiating table to have their interests secured. They are the silent instigators of the conflict and the silent beneficiaries of the narrow resolution.

As the dust of the mediation process settled, it became painfully obvious that little had changed in South Central Los Angeles. The tensions between the African American and Korean American communities became a part of the story of the Los Angeles rebellion. Six months after leaders from the two communities announced that they had reached a truce, the fight over the slice of pie resumed with tragic consequences. And in the aftermath of the rebellion, painfully little has changed in the priorities of the city's political and economic elite. Now, more than ever, it is clear that a comprehensive economic development plan for the South Central area must be instituted. The reliance on small business to re-invigorate the economy of the area is a naive, if not disingenuous, proposition. While it is surely true that external forces, such as the federal government, will have to bring resources to bear on the problem, the city of Los Angeles must re-examine its current prioritization of resources. Can a city whose inner-city population is swelling afford to continue a downtown corporate-led development strategy?

The city of Los Angeles needs to take a far more proactive approach to development, considering the needs of all segments of the city's population. Taking a cue from grassroots efforts already underway, the city should pursue a strategy that places a premium on satisfying the needs of the most neglected residents. One such effort involves the coming together of three umbrella organizations: The Multicultural Collaborative, which seeks solutions to inter-ethnic conflict in Los Angeles, The New Majority Task Force, which focuses on incorporating various racial groups in the economic development process, and the Coalition of Neighborhood Developers, which facilitates communication and activity among various non-profit economic development and community service organizations from low-income neighborhoods. According to a proposal (1993) submitted by the three groups , they have all come together to develop a new, comprehensive urban economic agenda. This multiracial collaboration of individuals offers a promising model of how to best pursue economic development, if avoiding interracial conflict is an important goal. The city should consider linking plans generated by efforts such as this to its negotiations with businesses seeking city subsidization for development. Instead of pursuing economic development strategies which reactively take leadership from the private sector, and more often than not ignore social welfare, the city would stand to benefit from offering leadership based upon a comprehensive development plan for all of Los Angeles. Such a plan should prioritize development projects by considering the needs of the city's residents as well as its business community. And any subsidization of private, for-profit endeavors should be linked to a guarantee that jobs will be created for local residents and that all projects seek a mixture of high-profit and low-profit ventures like day-care centers and low-income housing. While worries about the climate for business are real, guarantees such as these strike a balance between meeting corporate and human needs. Another rebellion and further explosive racial conflict bred from economic neglect can only serve to harm the business climate in Los Angeles.

As immigration patterns shift and the demography of those who live and work in South Central Los Angeles changes, it is likely that the conflicts will change as well. Unfortunately, the words of Annie Cho are indicative of how superficial this change is likely to be, "Yesterday it was Jews, today it is Koreans, tomorrow it may be Vietnamese or somebody else" (see note 1). Unless there is fundamental economic improvement in the lives of South Central Los Angeles residents, it is all too possible that only the faces of the conflict will change. The fight over the single slice of pie will simply begin anew.

Acknowledgment

I would like to thank Cathy Cohen, Michael C. Dawson, Douglass Dion, Phillips Freer, Rudell S. Freer, Wendell Freer, Kimberly James, Robin D.G. Kelley, Dominic Robbins, Steven Rosenstone, Jocelyn Sargent, Jefferey Spinner, and Terri Strodthoff for their helpful comments on this essay.

Notes

1. Interview with Annie Cho, Executive Director, Korean American Grocers Association, February 26, 1992.

2. The case of General Motors (GM) and the City of Detroit is exemplary of such failure to set up performance criteria. GM obtained public funds without any requirement to actually build their proposed project, nor pay back the city in terms of jobs or taxes (Clavel and Kleiniewski 1990).

3. Interview with Ralph Sutton, Media Director, Brotherhood Crusade, February 25, 1992.

4. Interview with Gary Boze, Special Assistant to Deputy Mayor, February 29, 1992.

References

Ando, Faith. 1988. "Capital Issues and the Minority-Owned Business." *Review of Black Political Economy*. Spring: 77-110.

Bakewell, Danny. 1991. *Pioneer of Black Achievement Award Dinner Program*. Los Angeles: Brotherhood Crusade.

Bluestone, Barry, and Bennet Harrison. 1982. *The Deindustrialization of America*. New York: Basic Books.

Bonacich, Edna. 1973. "A Theory of Middleman Minorities." *American Sociological Review*. 38:583-94.

Bong, Hwan Kim and Angela Eujin Oh. 1991. "Don't Fall for 'Divide and Conquer'." *Los Angeles Times*. 4, September: B7.

Boyarsky, Bill. 1991. "When Protest Edges Up to Racism." *Los Angeles Times*. 20, November: B2.

Chang, Edward Taehan. 1990. "Korean-Black Conflict In Los Angeles: Perceptions and Realities" in *Dreams and Realities*, edited by Kwang Chung Kim and E.H. Lee. Institute of Korea.

Connel, Rich. 1993. "City Hall Power Shifts to Eclectic Pragmatic Team." *Los Angeles Times*. 29, November: A1.

Curran, Ron. 1988. "Malign Neglect: The Roots of an Urban War Zone." *LA Weekly*. 30, December to 5, January: 8.

———. 1993. "The Deal Maker." *LA Weekly*. 21 May to 27 May: 18.

Davis, Mike. 1990. *City of Quartz*. London-New York: Verso.

Davis, Mike 1990. "The Redevelopment Game: The Rules, Players and History of the Biggest Game in Town." *LA Weekly*. 2 March to 8 March: 19.

Dominguez, John R. 1976. *Capital Flows in Minority Areas.* Lexington, MA: D.C. Heath and Company.

Estrada, Leobardo, and Sylvia Sensiper. 1993. "Mending the Politics of Division in Post-Rebellion L.A." Pp. 123-138 in *South Central Los Angeles: Anatomy of an Urban Crisis. Working Paper #6,* edited by Allen J. Scott and E. Richard Brown. Los Angeles: Lewis Center for Regional Policy Studies.

Glazer, Nathan. 1983. *Ethnic Dilemmas, 1964-1982.* Cambridge, MA: Harvard University Press.

Ice Cube. 1991. "Black-Korea." *Death Certificate.* Priority Records.

Johnson, James H., Jr., and Melvin L. Oliver. 1989. "Interethnic Minority Conflict In Urban America: The Effects of Economic and Social Dislocations." *Urban Geography,* 10, 5: 449-463.

Katz, Jesse, and Stephanie Chavez. 1991. "Blacks Seek to Channel Anger Over Sentence," *Los Angeles Times.* 17 November: A1.

Keller, Edmond. 1978. "The Impact of Black Mayors on Urban Policy," *The Annals of the American Academy of Political and Social Science.* Volume 439, September: 40-53.

Kim, Claire. *Crack in the Gorgeous Mosaic: Black- Korean Conflict and Racial Politics in New York City.* Unpublished dissertation. New Haven: Yale University.

Kim, Illsoo. 1981. *New Urban Immigrants: The Korean Community in New York.* Princeton: Princeton University Press.

Kim, Joan. 1990. "Southland Koreans Try Harder." *Korea Times.* 15 August: 1.

Kim, Sophia Kyung. 1992. "Annie Cho Leaps to Olympian Task." *Korea Times.* 26 May: 1.

Korean American Grocers Association. 1992. *KAGRO Newsletter.* Vol. 2, No. 11.

Krikorian, Greg. 1993. "The Bottleneck." *Los Angeles Times, City Times Edition.* 29 August: 14.

Labor/Community Strategy Center. 1993. *Reconstructing Los Angeles From The Bottom Up.* Los Angeles: Labor/Community Strategy Center.

Lee, Don. 1991. "Korean Americans See Need For Political Power." *Korea Times.* 26 May: 1.

Light, Ivan, and Edna Bonacich. 1988. *Immigrant Entrepreneur: Koreans in Los Angeles 1965-1982.* Berkeley: University of California Press.

Logan, John R., and Todd Swanstrom, eds. 1990. *Beyond The City Limits: Urban Policy and Economic Restructuring in Comparative Perspective.* Philadelphia: Temple University Press.

Los Angeles Times. 1991. "Diary of a War of Attrition in Volatile Urban Disputes," 2 July: A1.

Los Angeles Times, Editorial. 1991. "A Market Looking For Legitimate Businesses," 29 November: B4.

Needham, John. 1992. "Koreans May Lead Post-Riot Exodus," *Los Angeles Times.* 22 June: A3.

Oliver, Melvin L., and Thomas M. Shapiro. 1989. "Race and Wealth," *The Review of Black Political Economy*. Spring: 5-25.

Omi, Michael, and Howard Winant. 1986. *Racial Formations in the United States: from the 1960's to the 1980's*. New York: Routledge and Kegan Paul.

Payne, J. Gregory, and Scott C. Ratzan. 1986. *Tom Bradley: The Impossible Dream*. Santa Monica: Roundtable Publishing.

Peterson, Jonathan. 1992. "Rebuild L.A. Asks Residents For Their Input." *Los Angeles Times*. 5 November: A1.

Peterson, Paul. 1981. *City Limits*. Chicago: University of Chicago Press.

Rivera, Carla, and Dean E. Murphy. 1993. "Ueberroth Quits Rebuild L.A. Post." *Los Angeles Times*. 22 May: A1.

Rutten, Tim. 1991. "Unity Also a Victim of Shootings," *Los Angeles Times*. 21 June: E1.

Silverstein, Stuart, and Nancy Rivera Brooks. 1991. "Retail Exodus Short changes Consumer," *Los Angeles Times*. 24 November: A1.

Soja, Edward. 1987. "Economic Restructuring and the Internationalization of the Los Angeles Region." Pp. 178-98 in *The Capitalist City: Global Restructuring and Community Politics*, edited by Michael Peter Smith and Joe R. Feagin. Oxford: Basil Blackwell.

Sonenshein, Raphael. 1990. "Biracial Coalition Politics in Los Angeles," pp. 33-48 in *Racial Politics in American Cities*, edited by Rufus Browning, Dale Rodgers Marshall and David Tabb. New York and London: Longman Press.

Sowell, Thomas. 1980. *Ethnic America*. New York: Basic Books.

Stolberg, Sheryl, and Frank Clifford. 1991. "Danny Bakewell—A Taste for Street Politics, Business." *Los Angeles Times*. 20 October: A1.

Stone, Clarence. 1989. *Regime Politics: Governing Atlanta 1946-1988*. Lawrence, Kansas: University Press of Kansas.

Takaki, Ronald 1993. *A Different Mirror: A History of Multicultural America*. Boston, Toronto, London: Little Brown and Company.

Treadwell, David. 1991. "Hard Road for Black Businesses," *Los Angeles Times*. 20 September: A1.

Weinstein, Henry 1990a. "Vast Expansion of Rebuild L.A. Adds Minorities," *Los Angeles Times*. 27 June: A1.

——1990b. "Black Businessman to Manage Rebuild LA." *Los Angeles Times*. 28 June: A1.

Wilson, William Julius. 1980. *The Declining Significance of Race: Blacks and Changing American Institutions*. 2nd ed. Chicago: University of Chicago Press.

9

Community Coalition-Building

James A. Regalado

Mayoral Race 1993 brought the "City of Angels" a public leader whose private-sector background and leadership style are consistent with the business regime model of local governance associated more with Dallas, Texas (Elkin 1987) and Los Angeles in the first five decades of this century (Sonenshein 1993), than with Los Angeles over the last thirty years. Is a moderate to conservative Republican, a successful business leader and consummate insider on the city's governing coalition in the city's "Bradley years," truly "tough enough to turn L.A. around?" Richard Riordan's campaign theme has been commonly interpreted as the new mayor's recipe for preventing another riot while symbolically assuring a more tranquil existence for the city's middle and upper class voters. This would largely occur through placing 3,000 more cops on the beat while promoting ordinances that may be seen as further "gating" communities of color. The Riordan administration has proposed funding this "vision" through the selling of city assets (like LAX), contracting out city services and jobs to private bidders, and the anticipated largess of President Clinton's anti-crime urban agenda. Is this the tone-setting and tonic needed by a city whose various communities and groups are seemingly more at war with each other than in ongoing critical introspection and dialogue? Not according to L.A. writer Mike Davis (author of City of Quartz), who has contended that the city has learned little from the fires of Spring 1992, if the election of Richard Riordan as mayor is any indication (Mendez 1993).

Judging by Riordan's appointments to his inner-circle of Deputy Mayors and advisors as well as to Commissions and Departments running the city, the city's public leadership is becoming more class and race exclusive than it has been in the past twenty years (Connell

1993). The implication here is that the city's new mayor fashioned an electoral coalition components of which have become incorporated into the city's governing coalition. While the anchor of Riordan's electoral coalition was comprised of gentile and Jewish whites from the San Fernando Valley and the Westside, considerable Latino and Asian support was also evident. To illustrate this point, in his runoff election against former L.A. Council member Michael Woo, a Chinese-American, Riordan captured 67 percent of the White vote, 43 percent of the Latino vote, 31 percent of the Asian vote and 14 percent of the African American vote (Kaufmann 1994).

In terms of Riordan's key appointments, it becomes equally clear that there are more white and fewer "rainbow" elites involved on the "public" side of the city's governing coalition (see Los Angeles Times, 1993). Whereas, 42 percent of Bradley's Commission appointments were white, 24 percent African American, 18 percent Latino, and 11 percent Asian, Riordan's appointments have been 57 percent white, 15 percent African American, 14 percent Latino and 8 percent Asian (Connell 1993). Geographically, the exclusive public and private sector alliance running the city has now incorporated more wealthy and professional elites from the San Fernando Valley to join what had become a Downtown and Westside dominant coalition under Bradley (Mann 1989, Soja 1989, Regalado 1991). As this becomes better understood, what signals does it present to a city and region seemingly so nakedly divided? What hope does it offer for building a democratic fusion as well as inter-class and inter-racial dialogue?

And yet, Riordan is not alone in being apparently incapable of fashioning a sufficient understanding of the city's complexity, much less make a significant and unifying "call" on the city's diverse communities to coalesce. What of RLA (formerly Rebuild L.A.)? The grandiose abdication of public sector responsibility (Mann 1993b) for the riots and the "rebuilding" aftermath was symbolized in the very creation of this private sector driven entity, headed by 1984 L.A. Olympics titan Peter Ueberroth, to resuscitate and "rebuild" inner-city communities. Alas, it could not come close to living up to its early booster backing, much less its own press clippings. Advertised and self-promoted as a three-part coalition of equals involving private, public and community sectors (see Kinsey, et. al. 1992), RLA was never more than a private sector driven organization with minimal participation of public sector representatives and even more limited contact with community organizations and individuals. To underscore this point, when Ueberroth was pressed by State Assemblywoman Margarite Archie-Hudson during Assembly Speaker Willie Brown's 1993 Economic Summit in Los Angeles, to explain what RLA was accomplishing in South Central Los Angeles, he instead attempted to define the geographic proximity of South Central Los Angeles (the most engaged riot/uprising area and public point of RLA rebuilding focus) by referring to streets outside the parameters of South Central Los Angeles.

RLA, previous and current public officials like Bradley and Riordan, and some scholars (see Kotkin and Kinsey 1993) have defined RLA as an example of a multi-racial coalition. However, this is difficult to support, especially in terms of the organization's locus of day-to-day leadership, its top-down decision-making style and its devotion to secrecy. Additionally, Mann (1993b) argues that in advancing a corporatist definition of partnership, RLA is promoting an anti coalition-building ideology. Yet, by strictly looking at the roster of RLA's Board of Directors, one might indeed get the impression that all of the city's cultures, if not classes, are represented. However, RLA has a ninety-six member Board consisting of elites representing a number of constituencies and sectors, that is ideologically conservative to moderate, and which regularly follows policy leads and activity guidelines from its Directors. The organization has changed its focus from being the city's economic, race-relations and school district savior under Ueberroth to a more streamlined entity directing its energies to small-business assistance and start-ups in inner-city communities. This change was accompanied by a leadership change, as well. After Ueberroth's exasperated resignation in mid-1993, the Board opted for a symbolically appeasing four Co-Director experience (comprised of a Jewish White male, an African American male, a Latino male and an Asian Pacific woman—all representative of corporate sectors except for the Asian) in late 1993. More recently, and under strong prodding from Mayor Riordan and others in the city's governing coalition to form a more singular and cohesive management team, the Board selected ARCO President Lodwrick Cook who hand-picked Linda Griego (owner of an "inner-circle" downtown restaurant and former Deputy Mayor for economic development under Tom Bradley) to be the agency's Executive Director, in forming the organization's current Co-Director leadership. However, the organization's future success and longevity are anything but assured. What is clear is that RLA may be many things, but an example of community-oriented multi-racial coalition-building it is not (see Proffitt 1994, Feldman 1994).

Finally, combined with slow and halting beginnings on the part of both RLA and the Riordan public stewardship of the city, traditionally powerful economic and community development entities such as the City's Community Redevelopment Agency (CRA-LA) and, to a much lesser extent, the City's Community Development Department (CDD) and the County's Commission on Economic Development (CED) are attempting to "rediscover" and "reinvent" themselves in the wake of the L.A. uprisings and riots, on the one hand, and new urban overtures from the Clinton Administration, on the other (see Spring 1993b, Fulton 1992). Whether this means that these entities, especially CRA-LA, will formidably serve to break away from top-down corporate-centered development strategies (see Regalado 1992, Dymski & Veitch 1992) in service of community-inclusive models patterned to housing and small-business needs of inner-city communities remains a hot topic of concern (Spring 1993b). These entities have little history of working with community coalitions and grassroots groups in devising specific strategies and projects based on common need.

Within this backdrop, many of the city's residents and observers feel than unless formidable political reforms are adopted (Kayden 1992) and economic assistance arrives which deliver both an increased tax base to fund services to, and widespread job growth within and around inner-cities throughout the metropolitan region (Feldman 1993), relations among the City's communities and groups, long-divided along class and race/ethnic lines, will improve little, in spite of the nature of the "calls" (Davis 1993). These points were underscored in the "Webster Commission Report" (1992) on the causes of the '92 riots and in its prescriptions for "healing." However, others argue that the calls for coalition-building among culturally and racially diverse individuals and groups must continue, or begin anew, in order to pursue two objectives: present common-front agendas to traditionally "unfriendly" public and private institutions and reduce tension levels among communities of color.

This chapter will examine selected literature on, and theoretical applications of, multi/bi-racial coalition building and race relations that have relevance to what has occurred in Los Angeles' recent history. The chapter will also critically assess a number of multi/bi-racial coalitions, most created before the events of Spring '92, that have attempted to overcome tensions and conflicts among communities of color and/or promote common front strategies to secure policy and other political gains. The case studies will serve to (1) explore the focus of the coalitions before and after the uprisings, (2) determine their organizational response to the riots, and (3) assess the strengths and weaknesses of the coalitions in terms of "meeting the call." The chapter will conclude by arguing that successful coalition formations must meet certain criteria. Most formidably, formation "calls" for healing and progressive action must begin with increasing critical awareness of what bedevils us. In this regard, it is notable that the mass media has continued to report on the events of Spring '92 in a very similar black-white, dual society style with which they covered the urban riots and rebellions of the 1960s. However, where the mainstream media still discuss and report on the '92 civil disorder simplistically as a "South Central L.A. paradox," other voices have underscored the enormous complexity of the unrest by defining it as part bread riot, part rage against the police, and part racial antagonism between African and Korean Americans. However, antagonisms between African and Latino Americans and among other racial and ethnic groups was also discernible.

Literature Review

While it is widely acknowledged (most recently by Freer 1993, Sonenshein 1993, Calderon 1993, Regalado 1992, and Munoz and Henry 1991) that few theoretical works exist on the creation of biracial, much less multiracial, coalitions beyond the African American and liberal White models, a number of works exist which served to provide theoretical groundwork for applications over the past several years. Such models have, for the most part, been applied to explain an African American political incorporation thesis. However, for coalition-building spread more broadly among communities and groups of color, few scholarly works exist. Within that limiting context, several of the more significant works on coalition-building and race relations among communities of color of particular relevance to this chapter will be briefly addressed in this section.

King (1967) argued that political alliances (coalitions) among people of color must be honestly and openly based on some self-interest of each participant and group as well as on a common interest into which they merge as a larger group. His vision, created in and through the civil rights movements of the 1950s and 1960s, was that of an ideologically-based union of people of color, liberal and progressive whites, organized labor, and liberal clergy for the larger purpose of advancing civil rights agendas. Where King made general coalition calls based on good will, Carmichael and Hamilton (1967) became more specific. They suggested that four issues must be understood and resolved in building successful multi-racial coalitions. First, all parties involved must recognize the self-interest of each party/participant. Second, there must be an accompanying mutual belief that each party to the coalition stands to benefit from allying with others. Third, there must be broad acceptance that each party has its own independent base of power and external decision-making.

Fourth and finally, there must be widespread agreement that the coalition must deal with specific and identifiable goals and issues, as opposed to theoretical abstractions. I believe these criteria to be valid tests of contemporary efforts to build multi/bi-racial coalitions of color.

Dymally (1970) represented a small number of highly visible African-American and Latino leaders in the late 1960s and early-to-mid 1970s pushing for bi-racial coalition-building among African and Latino Americans. He argued that so many similarities existed between Black and Brown (primarily Chicano) working class communities that it made little sense to focus on the minor areas of difference which had become major impediments to coalition-building among the two communities. His argument, framed largely in a "poor peoples" theory of coalescing of the "have and have-not" rhetoric of the day, resonated well among liberals and progressives around issues of employment, income, housing, medical care, environmental racism, public transportation, and economic development. Many contend that these are many of the same issues around which multicultural collaboration could develop today. However, then as now, economic and political competition, angry nationalism and provincial outlooks, and limited public space conducive to information exchange and dialogue, limit the degree to which collaboration has occurred.

Taking issue with calls for Black and Latino unison made by King and Dymally and, to a lesser extend, Carmichael and Hamilton, Soto Ortega (1970) and, more recently, Kamasaki and Yzaguirre (1991) assessed African and Latino American coalition possibilities from largely nationalist perspectives. All argued that several conditions must be met by African American leaders before significant coalescing can take place. Soto Ortega wrote that

> it will be incumbent upon the black community to demonstrate that they are willing to share and share alike in financial assistance and in economic and political power (182).

Such an argument suggests that African Americans are politically and economically empowered and dismisses Latino culpability in not working towards greater collaboration. Similarly, Kamasaki and Yzaguirre (1991) argue that three basic issues separate Latinos and African Americans: civil rights enforcement, political representation and immigration. While many would agree that the latter two are legitimate concerns and areas of conflict, the authors maintain that African Americans generally have had too much while Latinos have had too little. This line of reasoning became highly publicized in the competition for Rebuild L.A.-inspired reconstruction projects and corollary job development in the early aftermath of the fires of '92. Antagonistic nationalist rhetoric, which also took on tones of "whose time (politically) has come and whose has gone," was expressed perhaps most pointedly in media crossfires involving N.E.W.S. America's Xavier Hermosillo and The Brotherhood Crusade's Danny Bakewell (nationalist Latino and African American organizations respectively). However, such views are by no means exclusive to these players.

While Kamasaki and Yziguirre conclude with hopeful rhetoric that public education and increased dialogue might enhance coalition-building possibilities in the future, they return to more confining projections in contending that

> there is a growing feeling within the Hispanic leadership that Blacks cannot be relied on as protectors of Hispanic interests or as coalition partners. There is growing sentiment that an Hispanic-specific, quasi-separatist approach is the only viable was of achieving full equality" (18).

Johnson and Oliver (1989) provide a similar argument but one largely from African American circles. Although they propose a "new configuration" of intergroup conflict through establishing "interconnections underlying economic and sociopolitical forces which precipitate interethnic conflict in urban America" (450), their basic argument is not altogether new. They contend that the emergence of interracial/ethnic conflict stems from increasing Mexican and Latin American immigration, Latino immigrant movement into traditional African American communities, and the increasing competition for scarce and valued resources between this immigrant community and their African American neighbors. Thus, in something of a reversal from the previous authors, Johnson and Oliver suggest that Latino immigrants are the fundamental cause of increasing tensions among the two communities that inhibit coalition possibilities. They conclude by calling for additional educational programs as a remedy for stereotypes but realistically suggest that solutions must await finding solutions to larger urban issues (like immigration) which are associated with the "economic, social and demographic transformations occurring in American society" (459).

Shingles (1991), while acknowledging such arguments, is reminiscent of Dymally (1970) in suggesting a more optimistic scenario for Latino and African American coalition-building. He contends that Latino and African Americans have long been separated by "misunderstandings, cultural differences, competition for scarce resources, and conflicting perceptions of self-interest" (1). Taking soft aim at the Soto Ortega, Kamasaki-Yzaguirre, and Johnson-Oliver theses, he laments that each group continues to see "one another as competitors for jobs, public understanding, political power and government largess, not allies with a common agenda" (1). Echoing Dymally, his own thesis is that

> though important, differences between the two groups can be overdrawn, thereby concealing superordinate issues that would otherwise serve as the basis for coalition politics (6).

Citing the Browning, et. al., model of coalition-building leading to political incorporation, Shingles contends that Black-Latino battles over political representation bring damage to both communities. Only by building "winning coalitions" among Latinos, African Americans and "like-minded, progressive European-Americans," can minorities of color effectively exercise political power and overcome prejudice and vested interests" (19). His recipe for such multiracial coalition building is three-fold: (1) learn to appreciate one groups' differences from the other(s), (2) develop more sensitive curricula in public education, and (3) engage in mutual dialogue (19).

Peter Eisinger's (1976) study of African and White American coalition activity in Milwaukee broke new ground in coalition research in that it focused on assessing the "timeliness of black urban dwellers becoming desirable allies for some white groups in politics" (2). This was a particularly significant direction in a period of urban white flight amidst black population growth. Maintaining that the nature of interracial relationships in politics is characterized by both conflict and cooperation, he argued that intergroup political relationships can be arrayed across a continuum of varieties of conflict and cooperation. Coalitions represent a cooperative form. According to Eisinger, political conflict and coalition activity are increasingly structured by racial interests and racial blocs, points of departure picked up by scholars in the 1980s. Given his Milwaukee focus, he was not concerned to explore multiracial coalition processes and possibilities beyond African and white American linking possibilities. Indeed, in arguing that African Americans were ripe for coalition possibilities on the basis of their constituting "racial political communities... capable of independent and cohesive action" (6), he seemed to be excluding latter day applications elsewhere involving other "minority" communities (such as Latino and Asian) which have been less politically cohesive than African American communities in cities such as Los Angeles, where demographic shifts have at least symbolically diminished African American voting clout and, thereby, their coalition attractiveness (Stewart 1993, Davis 1993).

Building upon Eisinger's typology of coalition formations, Rufus Browning, Dale Rogers Marshall, and David Tabb (1984, 1986, 1989) developed a theory of minority political incorporation that has been applied to a variety of cities in the United States and abroad. In their study of ten Northern California cities (1984), they suggested that through bi-racial coalitions, communities of color have an enhanced chance of becoming politically incorporated into the city's dominant legislative coalition than by simply struggling on their own. Through a series of community mobilization stages moving from (1) demand and protest, (2) electoral mobilization, and (3) representation onto (4) incorporation into the dominant coalition of the policy-making body, the community/communities in question are on the road to sustained policy influence and, implicitly, political equality, an assumption questioned by Hero (1992). Coalition-building becomes the most crucial ingredient in this process. In this regard, the authors found that in order for the incorporation process to proceed, much less occur, the community of color in question must seek coalition partnership with at least one other group.

Most of the Browning model applications, including those in the city of Los Angeles by Sonenshein, found that a white liberal community, often Jewish, had become the favorite coalition partner begetting African American political incorporation. In their studies, Browning, Marshall and Tabb did not find a successful example of multiracial coalition activity that led to the incorporation of a community of color, although Hero found mixed results in his application of the model exploring Latino incorporation in Denver and Pueblo, Colorado (Hero 1990). Hero argues, in a 1992 work, that Federico Pena's two elections as mayor of Denver provide both agreement as well as disagreement with the Browning, Marshall and Tabb (BMT) approach. More specifically, Hero contends that the approach is an application of late pluralist theory which ignores the degree to which political and other institutions are structurally biased to reward individual minority group members (co-optation) while maintaining the larger class (community) in society's "second tier." In his view, the BMT approach does not lead to incorporation as the authors defined it, nor does he feel that the reliance of the approach on allocational policy decisions and outcomes equates well with the "equality-tinged" definition of incorporation offered and implied by Browning, Marshall and Tabb.

Sonenshein (1989, 1993) has applied the Browning, et. al., model of political incorporation to Los Angeles through the much heralded Jewish—African American electoral coalition. He argues that the coalition, a political necessity for both groups, was successful in empowering the two communities, laying claim to the unparalleled degree to which African American and Jewish candidates were elected to public office representing Los Angeles over a thirty-year period. While meeting the model's allocational criteria/test for incorporation in terms of gaining commission and department head appointments, minority business contracts and affirmative action city hiring, this application has been questioned by Regalado (1991) for dealing almost exclusively with a black-white approach to explain both electoral and governing coalitions that left little room to include other major coalition players, namely the downtown business community and organized labor, as well as for failing to determine what segments of L.A.'s African American community became politically incorporated. In other words, if incorporation has occurred, what has it meant for the African American community beyond those relatively few gaining jobs, positions and contracts? Similarly, Jackson (1990) found fault with Sonenshein's applications contending that the coalition was heavily biased toward Westside Jews while arguing that neither the coalition nor the coalition's public point person, Mayor Tom Bradley, did much for the African American community of Los Angeles. Although Sonenshein acknowledges that the city has greatly changed since the Watts Rebellions/Riots of 1965, the title of his latest work, *Politics in Black and White*, suggests a model better suited to explaining urban politics a generation ago. Still, this work is both significant and compelling in its historical bi-racial linkage explanations, incorporation model rupture thesis, and discussion of L.A.'s search for a dominant electoral coalition to replace Bradley's.

Uhlaner (1991) provides notes of caution on inter-racial coalition-building that blend with arguments made by Soto-Ortega, Kamasaki-Yzaguirre, and Johnson-Oliver. Reporting on her study of inter-racial/ethnic attitudes in Los Angeles, she found that although "clearly, a coalition of minorities must rest on some common ground" (340), discrimination, which most groups of color feel, does not necessarily lead to cooperation, much less coalition-building. Discriminating experiences, she writes, "might produce antagonisms instead of coalitions" (341). Whether or not this a defining variable for inter-racial antagonisms, clearly such antagonisms continue to abound in Los Angeles.

Stewart (1993), in a significant article exploring reasons for African American out- migration from Los Angeles, takes some issue with Johnson & Oliver (1989) and others in the African American community who tend to lay blame on Latino and/or Asian immigration as the root or immediate cause of diminishing African American political, economic and demographic capital and, thereby, potential for African, Latino and/or Asian American dialogue and collaboration. She argues that black out-migration itself is due more to "fears of gun violence, anguish over ever-deteriorating urban schools, and desires for home ownership, than it is to rejection of poor immigrants as neighbors." Many blacks also have dreams of realizing suburban breathing space (18). What is more, the Black exodus transcends class which implicitly argues against the notion that lack of Latino and black unity is predominantly a matter of the have-nots fighting over service delivery and low-wage jobs. Steward points to examples of "successful" organizing among groups keying on specific issues, irrespective of race, such as United Neighborhoods Organization, South Central Organizing Committee, Justice for Janitors, LEARN and RLA. She implies that African American class and race interests are linked in successfully coalescing with groups of like-mind on in-class levels. However, little attention is given to attempts to form coalitions bridging class distinctions and levels.

Davis (in Mendez, 1993) argues that America faces no greater crisis than "the decline and abandonment of its great cities" (27). Symptomatic of such are the desperate conditions of Latinos and African Americans in the slums of the city. The new progressive agenda for cities like Los Angeles will be for African and Latino Americans to build unity and coalition. In taking issue with Johnson and Oliver, Davis contends that problems in building such unity stem more from conflicts among African Americans and Chicanos than among African Americans and immigrants. In arguing against the Johnson-Oliver thesis, Davis contends that the locus of battle is primarily over the holding of political power, little of which Latinos have, not immigration. Believing Latinos to be the most crucial element in building a new progressive coalition, Davis argues that former Mayor Bradley's greatest sin was in ignoring and not incorporating Latinos and the Eastside. "The tragedy of L.A. (under Bradley) is that there could have been many linkages of different kinds," and because they did not take place in an historical period when they more easily could have, Davis is not optimistic on developing a new progressive coalition for L.A. in the near future. A major limitation of his own work, as well as in many others, is that his coalition scenario omits the Asian connection.

Finally, Davis has elsewhere (1993) argued that L.A. is symptomatic of a larger failure of American cities. In a context of federal "disinvestment" in its cities stretching back to the Carter

Administration, Davis joins Freer (1994) in arguing that accelerated tensions among a city's major racial and ethnic groups is directly tied to the accelerated decline of public sector involvement. On this point, he argues against Steward's (1993) thesis in contending that "an embittering competition over shrinking resources...has brought the black and Latino communities to the brink of open street warfare" (3). It is this scenario that projects his pessimistic assessments for future coalition-building.

Coalition Building Amidst "L.A. Realities":

That the Bradley electoral coalition was dying became clear during the former mayor's ill-conceived second gubernatorial campaign in 1986 and, more dramatically, in his final mayoral campaign in 1989. The more formal stamp of death of the essentially African-American Southside and Jewish Westside coalition came, however, in mayoral campaign 1993, without Bradley. The question then became what coalition-formation would become electorally successful (Sonenshein 1993, Regalado 1992). However, the search for a dominant electoral coalition, although perhaps part of the equation, is usually a far different undertaking than creating a multi-racial collaboration for the purpose of building common progressive fronts and/or reducing escalating inter-racial tensions. This latter call to a "higher purpose" in many ways transcends electoral politics. However, this is not meant to imply that electoral politics are irrelevant to the larger issues facing diverse communities in cities like Los Angeles, New York, Chicago and Miami. In fact, it was frequently argued that the 1993 L.A. mayoral campaign should have had much more to offer a city and region suffering from severe economic decline and related social inflammation.

During the mayoral primary campaign of 1993, candidates ranging from front-runners Michael Woo, Richard Riordan and Richard Katz to the less formidable candidacies of Nate Holden, Linda Griego, Tom Houston and Julian Nava (there were twenty-seven candidates at one point), provided simplistic law and order responses both to the cause of the previous year's racial uprisings mixed with "bread riots" (see Pastor 1993, Davis 1993) and to the likelihood of a similar event following the federal civil rights trial involving the LAPD and Rodney King. Most of their "recipes" for city healing focused on hiring and deploying more LAPD officers, targeting undocumented immigrants as alternatively being lawless and crime-driven as well as a drain on the economy and jobs for citizens, and promoting simplistic rhetoric devoted to building inter-ethnic group dialogue. In the mayoral runoff election pitting Councilman Michael Woo against businessman Richard Riordan, class, ideological, and policy choices abounded but were drowned out in a sea of ad hominem attacks and simplistic calls for "healing" (see Kaufmann 1994, Brownstein 1993, Clifford 1993).

Although in recent history there have been many well-intentioned and well-founded efforts (including conflict resolution/management programs, public forums, and attempts to coalesce) to prevent further disruption in relations among the city's predominant racial and ethnic groups (see Seo 1993), any suggestions that broad "healing" is underway are entirely premature. On a national scale, the Kettering Foundation and, more recently, State Humanities Councils have been sponsoring community "conversations" aimed at engaging designated communities and their residents in discussions concerning political participation, governance and community-to-community relations (see The Harwood Group, 1993). However, while such efforts are needed and should be applauded, such efforts have had only a marginal impact, at best, in large and diverse cities like Los Angeles. It is my contention that in order to more fully confront the major issues which divide major cities like Los Angeles around race and class, and which prevent broader and more pervasive multicultural understanding and more consistent and sustainable coalition-building, broad and diverse streams of citizenry need to more honestly and thoroughly confront a number of fundamental questions and issues in a series of ongoing public space interactions.

First, *the meaning and application of representative democracy* in a rapidly changing society, particularly in communities of color, must be critically examined and honestly rethought. This critical and interactive discussion should be developed around a practical understanding of policy processes, governing structures, the nature and identification of governing coalitions and of who governs at community, city and regional levels. A discussion of the relative importance or unimportance of local political activity should also be a central focus. This becomes especially significant in a context of the increasing reach and influence of global and national economies (Davis 1993, Stone & Sanders 1987), resulting impact on cities (Eisinger 1988, Peterson 1981) and decisions and competition faced at the local level over diminishing local resources, public sector disinvestment, voting rights and political representation (Regalado 1988, 1992).

The issue of political representation has engendered significant conflict among African and Latino Americans over related sub-issues of demographic flux (especially Latino population expansion into districts and communities of traditional African American dominance such as that occurring in South Los Angeles), redistricting, voting rights, political representation and zero-sum politics (see Stewart 1993, Estrada 1993, Regalado 1988). It has also been the subject of "positioning" conflicts involving Asian Americans as well (e.g., over demographic and representation shifts in the San Gabriel Valley, Koreatown splits in 1986 and developing "common fronts" for 1990s redistricting) (Regalado, 1989, 1991).

Finally, structural class and racial biases of local political systems, the degree to which cities like Los Angeles are governable, the practical meaning of political incorporation, where and how coalition-building becomes strategically important and necessary, should also be on the "table" (see Hero 1992, Browning, et. al. 1984, Davis 1993, Sonenshein 1993, 1989, and Regalado 1991).

Second, *the nature of economic "rebuilding" and develop-ment/redevelopment* must be examined, especially with reference to (1) a more inclusive (and democratic) role for residents in communities of color, (2) models of development which make such inclusion possible, and (3) holding the public sector more accountable for future development decision-making and project realization. Historically, local and regional policy makers have strongly endorsed corporate-center economic development approaches and strategies that minimized or totally ignored roles for and input from working, poor and middle-class community residents while depriving the city's most needy communities of economic development projects (see Mann 1993, Dymski & Veitch 1992, Regalado 1992, Pastor 1989). For example, although the city's Community Redevelopment Agency has 20 redevelopment areas spread throughout the city, out of 210 CRA projects completed between 1959 and 1990, 116 of them were located in the Central Business District and the adjacent Bunker Hills downtown development areas. The 5 redevelopment areas containing portions of the city most centrally involved in the 1992 uprisings were recipients of 42 generally modest projects in this period (Regalado 1992). This history, along with awareness of national, regional and local economic development realities, should be part of this process of examination. For example, Davis' (1993) unfavorable impression of public sector interest, much less commitment, to be part of the solution should be seriously contended with. Additionally, free market development ideas embraced by the Reagan, Bush and Clinton administrations need to be assessed and addressed, especially in the wake of more limiting public sector commitments to job growth amidst a private sector focus on job training but not job creation (Feldman 1993), manufacturing and factory flight (Lee 1993) and questionable "commitments" to rebuild the Southland (Krikorian 1993, Zellers 1993).

Third, key *issues of race and class*, which act both as personal and collective community barriers and divides, should be concretely defined, articulated and examined, including assessments of how they intersect and link. Ties with organized labor and other class-driven/membered organizations should be factored in. Part of this and the preceding discussion should include the geographic and political spatial issues that make coalition-building, much less finding nearby solutions, difficult. Understanding the complex nexus between and among geographic economic decision-making , demographic movement and socio-racial conflict has become increasingly important. This becomes even more crucial given historic class and racial biases structured into local political systems (see Modarres 1994; Stewart 1993; Davis 1990; and Hoch 1984,). Recent bi-racial or multi-racial coalition-building activities discussed in this paper have failed to be effective in large part due to the ignoring of such dimensions of the city's past and present reality.

Fourth, the very *meaning of multicultural pluralism*, beyond "L.A. symbolism," must be rethought, especially in this urban context so beset by fear, segregation and polarity. The false historic image that Los Angeles power elites paraded to the rest of the nation and world through "sunshine" strategies (see Klein 1990) was revisited during the 1984 Los Angeles Olympics through the "melting pot oasis" strategy. However, whatever credibility the city was receiving for this image was rudely shattered by the reality of the events of Spring, 1992. Stewart Kwoh, Executive Director of the Asian Pacific American Legal Center of Southern California, in a public forum address that preceded the '92 uprisings by four years, sounded a note of challenge to allow the city to become more inclusively a "pluralist multicultural democracy" (Kwoh 1989). Kwoh, a progressive Bradley loyalist, was very well aware that appointing a number of "rainbow elites" to commission and department positions, would not be sufficient to ensure the type of inclusion he was referring to, a point made more strongly in terms of co-optation possibilities by Eisinger (1986). These interrelated topics beg a series of sub-questions on co-existence, democracy and governance. Is L.A. governable as it presently exists in class-segregated and racially-divided form? Is pluralism desirable, much less possible? If so, how do we make the city more inclusive, interactive and governable? (See Chase, 1993.)

Fifth and finally, *the nature of provincialism* and "in-group" versus "out-group" racial, ethnic and cultural attitudes must be discussed in the context of being serious impediments to coalition building, collective agenda setting, and collaborative goal attainment activity. To what extent does nationalist ethnic/racial identity harm the "common good?" King (1967), Carmichael & Hamilton (1967), Dymally (1970), Eisinger (1976) and Shingles (1991), among others, have remarked on the dangers to multi/bi-racial coalition-building in a setting where nationalism and nationalist agendas are rampantly adhered to. Such settings have frequently been breeding ground for individual and organizational use of straw man and ad hominem arguments in belittling those a part of or belonging to, other groups.

It is my contention that tackling such questions can be used as a guiding framework for discussions and dialogue that may lead to the establishment of more sustainable coalition formations and, through such efforts, beginning policy and action guides. To some degree, the discussion of particular coalition formations which follows will assess the extent to which each formation has attempted to deal with such issues. In this regard, the following sections will attempt to determine success and weakness in coalition attempts to "ferret out" that which may unite and that which continues to divide communities.

In large part, the future of the city has always resided with a coalition of players who often controlled major economic decisions and the body politic as well. In the wake of the demise of the "Bradley coalition" (see Sonenshein 1993, Regalado 1991), on the one hand, and the riots and disorder of Spring '92, on the other, the time for fashioning innovative coalitions based on common concerns, goals and strengths is ripe. However, the "calls" must be made on the basis of focusing on an agenda of hard and relevant questions, issues and concerns.

Case Studies of Multi/Bi-Racial Coalition-Building in Los Angeles

Contrary to reports of the news media and city and county officials before Spring, 1992, Los Angeles has long been a class and racially segregated and polarized society. This is not to deny that the city has a progressive and coalition-building history as well (see Underwood 1994). However, within the "balkanized" metaphor that Los Angeles is, the society known as L.A. has also changed substantially. Old models, old explanations, and old analyses need to be either discarded or seriously updated. However, old messages and old "calls" for the city to "regenerate" still dominate most "rebuilding" designs. Witness the aforementioned title of Professor Raphael Sonenshein's impressive new book —*Politics in Black and White*—itself a throwback to a more simplistic view of the city's social and political troubles which never truly fit with the reality of the city's historic multicultural harmonies and disharmonies. RLA fits well into this pattern of the old with its top-down corporate (secretive) style of economic development decision-making among elites, as does the city's Community Redevelopment Agency, a fixture of top-down corporate-style decision-making. Although changes have taken place among the leadership of both entities, it is not clear that either will become more community-inclusive in its decision-making style.

Space and time limitations prevent a full quantitative and qualitative accounting of all significant bi-racial and multi-racial coalition formations that have developed in Southern California over the past decade. Those selected for review in this section are widely considered among those most significant and represent those the author has had most experience with. Each coalition was formed on the basis of a "call" to meet an identified need or set of needs affecting coalition partners. In general, the coalitions represented well-intentioned efforts based on shortsighted and, in some cases, clearly failed calls for multi/bi-racial coalescence since the mid-1980s. Among them, the Black-Korean Alliance and the Black-Latino Roundtable come immediately to mind. Both were created with assistance from, and guidance by, the Los Angeles County Commission on Human Relations in the 1980s, with the participation of approximately thirty "community groups" (albeit without the community). Both were disbanded shortly after the uprisings and riots of Spring, 1992.

Black-Korean Alliance (BKA): As reported by Doherty (1992), the "Alliance," as it came to be known, was the city's oldest organization (created in 1986) "dedicated to easing tensions between these two ethnic groups." Its membership was of professional middle class sectors and included religious leaders, human relations consultants, lawyers, political operatives and educators. Dedicated to easing tensions through dialogue and finding common ground in this restricted class setting, the Alliance could never get beyond an "elite" dialogue stage. This limitation became the primary reason for the Alliance's breakup. It became painfully obvious in the wake of Korean grocer Soon Ja Du's "exoneration" by a state court judge, after having shot and killed African American teenager LaTasha Harlins in 1991, and the Spring riots, that talk and dialogue were simply not enough. The Alliance's remove from issues affecting working and poverty classes and, relatedly, from other than professional and public sector elite constituencies became critical deficiencies.

Agreements among elites, even elites of color, as the uprisings and other physically conflictual events underscored, meant little at the neighborhood level where most conflicts occur. The serious class differences and issues to confront, and the grassroots community constituencies to be led, were nowhere to be found. On this point, neither Korean merchants nor residents from South Central Los

Angeles were involved in the Alliance or sought out for membership within. Other problems included lack of permanent staff, sparse meeting attendance, and an inability to forge a consensus on a number of issues, thereby negating key elements of successful coalition-building called for by Carmichael-Hamilton (1967), Eisinger (1976) and Shingles (1991), among others. Also, the Alliance could never get beyond the provincialism of individual member group and racial-group loyalties. Therefore, neither the common interest needs rising above the tide of provincialism called for in both the King and Carmichael-Hamilton approaches, nor the mobilized constituencies called for in the Browning model of incorporation, were met.

The *Black-Latino Roundtable* (BLR): Similar conditions afflicted the Black-Latino Roundtable, which was also created in 1986. This coalition among bi-racial elites has all but formally failed for many of the same reasons. Tensions and conflicts among the area's burgeoning Latino populations and its declining African American populations have long existed in the Southland (Hoffman 1993). However, they have been increasing at alarming rates, whether measured by housing project intimidation and gang violence, public school brawls, competition for reduced public services, competition over public and private sector employment opportunities, immigration, and/or redistricting and political representation issues (Lopez 1993, Katz 1993, Valle & Torres 1992). Ironically, many of these issues, which affect grassroots communities, are similar to those raised by Dymally as coalition-building points, on the one hand, and as points of conflict and division by Kamasaki-Yzaguirre and Johnson-Oliver, on the other.

The composition of the Roundtable was heavily membered and dominated by professional African and Latino Americans, although some such as recent former co-chairs Mark Ridley-Thomas (then representing the Los Angeles Chapter of the Southern Christian Leadership Conference) and Antonio Villaraigosa (then affiliated with a number of community organizations and United Teachers of Los Angeles), were sensitive to community groups and issues. The more recent Co-Chairs Olivia Mitchell, a Bradley loyalist employed by the City and Edward Negrete, Professor of Education at California State University, Los Angeles, sought a stronger collaboration although, as with the Alliance, without the community "troops."

The sometimes well-attended symposia and conferences sponsored by the Roundtable could not hide its failure to overcome provincial racial-group loyalties and suspicions of others on the Roundtable, its primarily elite membership, and its inability to mobilize grassroots community. In both coalition examples, members frequently could not get beyond the narrow nationalism and racial-group loyalties necessary to bridge gaping community wounds and divides. This reality failed the Carmichael-Hamilton criterion of the necessity for each party to the coalition to understand that it would benefit in allying with others. As a result, broad consensus on important and timely issues was seldom reached. This formation failed to clearly and, for the most part, honestly articulate points of member, self, and mutual interests. In the process, it also failed to meet the criterion of rising above provincial agendas and suspicions. Like the BKA, the BLR did not have an organizational response to the '92 riots. The reality that the Roundtable was not equipped to respond to a series of conflicts and the events of Spring '92 underscored the class and constituency limitations of the coalition even though Latino and African American tensions and conflicts continue to grow. Evidence of unequal partnerships and mistrust, suggested by Soto-Ortega and Kamasaki-Yzaguirre, were membership realities as well.

The Ethnic Coalition (TEC) and the New Majority Task Force, are, unlike the examples of the Alliance and the Roundtable, not tied to a public sector sponsor and continue to pursue multi-racial/ethnic goals from different ideological perspectives and political approaches. Formed in 1987 primarily by African American professional activists, TEC is traveling a more familiar route than the New Majority Task Force in attempting to reach multi-racial consensus goals. Created in the hope of becoming a powerful forum for multi-cultural policy issues and membered by a professional "who's who" of local African Americans, Latinos and Asians, the Coalition reflects a mainstream approach by essentially well-meaning professionals of color. Comprised of forty-five board members who break down into three fifteen-member caucuses (African, Latino and Asian American), TEC is ideologically moderate with a focus on four dominant issue areas: land use, transportation, environment, and governance. However, most of its energies have been incorporated into holding occasional forums, providing public policy perspectives, and lobbying policy makers at both state and local levels on an array of public policy issues related to these four areas. It became involved in pushing, at an elementary stage, single-member district inclusion models of representation on regional governmental and planning bodies, and, more recently, in expressing concern over environmental racism. Additionally, one of its most prominent members, Rae James, was appointed by L.A. Mayor Riordan to serve as a Deputy Mayor for Economic Development while a more recently appointed Deputy Mayor for Finance, Latina businesswoman Sofia Garcia-Conde Zuckerman, is being courted by TEC to fill a vacant seat, thereby setting up potential incorporation possibilities for TEC. However, at the same time TEC's Latino members have been expressing concern and frustration at the erosion, under Riordan, of Latino Commission and Board appointments they had in the City under Bradley.

The coalition has neither a strong organizational structure nor permanent staff members. Currently going through internal restructuring and policy issue focus determination, TEC's organizational and constituency-related weaknesses became apparent with the L.A. riots/uprisings, to which it did not offer an organization response or activities. Also, it has become apparent that in its attempt to build a consensus agenda, important issues (such as immigration) which are perceived to cause divides among it caucuses do not get seriously considered, although this may be changing.

TEC should not be dismissed but as the events and aftermath of Spring 1992 have made clear, its membership does not presently reflect a capability of rising above its intellectual and professional middle class membership roster and origins. Again, the assumption may be made that it does not connect with grassroots class and community diversity where much, if not most, of the inter-racial/ethnic tensions exist. Additionally, it does not link with progressive groups and coalitions thereby inhibiting its effectiveness and attraction. A membership dues requirement of $100 per year adds to the exclusive nature of the coalition. New members must be recruited by each caucus as slots become available. As with many of the coalitions referenced in this chapter, the average age of coalition members is "forty-something," significant inasmuch as inter-racial conflict in the city is primarily located at youth and young adult levels. Furthermore, Asian TEC members are exclusively Japanese Americans while Latino members are all Chicanos. In other words, the membership base is a backstep into the L.A. of twenty years ago. Neither newer Asian immigrants (Chinese, Koreans, Vietnamese, Cambodians) nor more recent Latino immigrants (namely Central Americans) are represented. As a result of these coalition realities, TEC seems to be mired in a socio-demographic "time warp" which does not link well with much of what Los Angeles has become over the past two decades. Although it bears some similarity to the "liberal" coalition depicted by Holloway (1968) and Browning, Marshall & Tabb (1984), it does not link well with the type of progressive coalition King called for and its agenda and style of work appear to be much broader and more diffuse that the focus on specific agendas and issues within that agenda stressed by Carmichael and Hamilton. Mass based coalition-building strategies called for by Carmichael and Hamilton as well as Browning, et. al., are altogether absent.

The New Majority Task Force (NMTF) is the most politically progressive of the bi-racial or multi-racial "coalitions" yet referenced. Created in a founding conference in 1989 to develop inclusive and community-based economic development models as alternatives to the top-down corporate-centered models and strategies thoroughly associated with the Bradley years in Los Angeles, its multi-cultural membership is a mixture of professional, intellectual and community representatives. In terms of its membership, three differences are distinguishable from previously mentioned coalition formations. First, the membership makeup of the Task Force is decidedly more politically left-of-center, that is, more obviously progressive. Second, and relatedly, the membership of the Task Force more clearly represents an inclusive economic development agenda for the city and region and a direction for the coalition. Thus, it has the more tightly focused agenda concentration, than the groups referenced above, as called for in the Carmichael-Hamilton thesis. Third, much of its membership links with community constituency organizations (e.g., Coalition of Neighborhood Developers, Southern Christian Leadership Conference, Holman Methodist Church, Barrio Planners).

The Task Force has been effective in getting one of its founding members (Mark Ridley-Thomas) elected to the L.A. City Council, on which it considers him to be its policy "lightning rod." In this regard, the Task Force might be considered to be incorporating itself politically into the politics of the city, including City Hall. Although Browning, et. al., (1984, 1989), addressed its incorporation approach to specific communities of color (mass level), it may also be argued that in order for incorporation to occur in a broader "rainbow" coalition context, the coalition must remained organized, mobilized, and in influential contact and interaction with the dominant coalition on the City Council, which in Los Angeles has become more clouded in the wake of the Riordan victory. Many see a developing moderate-to-conservative coalition of dominance on the Council that does not bode well for either Ridley-Thomas or the agenda of the Task Force.

Until the '92 riots, the Task Force had been sporadically meeting incorporation criteria. For example, it met irregularly and although its academic and professional members conducted important policy-related studies concerning public housing, practices of inner city lending agencies, and enterprise zones, the organization has been also beset by lack of direct and actual membership from neighborhoods it seeks to serve. However, these links are more clearly in place in comparison with the previously mentioned coalitions. Membership is open and fluid. To its credit, differing class perspectives are noted and discussed and guide much of its work. Since Spring '92, and in response to the riots, the Task Force has, once again, begun meeting regularly, filled part-time staff positions through member organization internships, linked with grassroots activist coalitions, and begun preparing for a policy-driven community economic development summit. In preparation for this "Summit," out of which a number of community economic development policy initiatives are expected to be generated, a series of educational forums have been held over the past year largely focused on trends in and implications of national and regional economic developments on local and neighborhood development initiatives and planning. For some members, however, this process has been overly intellectual, catering primarily to a progressive array of university professors and less to city planners, human relations staff, religious leadership and representatives of community based organizations concerned with economic development. This has become a limitation of omitting, albeit apparently unintentionally, community voices in planning processes associated with this organizational mega-event.

Although the coalition indeed places a premium on inclusive community economic development strategies and planning ("economic democracy"), issues of race and class, and avoidance of parochial organizational and individual attidudes, it has not devoted itself to the practical nature of politics, political structures and representation issues. This omission has become a limitation when coalition conversations and planning become more policy-oriented and policy-inclined.

The *Multicultural Collaborative* (MCC) is the most recent coalition formation and the only entity referenced in this chapter formed after the uprisings of 1992. The Collaborative is seeking to get beyond the failures of the Alliance and Roundtable as well as the limitations of the Ethnic Coalition, in part by focusing on key issues involving race and class, in part by assessing neighborhood needs in a variety of communities of color, in part by developing a grassroots organizing component, and in part by having full-time staff members and organizers. The three Co-Directors are comprised of a Latino, a Korean and an African American. The Collaborative's policy-making and multi-racial Board of Directors is made up of a number of organizations which are constituency and resource- based and which have histories of seeking solutions to inter-ethnic conflicts in Los Angeles. The Southern Christian Leadership Conference, Asian Pacific American Legal Association, Korean Youth and Community Services, and the Central American Refugee and Community Center (CARECEN) are among the Board's organizational representatives. Funded by private foundations at significant levels for its first two years, the Collaborative has begun participating in joint ventures with the New

Majority Task Force, the Coalition of Neighborhood Developers, and other community organizations. It has focused most of its recent attention in three program areas: neighborhood economic development, public education (developing curricula in high schools dealing with racial tensions), and media relations (providing openings for alternative access, voices and views). MCC members are trained to impart interpersonal, dialogue and problem-solving skills in designated communities and schools. However, as is true of any new coalition formation, MCC continues to grapple with process, that is, with how to most effectively carry out its three primary objectives in an area so vast and with problems so enormous. It continues to build relations with community groups and organizations.

The *Southern California Civil Rights Coalition* (SCCRC) was formed in 1990 ostensibly to develop support for the 1990 and, subsequently, 1991 Civil Rights Act. It is the umbrella for over fifty local organizations for the advancement of national, regional and, more recently, local concern on the civil rights front. Its membership reflects a "rainbow" of organizations that cut across racial and cultural lines and distinctions. However, with the passage of the Civil Rights Act of 1991 and in conditions similar to those coalitions represented in the Civil Rights Movement of the 1950s and 1960s after the passage of the Civil Rights Act of 1964 and the Voting Rights Act of 1965, the Coalition has been floundering largely as an umbrella coalition in search of issues to keep it alive, thereby "violating" one of the coalition-building principles called for in the approaches of Browning, et. al., Eisinger and Carmichael-Hamilton. This "search" is similar to the ongoing issues-searching process at TEC. Since the L.A. riots, much of the energy of SCSSC's most consistent member group representatives was spent debating whether it should disband or remain alive in altered and streamlined form. The latter was decided and although it has become primed on specific issues such as immigration and immigrant-bashing, its future is still open to question. This coalition formation is much more amorphous than either the MCC or the New Majority Task Force. In fact, this feature bears closer similarity to The Ethnic Coalition, although its membership is more class varied and more progressive politically.

Finally, the *United Neighborhoods Organization* (UNO) and the *Southern California Organizing Committee* (SCOC) might be described, in taking issue with Stewart's (1993) depiction of them as multi-racial coalition formations, as organizing coalitions with strong grassroots links. Both UNO and SCOC employ Alinsky-style strategies of confrontational politics to achieve their agendized objectives. At one time, each coalition represented near-exclusive working class memberships of Latinos (UNO) and African Americans (SCOC). Over the past several years, however, the membership of each has become more racially mixed, particularly SCOC. The coalitions have directed membership energies to such issues as public school reform, environmental injustice and racism, raising the minimum wage, inner-city prison locations and gang violence.

On this last issue, the nature of these organizational coalitions became most apparent with a recently-funded project. Hope in Youth is a multi-million dollar, multi-year anti-gang project funded through the (Catholic) Archdiocese of Los Angeles by L.A. City and County government, which the Church, UNO and SCOC lobbied extensively. UNO and SCOC are coalition partners with the Archiodcese in the Hope Program and, indeed, they were relied upon heavily by the Church in carrying out aggressive activities aimed at attempting to alternately influence and embarrass Mayor Bradley and his City Council supporters who were decidedly against using the city's coffers to pay for a church-related program. Cool relations had prevailed between the Archdiocese and Bradley as well as with Bradley allies such as organized labor leadership, even before the issue of Project funding arose. However, that relationship scenario changed when (Archdiocese chief) Cardinal Roger Mahoney's good friend Richard Riordan became Mayor.

The leadership and influence of the Church in this project, which is developing through UNO and SCOC organizing satellite community programs centered around local parishes in East Los Angeles and in South Central Los Angeles, has not been lost on those studying coalition politics. On other issues, these organizations have become involved in ad hoc and short-lived coalitions with other organizations such as the Southwest Voter and Education Project, NAACP local chapters, MALDEF (Mexican-American Legal Defense & Education Fund), NAACP-Legal Defense Fund, SCLC (Southern Christian Leadership Conference), and area churches. However, because of their often abrasive style and because they are widely perceived to dominate the coalitions they join, their coalition ventures tend to be limited. Additionally, these organizations are seen to be less independent than the coalitions referenced earlier because of their close relationship with, and frequent monetary dependence on, the Catholic Archdiocese of Los Angeles and/or other area churches.

Conclusions

In this chapter, I briefly explored selected theories of race relations and inter-racial coalition-building, applying tenets of those theories to selected coalition formations created since the mid-1980s ostensibly to work and link together on behalf of common political goals as well as to confront increasing racial polarization and inter-racial hostility in the City of Angels.

In finding agreement with Davis (1993) and Doherty (1993), it has become obvious that the public sector lacks the will and resources to commit to bridging serious divides in "human relations" in the city. In part, this is revealed by the extremely limited staffing of both the City's Department of Human Relations and the County's Commission on Human Relations. For example, the City of Los Angeles, with a population well beyond three-million residents, employs a single full-time person in its Department of Human Relations. The County of Los Angeles, with a population closing in on ten million residents, employs a staff of fifteen "consultants" to deal with conflicts among racial and ethnic groups in its jurisdiction. This lack of public sector resolve was perhaps most acutely demonstrated by the turning over the area's economic development and rebuilding responsibilities and obligations, especially on the part of the city and state, to the private sector driven, and secretive, RLA, where there is no public accountability or recourse.

The numerous calls to "join together," made both before and after the events of Spring '92, to heal the wounds which badly separate racial and ethnic groups in the city and region, have been both restrictive and, for the most part, shortsighted. Most unity calls, since the mid-1980s, have been aimed at bridging "dialogue gaps" between Korean and African Americans (see Norman 1992, Freer 1993, Sonenshein & Davis 1993). Fewer calls have been made to bridge dialogue and other gaps separating Latino and African Americans (see Calderon 1993, Hoffman 1993), while still fewer have been made to bring Latino, Korean and other Asian Americans together. Jewish and gentile Whites have been largely left out of the picture underscoring the degree to which many of the "calls" have been limited.

The commonalty of these calls, whether many or few, has been to begin the processes of discussion and dialogue, locate and build on presumed common ground, negotiate in good faith, and enjoy the inevitable healing that would result, in building towards the multicultural-cultural plurality the city had (only symbolically) become before the events of 1992. I contend that, based on simplistic analyses of fundamental problems responsible for much of the segregation and polarization found in both the city and county of Los Angeles, the calls (such as those of Starr, 1993 and Kotkin & Kinsey, 1993) for more and more discussion, dialogue and coalition-building without critical class and class mixture assessments, much less structural disjunctures and structural reforms, are similar to the bland messages of the L.A. mayoral candidates in election '93.

It is the view here that coalition failures in this period have been due to a combination of conceptual, structural and organizational problems: (1) improperly understanding the complexity of race and class relations and issues in Los Angeles, inclusive of a reliance on and not going beyond building middle class memberships and constituencies; (2) becoming too comfortable with critically unchallenged concepts of pluralism and multiculturalism; (3) being oblivious to the degree to which traditional theories and beliefs of representative democracy and public policy formation are not working for communities of color; (4) failures to broadly recognize and confront the degree to which anti-democratic corporatist approaches have failed those most in need of economic development and job creation; (5) failure to set clear and strategic goals, realizable objectives, and targeted activities and outcomes; and (6) being unwilling to overcome provincial outlooks and agendas.

Social class and other critical issues referenced in Section III are largely absent from the perspectives and analyses of most of the "coalition" efforts responding to increasing calls to unite the city. This absence factored heavily into coalition failures mentioned in the previous section. Additionally, limited constituency bases, narrow foci restricted to some magical notion of dialogue, unclear generalized goals, and membership made up largely of middle-aged professionals with few ties to youth groups and young adults, also helped to preempt their efficacy and longevity. As such, they became part of the failed elite vision that had prematurely labeled Los Angeles as already being a model of multi-cultural pluralist inclusion and democracy. As argued in this chapter, the events of Spring, 1992 thoroughly exposed this as merely symbolism and charade. Also exposed was the notion that dialogue opportunities alone, especially in the absence of class and racial analyses, mixtures, and directed efforts, on the one hand, and sustainable agendas for structural innovations and changes in the city and county, on the other, cannot close the severe "racial" divides.

The coalitions seldom, if ever, intersect with one another. This is most pronounced among the most "professionalized" of the coalitions, past and continuing. Although all have operated programs in open space venues, with few exceptions the coalitions have not devoted themselves to a series of on-going demands and pressure for the public sector to devote more ongoing space dedicated to programming seeking critical dialogue and understanding. It should be noted that Cal State L.A. helped to provide a basis for interracial cooperation and coalition-building among Latino, African and Asian American community legal advocates through sponsoring a series of forums on redistricting, voting rights and political representation in the mid and late 1980s. It is a role that universities and communities should expand in providing neutral public space programs for serious exploration of key issues dividing communities. With the exception of the New Majority Task Force, none of the coalitions is membered by, or is in organized contact with, the few dispute resolution centers or teams in the city. With the many youth, race and class-related problems manifest in a variety of forms in the metropolitan area, it is difficult to believe these links have not been developed or explored.

With the above in mind, I contended in this chapter that the shape and substance of L.A.s' future resides, in large part, on the extent to which influential multi-cultural, class-sensitive coalitions are created and sustained. The building of such coalitions, in my view, must begin by asking and assessing key questions and critical concerns, such as those relating to the (1) practical meaning of representative democracy and political incorporation particularly among communities of color, (2) degree to which working class and poor communities can become incorporated into economic development planning and outcome scenarios in the city, (3) interlinked issues of race and class which act as communication barriers and socio-economic divides, and (4) practical meaning and application of multi-cultural pluralism as a goal for the city.

Of the coalitions referenced in this paper, only the New Majority Task Force and the Multi-Cultural Collaborative appear to meet most of the concerns and questions raised in this paper. However, their future is anything but certain in the complex and difficult terrain known as "L.A."

References

Browning, Rufus P., Dale Rogers Marshall and David Tabb. 1984. *Protest is not Enough: The Struggle of Blacks and Hispanics for Equality in Urban Politics*. Berkeley: University of California Press.

———. (eds.). 1989. *Racial Politics in American Cities*. (New York): Longman.

Brownstein, Ronald. 1993 (November 4). "Big City Voters Forge New Era of Pragmatic Mayors." *Los Angeles Times*. A1, 23.

Calderon, Jose. 1993. "Latinos and Asian Pacific Americans: The Role of Leadership and Strategy in Multi-Ethnic Coalition Building." An unpublished paper.

Carmichael, Stokely and Charles V. Hamilton. 1967. *Black Power*. New York: Vintage Press.

Clifford, Frank. 1993 (January 20). "Candidates Offer Tonics to Heal City." *Los Angeles Times*. B1.

Connell, Rich. 1993 (November 29). "City Hall Power Shifts to Eclectic, Pragmatic Team." *Los Angeles Times*. A1, 24.

Davis, Mike. 1990. *City of Quartz: Excavating the Future of Los Angeles*. (London): Verso.

———. 1993. "Who Killed L.A.? The War Against the Cities." *Crossroads* (June): 2-19.

Doherty, Jake. 1992. "Black-Korean Alliance Says Talk Not Enough, Disbands." *Los Angeles Times*. (December 24): A-1.

Dymally, Mervyn M. "Afro-Americans and Mexican-Americans: The Politics of Coalition." In Charles Wollenberg (ed.). 1970. *Ethnic Conflict in California History*. (Los Angeles): Tinnon-Brown, Inc. 155-71.

Dymski, Gary A. and John M. Veitch. 1992. "Race and the Financial Dynamics of Urban Growth: L.A. as Fay Wray." In Gerry Riposa and Carolyn Dersch (eds.), *City of Angels*. Dubuque: Kendall/Hunt. PP 131-57.

Eisinger, Peter K. 1986. "Local Civil Service Employment and Black Socio-economic Mobility." *Social Science Quarterly* 67, No. 1 (March): 169-175.

———. 1976. *Patterns of Interracial Politics*. New York: Academic Press.

Estrada, Leobardo F. and Sylvia Sensiper. 1993. "Mending the Politics of Division in Post-Rebellion L.A." In *South Central Los Angeles: Anatomy of an Urban Crisis*. Edited by Allen J. Scott and E. Richard Brown. Lewis Center for Regional Policy Studies. 123-38.

Feldman, Paul. 1994 (February 16). "Griego and Cook Take RLA Helm." *Los Angeles Times*. B1, 3.

———. 1993 (November 2). "Ready, Willing, Unable." *Los Angeles Times*. A22, 23.

Fulton, William. 1992 (December 20). "Break Up CRA to Best Rebuild L.A." *Los Angeles Times*. M1, 6.

Freer, Regina. 1993. "A Slice of the Pie: The Localization of Conflict and Mediation Between the African American and Korean American Communities in Los Angeles." A paper presented at the Annual Meeting of the Western Political Science Association, Pasadena, California.

Harwood Group. 1993. *Meaningful Chaos: How People Form Relationships with Public Concerns*. Dayton: The Kettering Founda-tion.

Henry, Charles and Carlos Munoz, Jr. 1991. "Ideological and Interest Linkages in California Rainbow Politics." In Byran O. Jackson and Michael B. Preston (eds.), *Racial and Ethnic Politics in California*. Berkeley: IGS Press. PP. 323-38.

Hero, Rodney E. 1992. *Latinos and the U.S. Political System: Two-Tiered Pluralism*. Philadelphia: Temple University Press.

Himmelman, Arthur Turovh. 1991. "Communities Working Collaboratively For A Change." Washington, D.C.: Community Information Exchange.

Hoch, Charles. 1984. "City Limits: Municipal Boundary Formation and Class Segregation." In William K. Tabb and Larry Sawers (eds), *Marxism and the Metropolis*. (New York): Oxford University Press. 101-19.

Hoffman, Adonis E. 1993 (October 18). "The Black-Latino Alliance Withers." *Los Angeles Times*. B7.

Jackson, Byran O. 1990. "Black Political Power in the City of Angels: An Analysis of Mayor Tom Bradley's Electoral Success." *National Political Science Review* 2: 169-75.

Jackson, Byran O. and Michael Preston (eds.). 1991. *Racial and Ethnic Politics in California.* (Berkeley): IGS Press.

Johnson, James H., Jr. and Melvin L. Oliver. 1989. "Interethnic Minority Conflict in Urban America: The Effects of Economic and Social Dislocations."

Kamasaki, Charles and Raul Yzaguirre. 1991. "Black-Hispanic Tensions: One Perspective." A paper presented at the 1991 Annual Meeting of the American Political Science Association. Washington, D.C.

Katz, Jesse. 1993 (December 26). "Clashes Between Latino, Black Gangs Increase." *Los Angeles Times.* A1.

Kaufmann, Karen. 1994. "Us Versus Them: A Group Conflict Analysis of the 1993 Los Angeles Mayoral Election. A paper presented at the annual meeting of the Western Political Science Association. Albuquerque.

King, Martin Luther, Jr. 1967. *Where Do We Go From Here?* New York: Harper and Row.

Kinsey, Bernard, Tony Salazar, Barry Sanders & Peter Ueberroth. 1992 (December 20). "The People's Effort Progresses." *Los Angeles Times.* M5.

Klein, Norman M. 1990. "The Sunshine Strategy: Buying and Selling the Fantasy of Los Angeles." In N. Klein & M. Schiesl (editors), *20th Century Los Angeles.* Claremont, CA: Regina Press.

Kotkin, Joel and Bernard Kinsey. 1993. "Beyond the Angry Rhetoric: An Overlooked L.A. Story." *Los Angeles Times* (September 19): M1.

Krikorian, Greg. 1993 (August 29). "The Bottleneck." *Los Angeles Times.* City Times: 15, 16.

Kwoh, Stewart. 1989. In Regalado, J. (Editor). *Political Battles Over L.A. County Board Seats: A Minority Perspective.* Los Angeles: PBI Publications.

Lee, Patrick. 1993 (November 29). "Factory Flight." *Los Angeles Times.* D1, 2.

Lopez, Robert J. 1993 (December 12). "LAPD Urged to Reduce 'Black-on-Brown' Crime." *Los Angeles Times.* City Times: 3, 4.

Mann, Eric. 1989. "New Coalitions for L.A.'s Future." *LA Weekly.* 11 (February 24 - March 2): 49.

———. (ed.). 1993a. *Reconstructing Los Angeles From the Bottom Up.* Los Angeles: Labor/Community Strategy Center.

———.1993b. "The Poverty of Corporatism." *The Nation* (March 29): 406-11.

Mendez, Carlos. "Metropolis Now." *LA Village View* (August 27-September 2): 26-7, 39.

Modarres, Ali. 1994. *Racial and Ethnic Structure of Los Angeles County.* (Los Angeles): PBI Publications.

Mollenkopf, John. 1989. "New York: The Great Anomaly." In Rufus Browning, et. al. (eds.), *Racial Politics in American Cities.* New York: Longman Press. PP. 75-87.

Norman, Alex J. 1992. "Black-Korean Encounter: Toward Understanding An Alliance." A paper presented at the Black-Korean Encounter Conference. Los Angeles.

Pastor, Manuel & C. Hayling (eds.). 1990. *Economic Development: The New Majority in Los Angeles*. Los Angeles: Occidental College.

———. 1993. *Latinos and the Los Angeles Uprising: The Economic Context*. Claremont: The Tomas Rivera Center.

Peterson, Paul. 1981. *City Limits*. Chicago: University of Chicago Press.

Proffitt, Steve. 1994 (February 27). "Linda Griego, Lodwrick Cook: Redefining RLA as an Engine of Economic Development." *Los Angeles Times*. M3.

Regalado, James A. 1991. "Organized Labor the Los Angeles City Politics: The Bradley Years." *Urban Affairs Quarterly* (September): 27, pp. 87-108.

———. 1992. "Political Representation, Economic Development Policymaking, and Social Crisis in Los Angeles, 1973-1992." In Gerry Riposa and Carolyn Dersch, *City of Angels*. Dubuque: Kendall/Hunt Publishing Company. PP. 159-79.

———. 1991b. "Reapportionment and Coalition-Building: A Case Study of Informal Barriers to Latino Empowerment in Los Angeles County." In Roberto Villarreal and Norma Hernandez (eds.), *Latinos and Political Coalitions*. New York: Greenwood Press. PP. 126-43.

———.1989. "Political Battles Over L.A. County Board Seats: A Minority Perspective." (Los Angeles): PBI Publications.

Seo, Diane. 1993 (July 18). "The Go-Betweens." *Los Angeles Times*. City Times: 14-16, 19.

Shingles, Richard D. 1991. "Relations Between Americans of Latino and African Decent: A Comparative Framework for Understanding Differences and Commonalities." A paper presented a the Fourth Annual Conference on Latino Issues. Wayne State University.

Soja, Edward W. 1989. "New Economic Order: When the First and Third Worlds Meet." *LA Weekly* 11 (February 24 - March 2): 21-26.

Sonenshein, Raphael J. and Corecia J. Davis. 1993. "The Battle Over Liquor Stores in South Central Los Angeles." A paper presented at the 1993 annual meeting of the Western Political Science Association. Pasadena, California.

Sonenshein, Raphael J. 1993. *Politics in Black and White: Race and Power in Los Angeles*. Princeton: Princeton University Press.

Stone, Clarence N. and Heywood T. Sanders (editors). 1987. *The Politics of Urban Development*. University of Kansas Press.

———. 1989. "The Dynamics of Bi-racial Coalitions: Crossover Politics in Los Angeles." *Western Political Quarterly* (June): 42, 333-53.

Spring, Greg. 1993a (August 16). "Certified Commissioners." *Downtown News*. 1, 4.

———. 1993b (August 9). "Whither the CRA Now?" *Downtown News*. 4, 6.

Soto-Ortega, Samuel. 1970. "A Chicano Response." In Wollenberg (cited). 173-82.

Starr, Kevin. 1993. "For L.A., There Is No Destiny Without Unity." *Los Angeles Times*. (October 24): M1.

Stewart, Jill. 1993. "Black Flight." *LA Weekly* (October 29-November 4): 18-28.

Underwood, Katherine. 1994. "Pioneering Rainbow Coalitions in Los Angeles: The Case of Edward Roybal and Gilbert Lindsay." A paper presented at the annual meeting of the Western Political Science Association. Albuquerque.

Uhlaner, Carole J. 1991. "Perceived Discrimination and Prejudice and the Coalition Prospects of Blacks, Latinos, and Asian Americans." In Byran O. Jackson and Michael B. Preston, *Racial and Ethnic Politics in California*. Berkeley: IGS Press. PP. 339-71.

Valle, Victor and Rudy D. Torres. 1992 (December 6). "Enough of the Great Melodrama of Race Relations." *Los Angeles Times*. M6.

Webster, William H. Special Advisor to the Board of Police Commissioners. 1992. "The City in Crisis." Los Angeles.

Wollenberg, Charles (ed.). 1970. *Ethnic Conflict in California History*. (Los Angeles): Tinnon-Brown, Inc.

Zellers, James. 1993 (January 28). "Third World Wages Won't Rebuild L.A." *Los Angeles Times*. B7.

10

Urban Rioting in Los Angeles: A Comparison of 1965 with 1992

David O. Sears

The nation is rapidly moving toward two increasingly separate Americas. Within two decades, this division could be so deep that it would be almost impossible to unite: a white society principally located in suburbs, in smaller central cities, and in the peripheral parts of large central cities, and a Negro society largely concentrated within large central cities.

—Kerner Commission (1968, p. 407).

I read [the] report. . . . of the 1919 riot in Chicago, and it as if I were reading the report of the investigating committee on the Harlem riot of '35, the report of the investigating committee on the Harlem riot of '43, the report of the McCone Commission on the Watts riot. I must again in candor say to you members of this Commission—it is a kind of Alice in Wonderland—with the same moving picture re-shown over and over again, the same analysis, the same recommendations, and the same inaction.

—Kenneth B. Clark (In Kerner Commission report, 1968, p. 29).

Many commentators have referred to the police brutality verdict and rebellion as a strong 'wake-up call'. . . . Sadly, our data provide no substantial indication that this 'wake up call' has been heard.

—Bobo et al. (Chapter 5).

Can we all get along?

—Rodney King, 1992

At 7 PM on August 11, 1965, a black man, Marquette Frye, having had several "screwdrivers" celebrating his brother's return to Los Angeles from military service, was weaving his way home down the freeway at a speed exceeding the legal limit. A motorcycle officer of the California Highway Patrol pulled him over at 166th Street and Avalon Boulevard, in the heart of the Los Angeles neighborhood known as "Watts." Frye's behavior was somewhat boisterous, though humorous and cooperative, but it attracted a crowd on a hot summer evening. Frye later became belligerent, as did the crowd, and other officers were summoned. His brother and mother arrived, and before long all three Fryes were on their way to jail, and the police departed leaving behind a wake of thrown rocks and bottles and bricks.

So began the "Watts riot" of 1965. Soon an area larger than the city of San Francisco was cordoned off by the National Guard as a "curfew zone." Nevertheless, the rioting continued for six days, leaving 34 dead, over 1000 injured badly enough to require treatment, nearly 4000 arrested, and 1000 buildings damaged or destroyed, at a probable loss, in 1965 dollars, of $40 million (Sears and McConahay, 1973). Local white officials denounced the rioters as inspired by "outside agitators," while black leaders tended more to see it as a racial protest.

Nearly 27 years later, on April 29, 1992, the acquittal in Simi Valley, California of four Los Angeles Police Department officers of charges related to the widely televised beating of Rodney King, a black motorist, set off more rioting in South Central Los Angeles. The police were wholly unprepared for the outbreak. The Chief was at a fundraiser in the posh suburb of Brentwood when it began, and did not leave it for some time. The police were wholly outnumbered and outgunned during the first evening, and lost control of great stretches of the city. After the first night, the entire city of Los Angeles was placed under a dusk-to-dawn curfew. Again the riot itself lasted six days. Nearly 14,000 law enforcement personnel from outside the city were required to stop it. Over 16,000 people were arrested, 52 lost their lives, and nearly $1 billion in property had been damaged or destroyed.

Initially the events seemed quite similar to those of the Watts riots in 1965, in that the rioters were predominantly black, the area of the rioting similar, the local police again quickly lost control and had to be supplemented by the National Guard, while the Chief of Police made hard-line, inflammatory statements about the rioters. As a result, initially the events were interpreted in familiar terms. Some once again saw street hoodlums (this time local gang members, not "outside agitators") as using the pretext of political events to pillage, loot, and injure the innocent, and so it was a "riot." Others saw another in a long line of black protests against social injustice, and so it was a "rebellion" or an "insurrection" of an oppressed people. But was it a 1960's ghetto riot all over again? Or was it, as some of these authors maintain, "a new form," "the first urban unrest of the 21st century"? This essay sketches out some of the similarities and differences between the two events, in an effort to understand both the meaning of the events themselves, and the social conditions underlying them.

Watts in 1965 and the Politics of Violence

Soon after the Watts riots of August, 1965, a group of social scientists at UCLA embarked on an ambitious multi-disciplinary research effort on the rioting. Much of it was published in a volume edited by Nathan Cohen (1970), the leader of the team. Our own account appeared in more detailed form as *The Politics of Violence: The New Urban Blacks and the Watts Riot* (Sears and McConahay, 1973). A simple approach to the comparison of these two events begins with a review of the main conclusions of the latter book.

Causes of the Riot

The theory of the riot's causes had three parts. First, we saw the broader white context as characterized by both a high degree of racial isolation and a new "symbolic racism" that had replaced the old-fashioned Jim Crow racism of the old South. A striking level of racial isolation did exist, due not to formal segregation but to the great geographical dispersion of the LA basin, the relatively small numbers of blacks, combined with the *de facto* segregation typical of Northern and Western American urban areas, and black invisibility in the media (Johnson, Sears, and McConahay, 1971). The new form of racism we proposed—symbolic racism—was described as a blend of traditional (and race-neutral) American values such as individualism with "the mild stereotyped white prejudice common to northern whites . . . " (p. 199). A second component was a collection of longstanding grievances widespread among blacks in Los Angeles, including police brutality toward blacks, gouging by merchants, perceptions of racial discrimination (especially in the schools), and the negative attitudes held toward the black community by such public leaders as the Mayor and Police Chief. These grievances tended not to divide along demographic lines among blacks; rather, they tended to be fairly widely distributed throughout the black community. The riot itself was triggered by "a typical `grievance,' involving an individual black who felt maltreated by an unsympathetic institution, largely managed and staffed by whites, following its standard operating procedures" (p. 198).

The third component was a theory of the "new urban blacks." The great migration of blacks from the South to Los Angeles had occurred during the 1940's and 1950's, so the first generation of young Los Angeles natives was coming into maturity only in the mid-1960's. This new generation of natives were urban and Northern-socialized, better educated and more politically sophisticated than their largely rural, Southern, and migrant forebears, and more angry, disaffected, anti-white, and proud of being black as well.

The data analysis indicated that the rioters tended to reflect these last two components: they were more aggrieved than non-rioters, and they tended to be young, Northern and urban-reared, anti-white, pro-black, disaffected, and frustrated. These data were interpreted as supporting the view that the rioting had been, to some substantial degree, a racial protest against bad local conditions, as well as reflecting more general support among the coming genera-tion of young Northern blacks for confronting racial inequality directly.

A series of other theories of rioting were also tested and rejected. Most prominently, the rioters did not fit the widely heralded profile of the "riff-raff" or urban underclass—they were somewhat more likely to be unemployed than non-rioters, but they were not less educated, or from broken homes, or Southern newcomers. Nor did they did not fit Banfield's (1970) "rioting for fun and profit" theory. They were not especially Southern-socialized; genuine discontents seemed to have motivated much of the rioting, rather than mere rampaging or foraying for pillage; and the "racial protest" interpretation of the rioting common throughout the area proved, as best we could tell, not to be mere post hoc rationalization. Whereas social contagion was no doubt widespread and accounted for some of the rioting, the data argued against its being the *principal* or primary explanation (p. 201).

The Legacy of "Watts"

The riot had a strongly polarizing effect on blacks and whites. Our analysis uncovered the spread throughout the black community, in the months following the riot, of what we called a "riot ideology"—the belief that it had been a racial protest founded on realistic grievances, that it was likely to have useful effects, combined with some sympathy for the rioters. This ideology was especially prevalent among the young, and indeed Southern newcomers seemed to be increasingly socialized to this new view of things.

Local white leaders at the time of "Watts" took a hard law

enforcement line, but the liberal Democrats then in charge of the state and federal government were more sympathetic. The white public responded with ambivalence: many also viewed it as a racial protest, and expected that it would lead to greater white awareness of blacks' problems, but supported the authorities and thought it would increase the gap between the races.

This presaged the ambivalent white response to the ghetto riots throughout the 1960's. On the one hand, elites often responded sympathetically, as in the McCone Commission report in Los Angeles or the Kerner Commission report nationally. These were followed by many active policy responses, such as school integration, affirmative action, and many efforts to reduce poverty in inner cities. Yet they also led to the spread of a strong "law and order" mentality among moderate and conservative whites throughout the country, and to the reactive conservative political campaigns of George Wallace and many local leaders (such as the then-Mayor of Los Angeles, Sam Yorty; see Kinder and Sears, 1981).

We concluded with four general predictions for the future:

1. Increasing ghetto tensions, based on the continuing existence of social conditions giving rise to realistic grievances, combined with increasing black sophistication.
2. Some continuing increase in violence as a strategy for dealing with those grievances, We did not expect further mass violence in the short run, but perhaps activities more akin to guerrilla action or conventional crime. We also anticipated increasingly creative and widely varying political strategies, and increasingly effective use of conventional electoral politics.
3. In terms of the white institutional response, we underlined the combination of anger and sympathy noted above. This threatened to make race an increasingly polarizing political issue (as it has become; see Carmines and Stimson, 1991; Edsall, 1993). And in doing so, we feared it might jeopardize one area of optimism shared by blacks in the 1960's—hopeful attitudes toward a federal government that had been favorably disposed toward blacks' aspirations through the administrations of FDR, Harry Truman, JFK, and Lyndon Johnson.
4. Finally, increasing racial isolation threatened America's urban areas, for two reasons: some increase in blacks' racial pride, and whites' fears of blacks (especially in terms of crime). School integration seemed at the time to be the most difficult looming issue.

What Had Changed? The Broad Context

So what, if anything, had changed in the intervening 27 years?

Blacks in South Central Los Angeles

The area of the rioting seems superficially similar: South-Central Los Angeles. To be sure, the heart of the rioting in 1965 was "Watts," an area around 103rd Street and Central Avenue, whereas in 1992, its heart was some distance to the northwest. But in both cases, the rioting was centered in areas that had been predominantly black since World War II.

Had the social and economic status of the black population improved in that period? Not dramatically. Americans in general were, in 1965, in the midst of the great postwar economic surge. It was an era that had finally and irrevocably integrated the European immigrant groups of the late 19th and early 20th century into mainstream American society, many into the middle class. Blacks were the major non-integrated group, and the most disadvantaged. In 1992 this was still true. More young black men were in prison than in college, unemployment was soaring, most black children were being raised in female-headed households, etc. etc. etc.

At a larger level, many macroeconomic changes had impacted severely on blacks in the area (and in most other inner cities as well). The globalization of capital and labor had resulted in the loss of hundreds of thousands of industrialized jobs in areas close to South Central Los Angeles in the 1970's and 1980's. As a result, unemployment and welfare dependency skyrocketed. Even the great economic development that had taken place in Los Angeles in that period had been concentrated downtown and in West Los Angeles, bypassing South Central. On top of all that, the Bush and Reagan administrations had systematically dismantled many public welfare and safety services, leaving the area with fewer resources for dealing with its serious social and economic problems.

Ethnic Change

But the area had changed more than this implies. As of 1965, the American population had been ethnically stable for many years, after the large flows of immigration from Eastern and Southern Europe were cut off in 1924. In 1965, South Central Los Angeles was almost all African-American, and had been for two decades. One source of cleavage was between the recent black migrants from the South and blacks who had been living there for a decade or more. But even the "newcomers" came from the same culture that the older residents (or their parents) had originally come from, and were of the same race.

In 1992, America was in the midst of another surge of immigration, most visibly from Asia, Mexico, and Central America, but from many other nations as well, as wide-ranging as Iran, Russia, and India. Los Angeles was in the front lines of this wave, and so its demographic makeup had changed sharply, from overwhelmingly white (71% in 1970) to decidedly mixed (41% white in 1990, 38% Latino, with as many Asians as blacks). And the change had been abrupt. Over the prior decade, the Latino population had increased by 1.3 million, and the Asian population had doubled, while the black population had remained about constant and the number of whites had actually diminished. South Central Los Angeles in particular had changed; by 1992, it was almost half Latino. Another major concentration of new Latino immigrants was in the Pico-Union district just to the north.

These changes generated considerable ethnic conflict. Latinos had long shared the conventional prejudices against blacks (e.g., Oliver & Johnson, 1984; also see Mexican-Americans' negative responses to the Watts rioting, in Sears and McConahay, 1973). But the recent massive influx of Latinos had exacerbated these tensions. They themselves had come from quite a variety of nations and cultures, not just Mexico. So the cultural clashes between blacks and groups moving into historically black neighborhoods were potentially even sharper than they might have been had the latter been of longer standing and from more familiar backgrounds.

And blacks and Latinos were struggling for the same piece of the small, and shrinking, economic pie in South Central Los Angeles—the flight of jobs, the influx of immigrants willing to work for less, and increasing demand for shrinking public services. In this struggle, Latinos seemed to have some advantages. Absent the legacy of slavery and a century of subsequent discrimination, they were less angry and violent, and whites often tended to trust them more. And they were often willing to work for lower wages and to forego unionization (Miles, 1992).

In 1965, the area's merchants had largely been either white (often Jewish) or black. By 1992 they came from a much greater variety of nations, including many from various Asian nations, especially Korea. Severe conflicts existed between blacks and Koreans, surrounding the latter's commercial successes (see Light and Bonacich, 1988). Blacks often felt Koreans exploited them, overcharging for goods and refusing to hire black employees, and were too ready to accuse blacks of shoplifting and other criminal behavior (Tierney, Chapter 7). The Asians rarely lived in South-Central (less than 1% was Asian in 1990), but inhabited a number of neighborhoods ringing that area, such as

"Koreatown," in the Wilshire District between South-Central and Hollywood. This exacerbated the tension: Asians were prominent as local shopkeepers, but did not live in the area or play any other role in it.

The black-Korean conflicts came to a head in 1991 with a Korean merchant's (ultimately televised) shooting of the black teenager Latasha Harlins in the back of the head, and then with the shooting of another black in a liquor store. In both cases the courts gave no jail time to the persons responsible for the shooting. This led to boycotts by blacks of Korean merchants. The blacks felt they were not respected by the Koreans; the Koreans felt outrage in turn because they felt little attention was paid to the dangers they faced, including the shooting of Korean merchants. The Koreans struggled with their own racism, but it was quite real, and blacks often did not understand or appreciate Korean culture. So cultural misunderstanding was rife. Underlying much of this conflict also was blacks' anger about being denied access to the American dream; once again African-Americans were being passed by, as ambitious immigrants from many lands and cultures found fertile economic ground in America.

Political Context

What about the political context? The rioting in 1965 occurred at the end of the civil rights decade's rollback of the centuries'-old system of white racial dominance in the South. Optimism abounded; the national government seemed sympathetic, as did much of the white population of the nation (at least outside the South). Locally, very little white support for formal segregation existed (Sears and Kinder, 1971), and nationally, (Schuman, Steeh, and Bobo, 1985) whites had become considerably more sympathetic to blacks' search for equality. Moreover, many whites understood the persisting impact of racial discrimination on maintaining racial inequality (Bobo et al., Chapter 5).

Moreover, by 1992 blacks seemed much more politically powerful than they had been in 1965. One of the most powerful political figures in the state was the black Speaker of the state Assembly, Willie Brown. Locally, the conservative midwestern white, Sam Yorty, had long since been replaced in the mayor's office by the moderate black, Tom Bradley.

Nevertheless, a number of warning signals existed. Racial isolation continued: "white flight" drove many white schoolchildren out of the mammoth Los Angeles school district in the 1970's and 1980's, and white adults followed. Conventional racial stereotypes damaging to blacks persisted: in 1992, blacks were regarded as the least intelligent and the most likely to be welfare-dependent of the four major ethnic groups, and the least welcome in Angelenos' own neighborhoods (Bobo et al., Chapter 5). The 1988 and 1990 national elections had presented blacks in their oldest and most degrading stereotypical form, in advertising such as the Willie Horton ad or in Jesse Helms' blunt attacks on affirmative action for blacks. The national administration seemed responsive to blacks only in putting a fervent black foe of affirmative action and civil rights on the Supreme Court. And Bradley's own support had waned somewhat, first in the black community as he cultivated Westside white liberals and the downtown business community in two decades of economic development, and then in the broader community as political scandals mounted.

Finally, the Los Angeles Police Department had been perhaps the single most aggravating element for blacks in 1965, particularly symbolized by its hardline longtime Chief, William Parker. Little had changed. The LAPD was responsible for the beating of Rodney King in 1991, and acquittal of those officers triggered the disturbances in 1992. The then-Chief, Daryl Gates, was fully as outspoken and uncompromising as Parker ever had been. The LAPD's investment in elite units rather than grassroots, community-based patrolling only exacerbated that.

The Events Themselves: Comparison with the Watts Riot of 1965

So how 1992 differ from the Watts Riot of 1965? First of all, the level of violence and scope of destruction were considerably greater, and the entire city was placed under curfew. Still, perhaps it is fairest to say bigger, but a similar event, in these terms.

However, the catalytic agent in 1992 was quite different, both more noteworthy and more sympathetic. The individual black drunk driver whose failed arrest by the CHP began the Watts riot was little noted and quickly forgotten. In contrast, Rodney King's beating was broadcast throughout the world, as was the jury verdict that stimulated the rioting. Opposition to the King verdict was overwhelming in all ethnic groups; over 60% of the whites in Los Angeles disagreed with it (Bobo et al., Chapter 5).

The participants in the rioting in 1965 were almost all black. Mexican-Americans were not seen as major players in the social drama. The small sample of Mexican-Americans interviewed after the 1965 rioting received only brief summary treatment, and in any case their attitudes were almost identical to those of whites (even exceeding whites' praise for the authorities' handling of the riot; see Sears and

McConahay, 1973, pp. 164-166). In 1992, by contrast, over half of those arrested were Latino (51%, with only 36% black; see Petersilia and Abrahams, Chapter 6). This change paralleled the dramatic increase in Latino residents of South Central Los Angeles (from 80% black to 45% Latino), though obviously it was not compelled by that demographic change.

The targets of looting and burning in 1965 were not thoroughly documented. But in 1992 the violence was obviously quite systematically aimed at Korean merchants. No other ethnic group came remotely close in terms of loss: 54% of those businesses that were totally lost had been owned by Koreans, of whom the largest number sold apparel (Tierney, Chapter 7). Some organized vigilante Korean defense forces literally fought off invaders at gunpoint, and other Koreans simply abandoned their properties in the face of the intense hostility toward them.

Attitudes toward the authorities were quite different in the two years. In 1965, the races polarized quite sharply, whites supporting them and blacks feeling they were ineffective or worse. Blacks were overwhelmingly unfavorable toward both the white mayor and the police chief (Sears and McConahay, 1973). In 1992, all ethnic groups felt the LAPD was ineffective, and were vehemently negative toward Police Chief Gates (e.g., only 18% of the whites supported him; see Sonenshein, Chapter 3). The mayor again polarized the races, but in the reverse direction: this time blacks supported the mayor, who was black himself. Most important, though, blacks' estrangement from the criminal justice system continued; most felt that it treated them unfairly (Bobo et al., Chapter 5).

In 1965, the dominant view in each ethnic group was that it was a black protest (though fewer whites than blacks used such political terms as "rebellion" or "insurrection" to describe it: 13% compared to 38%; see Sears and McConahay, 1973). In 1992, only blacks saw it as "mainly a protest" (68% did); whites, Asians, and Hispanics saw it mainly as "looting and crime" (Bobo et al., Chapter 5). Unhappily there are no day-by-day data on this point; many observers felt that it initially looked like as a racial protest of the King beating and verdict, but evolved into looting and chaos later on.

Finally, several of the immediate effects of the riots seem to me noteworthy. First, the King verdict seems to have increased blacks' belief in racial discrimination, greater belief that blacks are treated unfairly, and more black alienation. Blacks much more than other ethnic groups believe that the rioting was a racial protest (Bobo et al., Chapter 5). Second, Asians became more pessimistic and more negative toward blacks, and there is no evidence of a "wake-up call" having been received by whites. Blacks remained the group most often bearing the brunt of negative stereotypes and discrimination. Third, the entire community did show a marked loss of confidence in the police and especially Chief Gates, a loss of confidence that contributed to the passage of a later ballot proposition cutting the power of the police chief and increasing civilian control over the police (Sonenshein, Chapter 3). And fourth, the world wide news reporting capacities of CNN sped the word of the King verdict, the Denny beating, and the rest of the events around the globe in an instant. Yet, surprisingly, there was little spread of the rioting, much less than in, for example, 1967 or 1968. Perhaps these effects help us to understand the modesty of the "rebuilding" efforts that have occurred in the area subsequent to the riots.

Systematic Theories of the Rioting

The events thus soon turned from a stark and tragic but simple political stimulus, eliciting the usual interpretive suspects, to a vast and complex Rorschach card, yielding an equally diverse set of explanations for the rioting. This variety of popular theories is mirrored in the scholarly theories offered in this volume. Five stand out.

Social Contagion and Rioting for Fun and Profit

The version of social contagion theory that grew out of the 1960's ghetto riots was described as the "assembling process" (McPhail, 1971). Collective violence emerges from the assembling of crowds of people who simply happen to be close by. No crowds, no violence. Some of the current authors allude to this: the densely populated neighborhoods of South Central Los Angeles provided such crowds of available participants (Tierney, Chapter 7), with a "large number of young men at liberty", "with time on their hands," who could readily get caught up in some rioting (Morrison and Lowry, Chapter 2).

Edward Banfield (1970) popularized the notion that the ghetto riots of the 1960's were carried out "for fun and profit," by young men with excess energy who "rampaged" through the ghetto, taking such goods as liquor and television sets for pure pleasure. In 1992 the TV coverage of the riot gave rise to much of this, whether the wholly arbitrary and senseless and brutal beatings of innocents (such as Reginald Denny) or the pictures of healthy young men loading up their pickup trucks with any goods they could pry loose from retail stores. Morrison and Lowry saw the rioters as an available and unoccupied "pool of young men" hanging around the streetcorners in South Central Los Angeles; "the resulting explosion of human energy lacked political focus" rather than serving as the vanguard of an insurrection against abominable social conditions.

A related notion was the "criminal element" or "riff-raff" theory of ghetto riots so popular among conservatives in the 1960's. This theory alluded to the breakdown of the black community in the inner city, indexed by gangs, drugs, female-headed-households, illegitimacy, and crime. Various data are presented here to support this view: the arrestees were disproportionately adolescent and young adult males, had high unemployment rates, often lived in single-parent families, often had criminal histories, tended to be dropouts from school, and were asserted to have histories of drug and alcohol abuse (Morrison and Lowry, Chapter 2).

Whether or not the point is correct, these data are not very persuasive. There is rarely an appropriate non-arrested comparison group, there are no controls, there are alternative explanations in some cases, and so on. Yet some authors confidently conclude that these young men represented "a critical mass . . . [with] . . . little reason to feel bound by social rules", and that looting, rather than political rebellion, was their major motive (Morrison and Lowry, Chapter 2).

A Black Protest

Perhaps the dominant interpretation of the 1960's rioting was that they were black protests against police brutality, racial discrimination, poverty, and other social conditions that impacted particularly on them (see Sears and McConahay, 1973; Kerner Commission, 1968; McCone Commission, 1965).

At the outset, the 1992 Los Angeles riot certainly paralleled those earlier outbursts, and at least initially gave rise to a similar interpretation. The patent unjustness of the treatment of Rodney King himself (first his televised beating, and then his police assailants' walking free) were viewed as typical of a long line of outrages committed against African-Americans, whether slaveowners, lynch mobs, or brutal police officers. But to blacks in Los Angeles the King events had a special meaning, because the Los Angeles Police Department had a longstanding reputation for insensitivity to minority residents of the city (and indeed a rather insular and quasi-paranoid attitude toward the community as a whole). So, as Tierney (Chapter 7) notes, it (1) was triggered by an event highlighting conflict between blacks and the police; the King beating and verdict quickly became symbols of police misconduct toward blacks, (2) it was initiated within the predominantly black ghetto by blacks, (3) it resulted again in much burning and looting of local businesses, and (4) most of those killed were blacks. The local television coverage of beatings and burnings in South Central Los Angeles, most seemingly perpetrated by blacks, quickly gave rise to the impression that it was predominantly a black-white conflict.

But as time went on, the evident complexity of the events overwhelmed this interpretation. The Mayor was a black man, not the usual conservative white; he himself had denounced the unfairness of the jury verdict, and was openly critical of the Chief of Police. After the first night, intensive television coverage of the looting and burning revealed the extensive participation of Latinos, not all poor and oppressed, but backing innumerable vans and pickup trucks up to store after store and relieving them of truckloads full of merchandise. And the rioting quickly reached a scope far beyond the evening of any conceivable local scores; the longstanding poverty of East Los Angeles, entry point for generations of immigrants to Los Angeles, gave rise to very little destruction and looting, whereas numerous commercial establishments in Hollywood, some distance from any real poverty areas, were stripped clean; and the widespread attacks on relatively new and quite modest Korean-owned businesses seemed inconsistent with a rebellion against longstanding white racism. So with time, the "black protest" interpretation too looked more and more like an over-simplification.

The Rainbow Coalition

This evidence of broad participation of Latinos as well as blacks then suggested to some a "bread riot" engaged in by the disadvantaged of all minority groups, the coming together of a rainbow coalition of all people of color, who truly needed the food, the diapers, and everything else that was taken. Perhaps this was the harvest of a decade-long orgy of self-aggrandizement participated in by the white capitalist class, protected and encouraged by the Reagan administration, that progressively impoverished minorities and the working class, while redistributing wealth up the social pyramid.

As Sonenshein (Chapter 3) notes, though, there were two major problems with this explanation. Whereas minorities may all have had dissatisfactions, they were quite divided politically; both the long history of black-Latino conflict and the short history of black-Asian conflict have been alluded to, to say nothing of sharp conflicts among Latinos on both political and nationality grounds, and great differences among Asians from different nations. Moreover, whites were quite unlikely to coalesce around a politically conservative position. Of all the major groups in Los Angeles, whites are the most split ideologically, with the most educated whites the most split. In fact white liberals formed the core of the coalition that had succeeded in electing, and reelecting four times, the first black mayor in Los Angeles. So the "rainbow coalition" theory does not fit the actual data very well, either.

The Bladerunner Scenario

The "Bladerunner" syndrome heralded the final breakdown of civilized society, finally driven into criminal anarchy by the racial underclass, drug lords, and hardened criminals. Not only were the streets no longer safe at night in some neighborhoods, but the entire city had been taken over by street criminals, mostly but not exclusively racial minorities. Since the "Bladerunner" metaphor models reality on a movie, there is the inescapable and ever-popular "blame it on television" variant: blacks took the King videotape as the "smoking gun" they had long awaited to nail the LAPD where it lived.

Yet this scenario should not be dismissed too readily. It does reflect a more general fear of the breakdown of the American political system. As turnout sags, and public cynicism grows, and whites, money, and power flee to the suburbs, and even a black mayor is seen as a sell-out to downtown business interests, the process of electoral politics is often seen as irrelevant to the problems of the inner city and the poor. The Los Angeles Police Department gave fuel to this scenario by its quite evident lack of preparedness for the events, symbolized by the Chief's Nero-esque fiddling at a fundraiser throughout the first evening of the riots while his police force swiftly lost control of major portions of the nation's second largest city. And television technology had made enormous strides since 1965, reflected in both the King videotape and the zoom lenses in helicopters that allowed for close-up coverage of the rioting from a safe distance.

Multiethnic Conflict

Others saw it as an interethnic conflict. To be sure, Rodney King, a black man, was beaten badly by white officers of the LAPD, who then were acquitted of any wrongdoing. But many blacks attacked Korean-owned stores, and indeed engaged in pitched battles in the streets with Koreans. And more Latinos than blacks were involved in the rioting and looting and burning. The triggering grievances were not only the black-white conflicts surrounding Rodney King, but the black-Korean conflicts manifested in the shooting of Latasha Harlins. The Koreans in turn emphasized their roles as hard-working and misunderstood immigrants targeted by street criminals. The growing role of Latinos in Los Angeles, displacing blacks from traditional black neighborhoods and from traditionally black-held jobs, also began to receive some attention.

These facts led some (e.g., Tierney, Chapter 7) to talk about the riots as "a new form," "the first multiethnic riot," or "the first urban unrest of the 21st century." Other described it as a "violent inter-minority confrontation" (Sonenshein, Chapter 3). The local demographic situation was "ripe for unrest" (Morrison and Lowry, Chapter 2). In the end this led many to a realistic group conflict explanation (see Olzak, 1986, and others). The notion of "ethnic enclaves" (Tierney, Chapter 7) or "territorially-based ethnic tensions" (Morrison and Lowry, Chapter 2), is described as "the future" (Tierney, Chapter 7). True, the intense fighting between blacks and Korean merchants had some parallel to the attacks on Jewish shops in the black ghetto of the 1960's, but somehow the level of violence against the Koreans themelves, not merely their shuttered and empty shops at 2 AM, took it to another level.

It seems apparent to me that no simple or single interpretation fits the 1992 events very well. It might be more appropriate to describe the events as several riots of different kinds occurring more or less simultaneously, rather than trying to fit any one theory to them. In that sense each of these theories probably has some merit. This is not to open the door to post-modernist license, wherein any configuration painted on an empty canvas is regarded as equally valid (see several essays in Gooding-Williams, 1993, for expressions of a contrary view). Rather, it is to recognize the true complexity of the events and of the circumstances that gave rise to them.

Conclusions

What are the lessons to be learned from the rioting in Los Angeles? In one sense, they may be rather limited; the rioting did not spread much beyond Los Angeles, for example, and there is reason to believe that much of it was specific to the particular actions and reputation of the Los Angeles Police Department regarding the black community in Los Angeles.

But there are broader lessons in it. One is surely to underline the difficulties that American cities are facing. The globalization of labor and capital often referred to in discussions of Los Angeles affect all cities, and in similar ways: high levels of unemployment among unskilled, semi-skilled, and skilled blue collar workers; deterioration of such infrastructural elements as public school and public health systems; family disorganization, and so on. The squeeze on public sector revenues induced nationally during the Reagan years, and in California by recession and a series of short-sighted ballot measures, has further drained resources that might help rejuvenate the cities.

A larger lesson might be of the precariousness of public order, perhaps a lesson that needs to be relearned by every generation in every nation anew. Nothing so destructive as the ethnic cleansing in Bosnia occurred in Los Angeles, but for a few days we all got a taste of how close to the precipice we always live.

Finally, it seems evident that one cannot simply describe the rioting as a "black protest" and stop there. But there is some truth to that characterization. And the comparison with the Watts riots of 1965 must lead us to think in longer historical terms than if we focused solely on the cruelties and indignities visited on Rodney King. So another major lesson continues to be the tragic legacy of slavery.

It is not written in stone that the descendants of Africans must be poor, violent, rejected. They are not all, nor are they always, nor are they everywhere and in every context. Yet it is a powerful truth that in America, they are more at risk than any other group in almost every respect one can think of—for incarceration, educational failure, hypertension and heart disease, murder, teenage pregnancy, alcoholism, drug addiction, racial discrimination, police mistreatment. And now comes "the chosen alternative" from Mexico and Central America, less threatening and willing to work for less.

One of the great successes of black life in this country was the overthrow of Jim Crow segregationism in the South in the 1950's and 1960's. One of the ironic side effects of that success was that it quickly became the model for a whole host of other claimants, groups of every stripe claiming they had been oppressed through the centuries just like blacks. This came at an unfortunate time, when America intellectuals were just beginning to shake off the self-censuring effects of a generation of World War patriotism and anti-Communist vigilantism. A lot of family skeletons suddenly came to light, perhaps distracting many from the close scrutiny required to distinguish true cadavers from mere odoriferous embarrassments.

In many quarters, blacks became thought of as just another complaining special interest group that really should just get a hold of themselves, work hard, and get ahead. But blacks are not just another special interest group. Article I, Section 2 of the United States Constitution placed them in a separate category from other Americans: free persons were to be counted as whole persons, and African slaves at three-fifths apiece.

We continue to reap the diseased harvest of decisions made in the 17th and 18th century. And American society has not, in over 300 years, figured out what to do about it. We have on our hands a very longstanding, very difficult, and terribly costly social problem. The society at large has played a large role in creating the problem and continues to play a large role in nurturing it, in many and complex ways. So the society at large has to take an equally large role in trying at least to ameliorate its worst effects. Many writing about the rioting somewhat wishfully describe it as a "wake-up call." Well, maybe. Somebody keeps pushing the snooze button. And what we cannot afford is trying to wish it away, or the illusions either that segregation will work or that black self-help will be sufficient. There is no simple solution. But it is a serious problem, and it will not go away all by itself.

References

Banfield, Edward C. 1970. *The unheavenly city.* Boston: Little, Brown.

Carmines, E. G., and J. A. Stimson, 1989. *Issue evolution: Race and the transformation of American politics.* Princeton, N.J.: Princeton University Press.

Cohen, Nathan (Ed.) 1970. *The Los Angeles riots: A socio-psychological study.* New York: Praeger.

Edsall, T. B., with M. D. Edsall, 1992. *Chain reaction: The impact of race, rights, and taxes on American politics.* New York: W. W. Norton.

Gooding-Williams, Robert (Ed.) 1993. *Reading Rodney King reading urban uprising.* New York: Routledge.

Governor's Commission on the Los Angeles Riots [McCone Commission] 1965. *Violence in the city—an end or a beginning?* Los Angeles: College Book Store.

Johnson, P. B., David O. Sears, and John B. McConahay, 1971. "Black invisibility, the press, and the Los Angeles riot." *American Journal of Sociology, 76,* 698-721.

Kinder, D. R., and David O. Sears, 1981. "Prejudice and politics: Symbolic racism versus racial threats to the good life." *Journal of Personality and Social Psychology, 40,* 414-431.

Light, Ivan and Edna Bonacich, 1988. *Immigrant entrepreneurs: Koreans in Los Angeles, 1965-1982.* Berkeley and Los Angeles: University of California Press.

McPhail, C. 1971. "Civil disorder participation: A critical examination of recent research." *American Sociological Review, 36,* 1058-1073.

Miles, J. 1992. Blacks vs. Browns. *Atlantic Monthly,* October.

National Advisory Commission on Civil Disorders [Kerner Commission] 1968. *Report of the National Advisory Commission on Civil Disorders.* Washington, D.C.; U. S. Government Printing Office.

Oliver, Melvin, and James H. Johnson, 1984. "Inter-ethnic conflict in an urban ghetto: The case of blacks and Latinos in Los Angeles." *Research in Social Movements. Conflict and change. 6*, 57-94.

Olzak, Susan 1986. "A competition model of ethnic collective action." pp. 17–46 in S. Olzak & J. Nagel (Eds.), *Competitive ethnic relations*. Orlando: Academic Press.

Schuman, Howard, Charlotte Steeh, and Lawrence Bobo, 1985. *Racial trends in America: Trends and interpretations*. Cambridge, MA: Harvard University Press.

Sears, David O., and D. R. Kinder, 1971. "Racial tensions and voting in Los Angeles." In W. Z. Hirsch (Ed.), *Los Angeles: Viability and prospects for metropolitan leadership*. New York: Praeger.

Sears, David O., and John B. McConahay, 1973. *The politics of violence: The new urban blacks and the Watts riot*. Boston: Houghton-Mifflin.

About the Book and Editor

The Los Angeles riots in the Spring of 1992 were among the most violent and destructive events in twentieth-century urban America. This collection of original essays by leading urban experts offers the first comprehensive analysis of the unrest that took place after a jury acquitted the police officers who were accused of using excessive force in the Rodney King beating.

This book addresses three questions: What were the causes of the Los Angeles riots, what actually took place, and what are the consequences and meaning of the riots for U.S. cities? The findings presented throughout this volume provide strong evidence that the existence of an inner-city "underclass," the persistence of black-white tensions in U.S. society, and the emergence of inter-ethnic hostilities in urban neighborhoods are critical to understanding the Los Angeles riots and their implications.

While sounding an urgent warning signal to the governments and citizens of other U.S. cities, *The Los Angeles Riots* presents solutions and policy recommendations for avoiding a repeat of such unrest in the future. The book is crucial to everyone's understanding of the contemporary urban environment and will be ideal as a supplementary text in urban politics, sociology, and urban planning and policy courses as well as in current affairs.

Mark Baldassare is professor and chair of Urban and Regional Planning in the School of Social Ecology at the University of California, Irvine.